D0231065

RESTAURANT
DISHES
OF THE WORLD

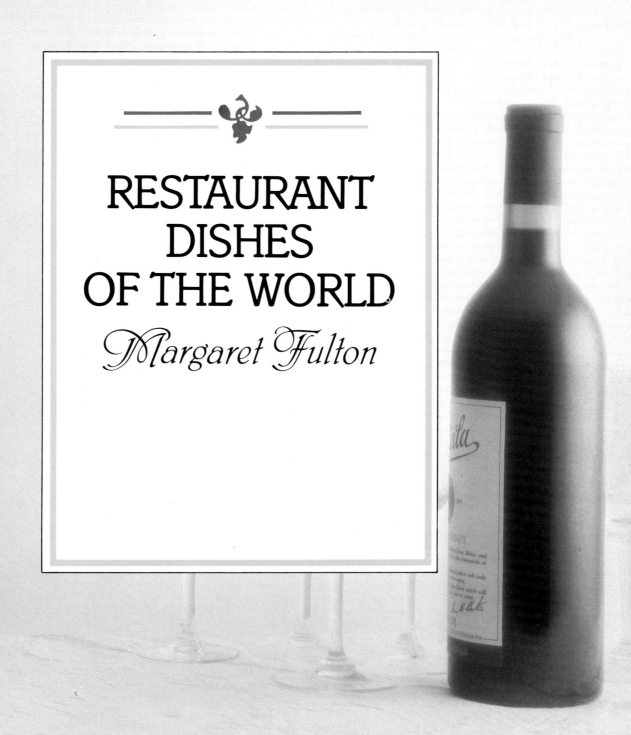

RESTAURANT DISHES OF THE WORLD

Margaret Fulton

Note

Restaurants often change hands and individual dishes come and go on menus, so specific place names are not always included with the recipes. However, all the dishes are representative of those you can look forward to in restaurants in the country or area mentioned.

This edition first published in 1984
by Octopus Books Limited
59 Grosvenor Street, London W1

© Octopus Books Limited 1983

ISBN 0 86273 149 6

Produced by Mandarin Publishers Limited
22a Westlands Road, Quarry Bay, Hong Kong

Printed in Hong Kong

Restaurant Dishes of the World was previously published in 1983
in hardback

CONTENTS

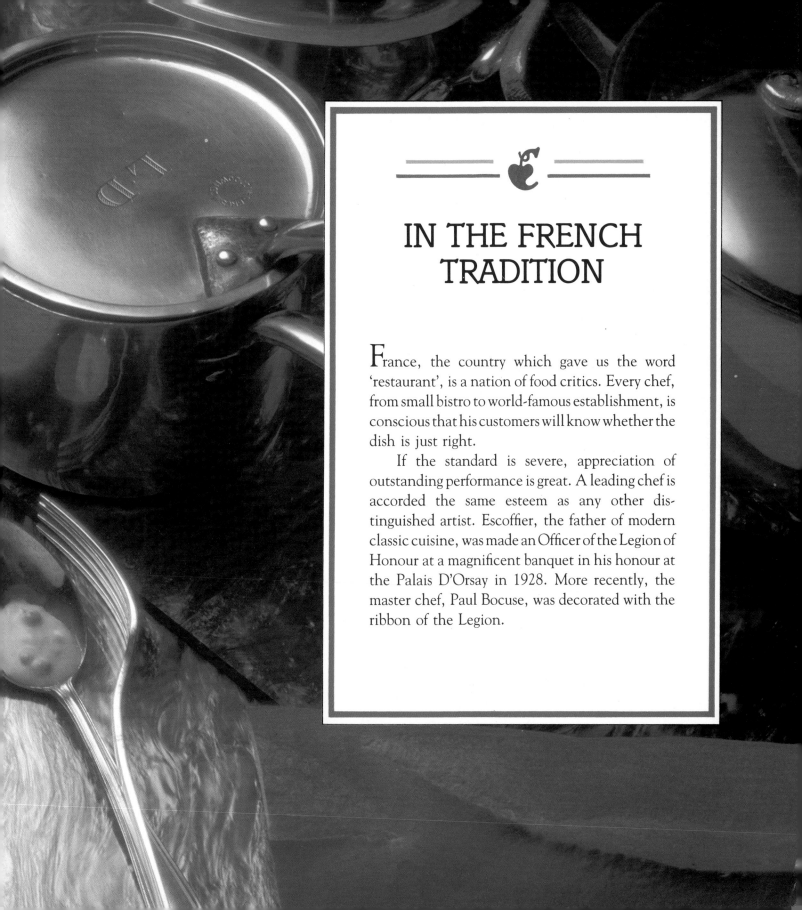

IN THE FRENCH TRADITION

France, the country which gave us the word 'restaurant', is a nation of food critics. Every chef, from small bistro to world-famous establishment, is conscious that his customers will know whether the dish is just right.

If the standard is severe, appreciation of outstanding performance is great. A leading chef is accorded the same esteem as any other distinguished artist. Escoffier, the father of modern classic cuisine, was made an Officer of the Legion of Honour at a magnificent banquet in his honour at the Palais D'Orsay in 1928. More recently, the master chef, Paul Bocuse, was decorated with the ribbon of the Legion.

From the point of view of the rest of the world, among France's most important exports are her chefs. They have taken their techniques and methods to almost every country, and, equally important, they have taken their conviction that a dish or a meal must be a harmonious whole – that it must show the balance and refinement that Escoffier summed up as 'elegant simplicity'. Some of the famous dishes are complex, more suited to a professional kitchen than a home one, but there are hundreds of others in the classic repertoire which are well within the scope of the home cook. Then there are the thousands of 'provincial' dishes, with their origins in the countryside rather than in a chef's inspiration. These dishes are prepared in millions of French homes and small eating-houses every day. They embody the same well-learned principles, the same respect for ingredients and attention to detail as are applied by the great chefs. You have only to go into a little country eating place and see the serious attention with which the meal is chosen and the dishes discussed . . . or go to the market and watch a housewife reject 20 *Bries* before she finds the one she wants . . . to understand that love, care and respect for food come from the very heart of the French people.

Quenelles de Brochet
Fish mousse with mushroom purée

La Tour d'Argent restaurant in Paris goes back to the 16th century. It is no wonder that amazing events stud the records of 'The Tower of Silver', named for the silvery stone from which it is built.

It is here the first fork was used, the first coffee drunk by Europeans . . . and where traditional standards of excellence have never wavered. This delicate dish of quenelles with mushrooms and cream sauce was given to me by owner M. Claude Terrail, who has added his own inventive genius to the fabled history of 'La Tour'.

1 quantity Fish Mousseline (page 12)
500 g (1 lb) button mushrooms, finely chopped
75 g (3 oz) butter
salt and freshly ground white pepper
120 ml (4 fl oz) double cream
450 ml (¾ pint) Béchamel Sauce (page 20)
125 g (4 oz) freshly grated Gruyère or Swiss cheese

Shape the mousseline into quenelles and poach as directed on page 12.

Meanwhile, cook the mushrooms in butter over moderate heat until very soft, stirring frequently, about 8 minutes. Season with salt and pepper, then purée with the cream in a blender or food processor fitted with the steel blade. Place a layer of mushroom purée in each of 6 individual heatproof dishes. Place 2 quenelles on top and cover with a layer of béchamel sauce. Sprinkle with grated cheese and place under a preheated hot grill until the cheese is lightly browned. Serve very hot. SERVES 6.

La Tour d'Argent is the oldest restaurant in Paris and one of the most celebrated in the world—famous both for its superlative food and its total ambience, which includes a marvellous view across the river to the Cathedral of Notre Dame. Some of the famous names of past and present are to be found in its 'Golden Book' of guests.

Provençal Poached Fish Thuilier

At *L'Oustau de Baumanière* in Provence, you might eat this fish dish looking out over the gardens, the swimming pool and the magnificent Provençal landscape. Chef Raymond Thuilier gave me the recipe, which he describes as having all of the Mediterranean and Provence in your plate. In the absence of red mullet (which is not related to grey mullet and is non-oily), choose other fine whole fish such as bream, snapper or whiting, or fillets of any good white fish.

4 whole fish, each weighing about 225 g (8 oz)
    or 4 large fillets
2 kg (4½ lb) mussels, beards removed and
    scrubbed
fresh basil, to garnish
SAUCE
300 ml (½ pint) olive oil
1 clove garlic, crushed
1 tomato, skinned, seeded and chopped
1 teaspoon finely chopped fresh fennel leaves
½ teaspoon finely chopped fresh rosemary
1 tablespoon finely chopped fresh basil
pinch of paprika
pinch of ground coriander
salt and freshly ground pepper
COURT BOUILLON
350 ml (12 fl oz) dry white wine
1 tablespoon wine vinegar
450 ml (¾ pint) water
pinch of salt
freshly ground pepper
bouquet garni (page 16)
sprig each of rosemary, basil and fennel
2 slices of orange
2 slices of lemon

Make the sauce 2 or 3 days in advance. Mix all the ingredients together, seasoning to taste with salt and pepper. Cover and leave in a cool place (but not in the refrigerator) until needed.

    Put all the ingredients for the court bouillon into a shallow pan big enough to hold the fish in one layer. Bring to the boil, partially cover and simmer very gently for 1 hour. Add the fish and mussels, cover and poach (the water should shiver but not bubble) for 5 minutes or until mussels open (discard any that do not open). Remove mussels and keep warm; continue cooking fish, if necessary, just until the flesh turns white and flakes at the touch of a fork.

Lift the fish out carefully with a slotted fish slice and arrange on a large, heated oval platter. Arrange the mussels in their shells round the platter, garnish with fresh basil and pour the sauce over the fish. Serve immediately. SERVES 4.

Les Crêpes Vonnassiennes
☙*Potato Pancakes, Vonnas Style*

One of the most famous restaurants in the province of Bresse, and considered one of the finest in all France, is *La Mère Blanc* at Vonnas, which presents an irresistible mixture of traditional cuisine and the new ideas of owner-chef Georges Blanc. Georges, who says he was 'born with a casserole in his hand', is the fourth generation of his family at *La Mère Blanc*, and it was while he was only 30 that his restaurant received its third Michelin star—a rare honour. Georges' recipe for potato pancakes, which he was kind enough to give me, is a particularly versatile one; they can be served with the meat course, or as a dessert with caster sugar and a fresh fruit purée.

500 g (1 lb) potatoes
4 tablespoons boiling milk
4 tablespoons flour
3 whole eggs
4 egg whites
4 tablespoons double cream
salt
clarified butter (ghee) for frying

Boil the potatoes in their skins and, when cool enough to handle, peel and mash them. Beat in the boiling milk and cool completely.

    Beat in the flour with a wooden spoon, then beat in the eggs and egg whites (without beating them first). Stir in the cream. Season lightly with salt and beat the mixture until it is very smooth; it will be thicker than the usual crêpe batter.

    Heat enough clarified butter to cover the base of a heavy frying pan. When it begins to give off a slight haze, drop in tablespoons of the batter, a little apart so they have room to spread. Cook on high heat until the underside is browned, turn and cook the other side, and remove. Add a little more butter and repeat until all the batter is used. Keep the pancakes warm between the folds of a tea-towel in a cool oven until all are made. Serve the pancakes very hot. SERVES 6.

<u>Boil, Simmer, Poach</u>
Every chef knows it is important to understand the difference between boiling, simmering and poaching. A liquid is boiling when many bubbles rise vigorously to the surface; it is simmering when the surface shudders and bubbles rise one at a time; it is at poaching temperature when the surface shivers but no bubbles rise.

Bavarois de Saumon Fumé
🍂 *Smoked Salmon Mould*

Chiberta, on the short rue Arsène-Houssaye at the Étoile end of the Champs Élysées in Paris, has a superlative host in Louis-Noel Richard and one of the new innovative young chefs, Jean-Michel Bedier. This provocative *bavarois* is a perfectly delicious way to start a meal, and a simple dish to reproduce when a visit to *Chiberta* is out of reach.

125 g (4 oz) smoked salmon, thinly sliced
120 ml (4 fl oz) Crème Fraîche, well chilled (page 21)
1 tablespoon red salmon roe
¼ teaspoon cayenne pepper
TO SERVE
fresh tomato purée
snipped chives

Rinse 4 individual soufflé dishes 8–10 cm (3–4 in) in diameter. Line the moulds with smoked salmon; trim off any overhanging salmon and purée it in a blender or food processor fitted with the steel blade.

Beat the chilled crème fraîche in a small bowl until it forms soft peaks. Lightly mix the puréed smoked salmon, salmon roe and cayenne and gently fold in the crème fraîche. Divide the mixture evenly among the soufflé dishes. Chill well.

Run a thin knife round the sides of each mould. Place an inverted plate over each dish, hold plate and dish firmly together and turn over. Rap the plate sharply on the table to release the mould and lift the dish off carefully.

Spoon fresh tomato purée in a cordon round each mould and sprinkle the mould with snipped chives. SERVES 4.

The baroque, beautiful, legendary *Maxim's* of Paris was launched in 1893, replacing an icecream parlour that formerly occupied the site in the Rue Royale. Business was slow at first, but popularity arrived overnight when the great Paris Exhibition of 1900 drew crowds of hungry, wealthy sightseers. By good fortune, its entrance gates were only a soufflé's throw from *Maxim's!* Ever since, the restaurant has maintained its position as one of the finest in the world. As the French put it: '*Maxim's* will always be *Maxim's!*'

Crayfish au Chardonnay

This recipe is from the elegant *Auberge de la Côte 108* restaurant at Berry-au-Bac near Reims in France. Naturally, chef Serge Courville specifies Charles Heidsieck Blanc de Blancs de Chardonnay in his dish, for Reims is the home of world-famous Heidsieck champagnes and fine wines. If you cannot get hold of or afford this, use any champagne. Green prawns may also be used in place of the freshwater crayfish in this beautifully flavoured main course casserole.

1 medium carrot, thinly sliced
2 medium onions, thinly sliced
3 spring onions, chopped
½ bottle champagne
½ bay leaf
1 sprig of fresh thyme
1 stick of celery, with leaves
2 sprays of parsley
salt and freshly ground pepper
24 crayfish or green prawns, cleaned
125 g (4 oz) butter, softened
2 ripe tomatoes, skinned, seeded and cut into
   small dice
1 tablespoon snipped chives

Place the vegetables, champagne and flavourings in a saucepan, bring to the boil and cook until vegetables are tender, about 20 minutes. Drop the shellfish in and cook for 3 minutes. Take out shellfish and aromatic leaves (bay leaf, thyme, celery, parsley). Remove the flesh from the tails and claws of the crayfish or devein the prawns and set aside. Discard the leaves.

Heat a small knob of the butter in a saucepan and cook the diced tomato until it is soft and the liquid has evaporated, about 3 minutes. Press liquid and vegetables used to cook the shellfish through a sieve, then return to the rinsed-out saucepan and cook, uncovered, over high heat until reduced to about 1½ cups. Reduce heat to moderate and whisk in the remaining softened butter in small pieces. Add the tomatoes, snipped chives and taste for seasoning, then add the shellfish and gently heat through. Spoon into 4 heated individual casserole dishes and serve at once. SERVES 4.

Crayfish au Chardonnay

Chez Barrier at Tours is the total creation of Charles Barrier, one of the most honoured chefs in France. No detail is too small to escape this remarkable man.

His fish arrives fresh each morning from Brittany or the Atlantic coast, goes into a high humidity cold drawer, packed with specially rounded ice cubes that do not pierce or pinch the skin. There are separate cold rooms, with individually adjusted temperatures, for his bread, soft fruits and vegetables, meats, fish, pâtisseries and ices. No wonder the food at *Chez Barrier* has been described as 'perfection'.

Scallop Mousseline

One of the glories of classic French cuisine is the featherlight mixture called *mousseline*, used as a stuffing, to shape *quenelles*, poached in little moulds, or served as a course on its own with an interesting sauce. Master this basic recipe and you will be ready to try many variations.

350 g (12 oz) fresh scallops, cleaned and dark beards removed
1 teaspoon salt
freshly ground white pepper
pinch of freshly grated nutmeg
1 whole egg
1 egg white
450 ml (¾ pint) double cream
2 teaspoons melted butter

Remove the coral from the scallops and set this aside. In a food processor fitted with the steel blade, purée the white meat of the scallops for 3–4 minutes. Season with salt, pepper and nutmeg. Add the whole egg and the egg white. Blend for a further minute. Put the container in the refrigerator and chill for 30 minutes to firm the mixture.

Return the container to the processor, add the cream and blend for a few seconds—take care not to over mix. Return the container to the refrigerator and chill for 1 hour.

Brush 6 *oeuf-en-gelée* moulds, available from specialty kitchen shops, or 150 ml (¼ pint) moulds with melted butter. Fill them to the brim with the scallop mixture. Smooth the top of each mould, put the moulds in a large baking dish, and add enough water to come half-way up the sides of the moulds.

Bake the mousselines, covered with buttered foil or greaseproof paper, in a preheated moderate oven (180°C/350°F/Gas 4) for 10–12 minutes or until a skewer inserted in the centre comes out clean.

When the mousselines are cooked, turn them out on to hot plates and pour hot sauce (see individual recipes) over each to decorate. SERVES 6.

Note 1: The mousselines may be cooked as far as 24 hours ahead and chilled, covered. To reheat, put them in a baking dish, add enough water to come half-way up the sides of the moulds, cover with foil and place in a hot oven (200°C/400°F/Gas 6) for 10–12 minutes or until the mousselines are puffed and heated through.

Note 2: The coral from the scallops may be used in the accompanying sauce, or poached for 30 seconds in a little acidulated water (use wine or lemon juice) and used as a garnish, or a whole piece of coral is sometimes put in the centre of each mousse before baking.

Fish Mousseline (Salmon, Perch, Sole)
Use the basic recipe for Scallop Mousseline, but use fresh fish of your choice instead of scallops. Bone and skin the fish, weigh, then proceed with recipe as above.

Crayfish Mousseline
Use the basic recipe for Scallop Mousseline, substituting 350 g (12 oz) raw fresh crayfish, lobster or prawn flesh for the scallops.

Quenelles
Poached Fish Mousse

Use the mousseline mixture of your choice (see preceding recipes). To shape each quenelle, dip 2 tablespoons in boiling water, heap the mixture on 1 tablespoon and round off with the second spoon. Dip the second spoon again in hot water, slip it under the quenelle and slide into a deep buttered flameproof dish. Add enough hot water, or fish stock to float the quenelles and bring to a bare simmer (the liquid should quiver, but no bubbles rise).

Poach the quenelles over low heat for 10–15 minutes or until firm. Do not allow the water to boil or the quenelles will split. Remove them with a perforated spoon and dry on paper towels. They may be served at once, or can be covered and stored in the refrigerator for up to 24 hours.

To reheat quenelles: return them to the buttered baking dish, cover with hot water or stock and poach very gently for 6–8 minutes or until heated through. Serve 2–3 quenelles for each serving, masked with a good sauce, such as Velouté Sauce (page 21) or Beurre Blanc (page 15).

Blanquette de Poulet à la Tourangelle

> *Blanquette of Chicken Tourangelle*

I thank M. Barrier of *Chez Barrier* in Tours for supplying the recipe for this blanquette of chicken— so simple, yet superb when prepared correctly.

1 chicken, about 1.8 kg (4 lb), jointed
175 g (6 oz) butter
salt and freshly ground white pepper
6 spring onions, chopped
2 tablespoons Cognac, slightly warmed
250 ml (8 fl oz) Chicken Stock (page 90)
170 ml (6 fl oz) dry white wine
30 button onions, peeled
350 g (12 oz) small button mushrooms
1 clove garlic, crushed
1 tablespoon finely chopped parsley
4 egg yolks
120 ml (4 fl oz) double cream
juice of ½ lemon
½ teaspoon chopped fresh tarragon

Dry the chicken pieces with paper towels. Melt all but 1 tablespoon of the butter in a deep frying pan or flameproof casserole, add the chicken and cook very gently, turning the pieces until stiffened and white on all sides. Season with salt and pepper to taste.

Add the chopped spring onions and cook gently until they are soft. Add Cognac, set alight, and shake the pan until the flames die down. Add half the stock and the wine, cover and simmer for 30 minutes or until chicken is tender.

Meanwhile, place the button onions in a saucepan with remaining chicken stock and butter, cover and simmer very slowly for 25 minutes, rolling the onions in the saucepan from time to time. If all the liquid evaporates during cooking, add a spoonful or two of water. Add mushrooms, simmer for 5 minutes more and remove from heat.

When the chicken is cooked, lift it from the pan and keep warm. Add garlic and parsley to the liquid in the pan and boil, uncovered, until reduced to about 120 ml (4 fl oz). Beat the egg yolks with the cream, stir in a little of the hot liquid and return this to the pan, stirring over low heat until the sauce thickens and becomes glossy. Do not allow to boil. Taste and correct seasoning and stir in lemon juice and the chopped tarragon.

Return the chicken to the pan, add the mushrooms and onions and spoon the sauce over. Serve very hot from the casserole. SERVES 4–6.

Huîtres Chaudes aux Endives

> *Hot Oysters with Endives*

The three-star *Restaurant Pic* in Valence-sur-Rhone is one of the finest in France, but the warm and unpretentious Jacques Pic and Madame Suzanne Pic make it a delightfully friendly place with the atmosphere of a traditional family establishment. This oyster dish depends, like all Jacques Pic's cooking, on superb ingredients and unstinting attention to detail.

24 large oysters in the half shell
coarse sea salt
300 g (10 oz) Belgian endives (chicory)
25 g (1 oz) butter
salt
pinch of sugar
squeeze of lemon juice
170 ml (6 fl oz) double cream
1 egg yolk
pinch of curry powder

Leave oysters in the shell and arrange in a steamer. Steam for one minute, or until plump. Drain, reserving the juice, and set oysters aside. Wash the shells and arrange them on a bed of coarse sea salt to keep them level.

Wash endives and chop them finely. Melt the butter in a pan and toss the endives in the hot butter for a few moments. Season with salt, a pinch of sugar and a squeeze of lemon juice and moisten with 120 ml (4 fl oz) cream. Allow to cook for 3 minutes; drain, reserving the liquid, and set endives aside.

Make a liaison of 1 egg yolk and the remaining cream, beaten together.

Strain the oyster cooking liquid through fine muslin or a disposable cloth into a saucepan. Boil rapidly until reduced by half, then add the cooking liquid from the endives and return to the boil. Remove from the heat and add the liaison, stirring briskly. Stir in the curry powder.

Arrange the endives in the oyster shells and place oysters on top. Coat each oyster with the sauce and place the dish under a hot grill for a minute or so to glaze. Serve immediately. SERVES 4.

> *Fines Herbes*
>
> *This is the French term for a mixture of herbs used for flavouring omelettes, savoury butters and other foods. The traditional mixture is parsley, chervil, tarragon and sometimes chives, but other mixtures of fresh herbs may be used.*

Chicken Tante Célestine

This wonderfully simplé but delicious recipe for 'Aunt Celestine's Chicken' was given to me by M. Jean Delaunay, demonstration chef for Marnier-Lapostolle of Paris.

1 chicken, weighing about 1.5 kg (3½ lb)
flour, seasoned with salt and pepper
40 g (1½ oz) butter
3 tablespoons Grand Marnier
3 tablespoons Chicken Stock (page 90)
250 ml (8 fl oz) double cream
25 g (1 oz) toasted, flaked almonds
APPLE GARNISH (*see below*)
4 medium cooking apples (e.g. Granny Smiths)
40 g (1½ oz) butter, melted

Divide the chicken into 6 portions—2 legs, 2 wings with some breast attached, and the remaining breast cut in two. Coat in seasoned flour and shake off excess.

Heat the butter in a heavy frying pan and fry the chicken over medium heat until golden-brown, turning to brown evenly. Sprinkle with 2 tablespoons Grand Marnier and the stock, then cover tightly and simmer for 30 minutes or until tender. Remove chicken to a serving dish and keep warm.

Add remaining Grand Marnier and the cream to the pan, scraping up the brown bits from the bottom. Stir gently until heated through, taste for seasoning and spoon over the chicken. Serve garnished with apples and sprinkle with almonds. SERVES 6.

Apple Garnish

Peel and core apples and cut into bite-size cubes. Place in a shallow baking dish in one layer. Pour over the butter, tossing the apples lightly to coat. Bake in a preheated moderate oven (180°C/350°F/Gas 4) for 15 minutes, or until the apples are soft. Do not stir, to avoid breaking the apples. Use apple garnish hot.

Filet de Boeuf au Cassis et Poivre Rose

Beef Fillet with Blackcurrants and Pink Peppercorns

Beef and peppercorns are a classic combination. Jean-Luc Lundy of Sydney's *Bagatelle* gives it fresh interest for palate and eye with the addition of tart-sweet blackcurrants. It's a simple yet sensational idea for your next dinner party.

Jean-Luc suggests you order your beef from your butcher a day or so before. It should be from the thick end of the fillet, and free of any fat or gristle.

75 g (3 oz) butter
8 slices of beef fillet, each weighing about 90 g
  (3½ oz)
1 small jar pink peppercorns (see Note)
4 tablespoons wine vinegar
90 g (3½ oz) blackcurrants, fresh or frozen
4 tablespoons White Stock (page 77) or water
salt
tomato roses (page 84) and parsley sprays, to
  garnish

Heat half the butter in a large, heavy frying pan and sauté the beef slices on both sides until done to your liking. Remove to a plate and keep warm by placing in a slow oven (150°C/300°F/Gas 2) with the door open.

Rinse the peppercorns under cold, running water and drain.

Pour the fat from the pan and add the vinegar, stirring to get up the brown bits from the bottom (deglaze). Boil rapidly for 20 seconds or so until reduced, then add peppercorns, blackcurrants and stock or water.

Continue reducing until the sauce looks syrupy and season with salt to taste. Add the remaining butter in small pieces and swirl the pan to distribute it evenly.

Serve 2 slices of beef per person, with some of the blackcurrants and peppercorns arranged on top of each slice and the sauce spooned over. Garnish each plate with a tomato rose and a spray of parsley—preferably the flat Italian type. SERVES 4.

Note: Pink peppercorns are available in small jars from Continental delicatessens and many large supermarkets.

Beurre Blanc

This delicate buttery sauce is a superb one to serve with poached fish, seafood or quenelles. Bring 250 ml (8 fl oz) fish stock (page 81) and 4 tablespoons dry white wine to the boil and reduce by half. Turn heat low and gently beat in 125 g (4 oz) softened butter bit by bit. When the sauce is the consistency of cream, stir in 2 tablespoons cream and salt and pepper to taste.

Chicken Tante Célestine

Sherry Wine Vinegar Chicken, Gidleigh Park

Kay Henderson is the culinary artist behind the superb food . . . 'French in the modern idiom', as the Egon Ronay Guide calls it . . . at *Gidleigh Park Hotel Restaurant* near Chagford, in Devon. The Tudor building is set in 30 acres of grounds, and guests eat in a panelled dining room with an open view of the beautiful countryside. From cheeses to wines (which include selections from California and Australia as well as Europe), every detail at *Gidleigh Park* is personally supervised by Kay Henderson and her husband, who is in charge of service. They were kind enough to give me this recipe for a simple but unusual chicken dish.

olive oil
1.5 kg (3½ lb) chicken, cut into quarters
salt and freshly ground pepper
sherry wine vinegar (see Note)
3 unpeeled cloves garlic
250 ml (8 fl oz) Chicken Stock (page 90)
250 ml (8 fl oz) double cream
TO SERVE
boiled rice
turned and lightly cooked courgettes (or unpeeled, blanched cucumber) and carrots (see Note)

Heat enough oil in a heavy frying pan to cover the bottom of the pan. Add the chicken pieces and season with salt and pepper. Sauté over moderately high heat until browned on both sides. Reduce heat and sprinkle the chicken with sherry wine vinegar. Add the garlic cloves, cover the pan and cook until the chicken is tender, turning once, about 20 minutes. While the chicken is cooking, lift the lid every 5 minutes and sprinkle with a little more sherry wine vinegar. When the chicken is ready, remove and keep warm while making the sauce.

Discard garlic, add the stock to the pan of cooking liquid and boil over high heat until reduced by half. Stir in the cream and cook over moderate heat for 5 minutes or until slightly thickened. Stir in 1 tablespoon sherry wine vinegar and salt and pepper.

Arrange the chicken pieces on a bed of boiled rice, spoon the sauce over and surround with turned courgettes and carrots. SERVES 4.

Note: If sherry wine vinegar is unobtainable, add 1 tablespoon medium dry sherry to 120 ml (4 fl oz) white wine vinegar.

'Turned' vegetables are vegetables cut into finger lengths and the ends rounded with a sharp knife.

Soufflé aux Épinards, Sauce Anchois

Spinach Soufflé with Anchovy Sauce

Langan's Brasserie is a large, bustling French restaurant in London's Piccadilly. Though catering for 400 to 500 clients a day, it maintains a reputation for superb food and an infectiously friendly atmosphere. A highlight of my meal was the pretty spinach soufflé with its creamy anchovy sauce—a specialty of *Langan's*. My thanks to director Richard Shepherd for supplying the recipe.

75 g (3 oz) butter
75 g (3 oz) flour
400 ml (14 fl oz) warm milk
6 eggs, separated
4 tablespoons cooked spinach (see Note)
salt and cayenne pepper
freshly grated nutmeg
ANCHOVY SAUCE *(see below)*
250 ml (8 fl oz) Hollandaise Sauce (page 21)
1 small can flat anchovy fillets, drained

Grease 6 individual 150 ml (¼ pint) soufflé dishes and tie around each a collar of doubled, greased greaseproof paper to come 4 cm (1½ inches) above the rim. Set oven to hot (200°C/400°F/Gas 6) and place a baking tray on the centre shelf.

Melt the butter in a saucepan over low heat, add flour and stir for 1 minute. Remove from heat, cool a little and add warm milk. Stir until smoothly blended, then return to heat and stir until boiling. Boil for 30 seconds, then remove from heat and cool slightly. Add the egg yolks, one at a time, and stir in the spinach. Season well with salt, cayenne pepper and nutmeg. Whisk egg whites until they hold soft peaks. Add one-third of the whites to the yolk mixture, folding in well. Scoop remaining whites on top and fold in lightly.

Turn the mixture into the prepared dishes and arrange them on the heated baking tray. Immediately turn the oven down to moderately hot (190°C/375°F/Gas 5) and bake for 15 minutes, or until soufflés are well risen and brown on top. Serve immediately, with a separate bowl of anchovy sauce. SERVES 6.

Anchovy Sauce

Have Hollandaise sauce warm. Purée anchovy fillets in a blender or food processor, or pound in a mortar, adding a little water to make a smooth paste. Combine with the Hollandaise and serve at once.

Note: Approximately 225 g (8 oz) spinach will yield 4 tablespoons when cooked. If using silver beet, about

Bouquet Garni
This is a small bundle of herbs and aromatics, tied together, for flavouring stocks, soups and casseroles. The classic bouquet is made from a few parsley stalks, a small bay leaf, a sprig of thyme, a strip of celery and a strip or two of leek, but the ingredients may be varied according to the dish. If using dried herbs or other ingredients unsuitable for tying in a bundle, tie them in a square of muslin.

125 g (4 oz) should do. Remove white stalks and ribs from the spinach or silver beet and wash well. Steam, covered, in the water clinging to the leaves until they are just tender, about 3 minutes. Drain in a sieve, pressing on the leaves to extract as much moisture as possible. Chop or shred very finely and measure 4 tablespoons.

Le Caneton Rôti Marco Polo
🦆 *Roast Duckling with Green Peppercorns*

M. Claude's recipe for duckling is a specialty of *La Tour d'Argent* in Paris. It is one of the simplest but best ways to cook a young duck. (Illustrated on pages 6 and 7.)

1 duckling, weighing about 2 kg (4 lb)
3 tablespoons juice from canned green peppercorns
1½ tablespoons Cognac
2 tablespoons dry white wine
2 tablespoons green peppercorns
450 ml (¾ pint) veal and duck stock (see Note)
4 tablespoons double cream or Crème Fraîche (page 21)

Pull any loose fat from neck and body cavities of the duckling and wipe the bird inside and out with damp paper towels. Dry well and truss neatly (page 96). Place, breast side up, on a rack in a greased roasting pan and roast in a preheated moderate oven (180°C/350°F/Gas 4) for 1½ hours, or until the juice runs clear when thickest part of thigh is pricked with a fine skewer. (Prick skin of breast 20 minutes before end of cooking to release fat and crisp the skin.) When roasting is finished, leave the duckling in a warm place for 20 minutes before serving.

Meanwhile, make the sauce: place peppercorn juice, Cognac and wine in a small, heavy saucepan and reduce by half over gentle heat, adding peppercorns half-way through the process. Add the veal and duck stock to the saucepan, bring to the boil and turn off the heat. Let the sauce stand for 20 minutes and skim off any scum from the surface. Add the cream or crème fraîche and stir briskly over gentle heat until sauce is very hot.

Remove trussing strings from the duckling and place it on a hot serving platter. Spoon over enough sauce to coat it and serve remaining sauce in a heated sauceboat. Carve at the table. SERVES 4.
Note: If it is easier for you, the duck may be carved in the kitchen.

To make veal and duck stock, follow directions for White Stock (page 77), adding the duck neck and giblets for flavour.

Gigot d'Agneau en Croûte
🦆 *Leg of Lamb in Pastry*

In the heart of Provence in France is Raymond Thuilier's *L'Oustau de Baumanière*, a beautiful old château which is now a superb hotel with a fine collection of paintings, tapestries and antique furniture. In winter, giant logs of olive wood burn in the huge fireplaces. M. Thuilier, who is a talented painter as well as a noted chef, gave me these directions for his favourite way of preparing the first spring lamb.

75 g (3 oz) butter
6 lamb kidneys, skinned, cored and finely sliced
120 ml (4 fl oz) Madeira
125 g (4 oz) mushrooms, finely chopped
1 teaspoon each fresh thyme and tarragon, or
    ¼ teaspoon dried
½ teaspoon chopped fresh rosemary, or pinch of
    dried
salt and freshly ground pepper
1 small leg of lamb, boned, trimmed of fat and
    gristle
little extra butter
225 g (8 oz) frozen puff pastry, thawed
1 egg, beaten

Heat the butter in a heavy frying pan and briskly sauté the kidney for 2 minutes, stirring. Add the Madeira, mushrooms and herbs and simmer for 3 minutes on very low heat. Season with salt and pepper and allow to cool.

Stuff the lamb with the kidney mixture, re-shape the leg with your hands and sew it up with white thread. Rub with a little butter and place in a preheated hot oven (200°C/400°F/Gas 6) for 20 minutes. Remove from oven, allow to become quite cold and remove the thread.

Roll pastry out thinly, cut some fine strips for decoration and set aside. Wrap the lamb in the pastry, tucking the ends under neatly and sealing with beaten egg. Decorate with pastry strips and leaves cut from trimmings, securing the decorations in place with beaten egg.

Place pastry-wrapped lamb in the refrigerator for 30 minutes, then brush with beaten egg (avoiding cut edges of decorations). Bake in a preheated very hot oven (230°C/450°F/Gas 8) for 10 minutes, before carving across into thin slices. SERVES 4.
Note: This cooking time is correct for the tiny spring lamb available in France, cooked pink. You may wish to cook the lamb for an extra 10 minutes initially and an extra 15 minutes when wrapped in pastry. M.F.

🦆 Beetroot Dauphinoise
An exciting French approach to beetroot—excellent with roast meats. Peel and thinly slice 1 kg (2 lb) raw beetroot. Place in a saucepan with 350 ml (12 fl oz) chicken stock (page 90), 250 ml (8 fl oz) double cream, 2 chopped cloves garlic, 1 small chopped onion and salt and pepper to taste. Simmer for 2 minutes. Spread mixture in a buttered baking dish and sprinkle with 125 g (4 oz) grated Swiss cheese. Bake in a hot oven (200°C/400°F/Gas 6) until beetroot is tender, about 45 minutes. Serves 8.

Grand Marnier Soufflé

Grand Marnier is a beautiful orange-flavoured liqueur, and Jean Delaunay is the Paris chef with the enviable role of demonstrating Grand Marnier recipes in restaurant kitchens around the world. His Grand Marnier Soufflé is a classic dessert you can expect in many fine restaurants that follow the French tradition.

2 tablespoons caster sugar for dusting moulds
50 g (2 oz) butter
2 tablespoons flour
2 teaspoons cornflour
300 ml (½ pint) warm milk
2 tablespoons sugar
grated zest of 1 orange (see left)
3 tablespoons Grand Marnier liqueur
4 egg yolks
5 egg whites
1 tablespoon caster sugar

Grease a 1.1 litre/2 pint soufflé mould and tie around it a collar of doubled, greased greaseproof paper to come 4 cm (1½ inches) above the edge of the dish. Dust the inside of the dish with caster sugar, then turn it upside down and tap the base to remove excess sugar. Set oven to hot (200°C/400°F/Gas 6) and place a baking tray on the centre shelf.

Melt the butter in a saucepan over low heat, add the flours and stir for 1 minute. Remove from heat, cool a little, then add warm milk. Stir until smoothly blended, then return to heat and stir until boiling. Boil for 30 seconds, remove from heat and stir in sugar. Stir in zest, Grand Marnier and egg yolks, one at a time. Turn the mixture into a large bowl.

Whisk the egg whites until they hold soft peaks. Stir a large spoonful of the whites into the egg yolk mixture, then scoop remaining whites on top. Fold in with a large metal spoon or rubber spatula, using a down, up and over cutting motion and turning the bowl a little each time.

Turn the mixture into the prepared soufflé dish and place it on the heated baking tray. Immediately turn the oven down to moderately hot (190°C/375°F/Gas 5) and bake for 20 minutes without opening the oven door. Then open the oven door gently, sprinkle top of soufflé with caster sugar and bake for 10–15 minutes longer until soufflé is well risen and brown.

Place the dish on a heated serving platter, remove paper collar and take immediately to the table. To serve, spread the top apart with a warmed serving spoon and fork and serve some of the firm outside and creamy centre with each portion. SERVES 6.

❧ Zest

Zest is the coloured outer layer of the rind of citrus fruits, and contains the concentrated oils which flavour the fruit. The recipe may call for grated zest, or finely shredded or julienne zest (cut in matchstick strips). Whether grating or peeling, be sure not to include any of the white pith, which can give a bitter taste. A swivel-bladed vegetable peeler is useful for peeling.

La Mousseline de St. Jacques à l'Orange
❧*Mousse of Sea Scallop with Orange Sauce*

Guy and Lucette Mouilleron's *Ma Cuisine* is one of the smallest restaurants in London; it is also one of the best, for in Guy Mouilleron it boasts one of London's most talented chefs. 'Brilliant, . . . pure genius' is how he has been described by more than one top restaurateur.

M. Mouilleron is an innovative chef who does not deny the 'old cuisine', but wants to provide something different. This dish, based on a classic *mousseline* and a traditional *sauce vin blanc*, but with a subtle difference, is typical of the light, beautiful food served at *Ma Cuisine*.

1 quantity of Scallop Mousseline (page 12)
2 peeled, sliced oranges, to garnish
SAUCE
120 ml (4 fl oz) Fish Stock (page 81)
120 ml (4 fl oz) dry white wine
3 strips of orange zest (see far left)
2–3 tablespoons orange juice
2 egg yolks
125 g (4 oz) butter, softened

Prepare the mousseline and poach in six 120 ml (4 fl oz) moulds. Keep warm while making the sauce.

To make the sauce: place the fish stock, wine, orange zest and 2 tablespoons juice in a saucepan and cook over moderate heat until the mixture is reduced to about 4 tablespoons; strain. To this reduction add the egg yolks, one at a time, whisking over very gentle heat or over simmering water until the yolks thicken and the mixture has the consistency of cream.

Add the butter gradually, whisking until it is absorbed. The mixture should be thick and firm; it is brought to the right consistency with the remaining orange juice—just add enough to give the sauce a masking consistency.

To finish: turn warm mousses onto 6 hot plates, spoon sauce around and garnish with orange. SERVES 6. *Note:* if liked, tiny baked crescents of puff pastry may be added. At *Ma Cuisine* the top of the mousse is decorated with slivers of *bêche-de-mer* (sea cucumber), but a twist of julienne strips of orange would be a good substitute. For a more dramatic effect, use pieces of Chinese black cloud ear (a dried wood fungus), soaked in water for 20 minutes until they become glutinous and crinkly. Arrange small pieces on top of each mousse.

La Mousseline de St. Jacques à l'Orange

Omelette Lorraine

🍂 *Omelette with Bacon, Cheese and Herbs*

We all know Lorraine's own quiche, the savoury tart with eggs, cream, cheese and bacon. Some years ago when I was passing through this rich north-eastern province of France, I lunched pleasantly on an omelette made from these same products of the region, served with a glass of the local wine and a green salad.

15 g (½ oz) butter
3 rashers of bacon, derinded and cut into little
*   strips*
6 eggs
4 tablespoons double cream
50 g (2 oz) grated Swiss cheese
2 teaspoons chopped, mixed fresh herbs

Melt the butter in a small frying pan which can also go into the oven. Add bacon strips and cook slowly, turning once or twice, until lightly browned. Remove bacon with a slotted spoon and set aside. Turn up the heat under the pan.

Mix the eggs, cream, cheese and herbs with a fork just until well blended. Pour into the hot pan and place immediately in a preheated hot oven (200°C/400°F/Gas 6). Bake until the omelette is set underneath but runny on top, about 10 minutes.

Scatter bacon over the top of the omelette and continue baking for a few minutes until the top is just set. Serve immediately from the pan. SERVES 2.

Wherever in the world you find French chefs, emphasis is placed on the superb sauces that glorify meat, fish, chicken, vegetables and other foods. What would a tournedos be without Béarnaise Sauce . . . asparagus without Hollandaise or Beurre Blanc? The *Chef Saucier* in a restaurant kitchen is in fact second only in status to the *Chef de Cuisine* . . . he is honoured and he is indispensable.

Béchamel Sauce

Béchamel is perhaps the most widely used French sauce in cooking, both in restaurants and in the home. Its subtle flavour enhances many foods and it is the basis of other sauces such as cheese-flavoured Mornay (see below).

450 ml (¾ pint) milk
1 slice of onion
8 peppercorns
1 bay leaf
1 × 8 cm (3 inch) piece of celery
blade of mace
50 g (2 oz) butter
3 tablespoons flour
salt and freshly ground white pepper
freshly grated nutmeg

Heat the milk with the onion, peppercorns, bay leaf, celery and mace until bubbles form round the edge. Remove from heat, cover and stand 20 minutes. Strain.

Melt the butter in a heavy saucepan and stir in flour. Cook on low heat for 1 minute, stirring all the time, until the roux is a creamy colour. Remove from heat, cool a little and add warm milk. Stir until smoothly blended, then return to medium heat and stir until boiling. Season with salt, pepper and a hint of nutmeg. Simmer gently for 15 minutes, stirring frequently. MAKES about 450 ml (¾ pint).
Note: This recipe makes a sauce of coating consistency. For a flowing or pouring sauce, use 2 tablespoons flour to 450 ml (¾ pint) milk.
Mornay Sauce
450 ml (¾ pint) Béchamel Sauce (see above)
40 g (1½ oz) freshly grated Parmesan, Gruyère
*   or sharp Cheddar cheese*
pinch of dry mustard

Stir the cheese and mustard into hot béchamel sauce and remove from heat. If reheating mornay sauce, use low heat and do not cook for too long or the cheese will become stringy. Alternatively, reheat in a double boiler.

Hollandaise Sauce

This creamy sauce is the classic one to serve with broccoli and asparagus, poached fish and poached eggs. It is part of every good chef's repertoire.

2 egg yolks
1 tablespoon water
1 tablespoon lemon juice
125 g (4 oz) butter, cut into small pieces
salt
freshly ground white pepper

Simmer a little water in a saucepan over which a mixing bowl will fit. Place the egg yolks, water and half the lemon juice in the bowl and whisk over the simmering water until the mixture thickens a little—you will see the bottom of the bowl between strokes and the mixture will cling to the whisk.

Add the butter piece by piece, slipping it through your fingers to soften it slightly and whisking constantly. Incorporate each piece thoroughly before adding the next. If added too quickly, the sauce will not thicken.

When the butter has been added and the sauce is creamy, remove from heat and season with salt, pepper and remaining lemon juice to taste. MAKES about 120 ml (4 fl oz).

Note: Hollandaise should be served warm, not hot. It should not be kept longer than an hour, but may be reheated by placing the bowl in a pan of warm water and, just before serving, beating in 1 teaspoon lukewarm water.

Velouté Sauce

This classic sauce is used by French chefs with many fish and veal dishes, including *quenelles*, and is the base of other sauces. Use the appropriate stock according to the dish the sauce will accompany.

600 ml (1 pint) stock (chicken, fish or veal)
50 g (2 oz) butter
2 tablespoons flour
salt and freshly ground white pepper
few drops of lemon juice
2 egg yolks
2 tablespoons cream

Warm the stock and set aside. Melt the butter in a heavy saucepan, stir in flour and cook over a low heat, stirring constantly, until the roux is a creamy colour. Remove from heat, cool a minute, then add warm stock all at once and stir until smooth.

Return the saucepan to medium heat and stir constantly until boiling. Lower heat and cook very gently for 15 minutes, stirring often. Season with salt, pepper and lemon juice.

Stir the egg yolks and cream together in a small bowl. Add a little of the hot sauce, stir to combine, then return the mixture to the saucepan. Stir over low heat until the sauce is glossy and a little thicker, but do not allow to boil. MAKES about 450 ml (¾ pint).

Sauce Aurore
(Delicious with chicken quenelles.) Add 1½ tablespoons tomato paste and 1 tablespoon butter to 450 ml (¾ pint) velouté sauce made with chicken stock.

Sauce Vin Blanc
(Perfect with fish quenelles.) Combine 50 g (2 oz) chopped mushrooms, 250 ml (8 fl oz) each dry white wine and fish stock in a saucepan and boil rapidly until liquid is reduced to 5 tablespoons. Add 250 ml (8 fl oz) béchamel sauce, or velouté sauce made with fish stock, and season with salt and white pepper. Fold in 120 ml (4 fl oz) double cream or swirl in 50 g (2 oz) butter. Add a few drops of lemon juice and strain. Use to mask quenelles or serve with poached fish.

Béarnaise Sauce

The technique for making Béarnaise Sauce is almost the same as for Hollandaise, but the flavour is more piquant. Serve Béarnaise warm with grilled steak, fish or chicken.

4 tablespoons dry white wine or dry vermouth
4 tablespoons tarragon vinegar
1 spring onion, finely chopped
4 peppercorns, crushed
½ teaspoon dried tarragon
3 egg yolks
225 g (8 oz) butter at room temperature
salt and freshly ground white pepper

Place the wine or vermouth, vinegar, spring onion, peppercorns and tarragon in a saucepan and simmer until reduced to 2 tablespoons of liquid. Strain and cool slightly.

Place reduced liquid and egg yolks in a mixing bowl set over a pan of simmering water. Whisk until the mixture thickens a little, then beat in the butter piece by piece, slipping it through your fingers to soften it slightly and whisking constantly. When all the butter has been added, remove the sauce from the heat and season to taste with salt and pepper. MAKES about 120 ml (4 fl oz).

Note: Serve Béarnaise Sauce warm, not hot. Reheat, if necessary, as for Hollandaise.

✔ Crème Fraîche
A thick cream with a slightly tart flavour. It replaces thickeners in savoury sauces, and can be lightly sweetened to serve with desserts. To make, stir 1 tablespoon buttermilk and 450 ml (¾ pint) double cream over low heat until just tepid. Pour into a bowl, cover with plastic film and a tea-towel and leave in a warm place for 8 hours. Store in the refrigerator.

THE ITALIAN INFLUENCE

There are wonderful Italian restaurants all over the world—the Italian influence has spread far and wide. Some are grand, many are small family affairs. But whether you go out to eat in Naples or New York, Milan or Melbourne, you are aware of the same thing—an atmosphere as colourful and cheerful as the food.

Italian restaurants always seem to me especially happy places. No wonder they are the scene of so many romances on our cinema and TV screens and, of course, in real life! You just can't help feeling more creative, more full of zest, when you eat Italian-style.

Italian cuisine has long been called 'the mother cuisine' because of its influence on other western countries. Such delights as icecreams and other frozen desserts, cakes and pastries began with inventive Italian chefs, and many travellers still believe Italian food is the best in Europe.

One of its great attractions is the amazing variety! Every region in Italy has its favourite dishes based on local produce and tastes, and the best of them find their way on to restaurant menus. In the pasta-loving south you will still be able to try risotto and polenta dishes of the north. Along the coastline, seafood will be featured, but there will also be the great lamb, veal, ham and chicken specialties from other areas. Overall, you will be delighted with the freshness of Italian food. Chefs as well as home cooks still follow the age-old tradition of shopping once a day (sometimes twice). They are proud of their reputations for serving only the freshest vegetables, tree-ripened fruits, fish straight from the sea, new-laid eggs.

With all this freshness and variety—not to say the warmth of the atmosphere—is it any wonder so many of us have come under the spell of the Italian influence!

Butter is the preferred cooking fat in the Italian province of Lombardy—indeed, it is said to have been invented just a few miles from Milan. The story goes that Julius Caesar was the first great man to appreciate its use in cooking. Before that, butter was used by soldiers and athletes for greasing their bodies before sporting competitions and battles. Another reason to 'Hail Caesar!'

Prosciutto con Fichi
🍂 *Prosciutto with Figs*

Prosciutto is the raw, cured Italian ham always cut in paper-thin slices. It is saltier and tangier than ordinary boiled ham, and a perfect partner to fresh fruit. This is a favourite first course throughout Italy, and will also be found on menus of such superb Italian restaurants as *Mario and Franco's Terrazza* in London, *Agostino's* in Washington D.C., and *Beppi's* in Sydney.

12 paper-thin slices of prosciutto
6 ripe figs
crushed ice

Arrange the prosciutto on a chilled platter. Peel figs if desired (though Italians rarely do) and arrange over a bowl of crushed ice. Guests simply help themselves to ham and figs, eating them with a knife and fork. No extra seasoning is required. SERVES 6.

Pâté de Fegato di Vitello
🍂 *Calf's Liver Pâté*

A simple but superb pâté from the *Gritti Palace Hotel* in Venice.

25 g (1 oz) butter
2 tablespoons olive oil
2 medium onions, thinly sliced
350 g (12 oz) calf's liver, cut into bite-size
  pieces
3 tablespoons finely chopped parsley
salt and freshly ground pepper
225 g (8 oz) unsalted butter, softened

Heat the butter and the olive oil in a heavy frying pan. Add onions and stir over moderate heat until soft but not coloured, about 5 minutes. Add liver to the pan. Raise heat to moderately high and toss liver for 5 minutes; or until firm and brown outside but still slightly pink inside. Allow to cool, then stir in parsley and season well with salt and pepper.

Purée the liver mixture in a food processor fitted with the steel blade, then rub through a fine sieve into a bowl. (You may also purée it in a blender, in 2 batches.)

Return the purée to the food processor or blender and add the unsalted butter gradually, about a tablespoon at a time. The butter must be thoroughly incorporated and the mixture smooth.

Moisten a 35 cm (14 inch) piece of foil or waxed

paper and place the pâté mixture in the middle. Using a spatula, smooth it into a log shape about 20 × 5 cm (8 × 2 inches). Roll the foil or paper around the log, twist the ends together, and squeeze to expel air bubbles. Chill the pâté for at least 2 hours or until firm. Remove the foil or paper, transfer to a serving plate and serve with water biscuits or toast triangles. SERVES 4–6.

Pollo alla Diavola
➥ Devilled Grilled Chicken

Grilled chicken is on the menu of many restaurants in Italy. In Tuscany, it is sometimes basted with a peppery butter mixture as it cooks, and finished with a crisp coating of onion and parsley.

1.5 kg (3½ lb) chicken, cut into quarters
125 g (4 oz) butter, melted
2 tablespoons olive oil
1 small, dried red chilli, seeded and crushed
1 small onion, grated
2 tablespoons finely chopped parsley (preferably
  the flat-leaved Italian type)
1 fat clove garlic, crushed
1 teaspoon salt

Rinse the chicken in cold water and pat dry with paper towels. Place the butter, olive oil and crushed chilli in a small bowl and mix together. In another bowl, mix the onion, parsley and garlic. Add 1 tablespoon of the butter mixture to the onion and parsley and stir into a paste.

Preheat the grill. Brush the chicken pieces all over with the butter-chilli mixture (there will be some left) and sprinkle with salt. Arrange chicken pieces, skin side down, on a rack placed over the grill pan and grill about 10 cm (4 inches) from the heat for 5 minutes. Turn the chicken pieces skin side up, baste with remaining butter mixture and grill for another 5 minutes.

Turn the pieces twice more, each time basting with the buttery juices that have collected in the grill pan. The pieces should be cooked through in about 20 minutes altogether. Test by piercing with a skewer—if the chicken is cooked the juices will run clear, without a tinge of pink.

Turn the pieces skin side up and spread each piece with the onion-parsley paste, patting it on firmly. Grill the chicken for a further 4 minutes or until the coating is lightly browned. Arrange chicken on a heated serving platter and pour the remaining pan juices over. SERVES 4.

Spaghetti alla Boscaiola
➥ Spaghetti with Tuna and Mushrooms

Along the Mediterranean coast, many pasta dishes feature tuna in the sauce, and Italian canned tuna is justly famous for its flavour and quality. You can prepare this spaghetti in the time it takes to sip an *apéritif*—then imagine you are sitting in the sun in Sorrento.

500 g (1 lb) spaghetti
125 g (4 oz) best-quality tuna, packed in oil
120 ml (4 fl oz) olive oil
1 clove garlic, crushed
225 g (8 oz) mushrooms, finely sliced (including stalks)
1 teaspoon salt
¼ teaspoon freshly ground pepper
finely chopped parsley or shredded fresh basil, to
  garnish

Cook the spaghetti in plenty of boiling salted water until tender but still firm. Drain well. Meanwhile, turn the tuna into a small bowl and separate into flakes (do not drain).

Heat the oil in a heavy frying pan and cook the garlic and mushrooms over medium-high heat for 5 minutes, until the mushrooms are tender but still firm. Add the tuna and stir gently until the sauce is blended and piping hot. Season with salt and pepper.

Arrange the freshly cooked, hot spaghetti on a serving platter, spoon the sauce over and sprinkle with parsley or basil. SERVES 6.

Prugne Farcite
➥ Stuffed Prunes

The Calabrian area of Italy is famous for its honey, figs, almonds and dried fruits, which are exported all over the world. Use the best-quality dessert prunes you can find for this delicious Calabrian sweetmeat.

500 g (1 lb) large prunes
75 g (3 oz) walnuts, roughly chopped
125 g (4 oz) dark chocolate, grated

Soak the prunes in boiling water to cover for 5 minutes. Drain and pat dry. Make a slit in the side of each prune just large enough to extract the stone, then pull apart slightly to make room for the filling.

Mix together the walnuts and chocolate, fill the prunes with the mixture, then reform into shape.

Serve the prunes in small paper patty cases, or piled high on a serving dish. Superb with after-dinner coffee. SERVES 10–15.

➥ Pesto Pantesco

From Sicily, a bright variation of pesto sauce, to serve over freshly cooked pasta. Purée in a blender (or pound with a mortar and pestle) 2 chopped cloves garlic and 2 ripe tomatoes, skinned, seeded and chopped. Transfer the mixture to a bowl and stir in 6 tablespoons finely chopped fresh basil, 2 tablespoons olive oil, and salt and cayenne pepper to taste. Makes about 250 ml (8 fl oz).

Cold vegetables are often served with main courses in Italy. The chef will obligingly heat the vegetables for you on request, but try the hot-cold combination first—I think you will enjoy it. One of my favourites is spinach, the leaves left whole, lightly cooked, then sprinkled with olive oil and lemon juice.

❧ Prosciutto-Asparagus Appetizer

A delightful first course from Italy. For each serving, allow 1 large, paper-thin slice of prosciutto and 4–5 freshly cooked young asparagus spears. Arrange the spears on one half of the prosciutto, fold the other half over and sprinkle lavishly with grated Parmesan cheese. Place under a hot grill just until cheese melts— too much cooking will harden the prosciutto. Serve at once.

Pomodori alla Romana
❧ *Tomatoes Stuffed with Herb-Anchovy Rice*

Italian cooks are adept at making remarkable dishes from their beautiful vegetables and just a little meat or fish. They may have originated from a need for economy, but have now become restaurant favourites—even in hotels as grand as the *Hotel Hassler* in Rome.

4 large, ripe tomatoes
salt
225 g (8 oz) cooked, long-grain rice
2 tablespoons finely chopped parsley
25 g (1 oz) chopped, fresh basil or 2 tablespoons dried basil with extra 15 g (½ oz) parsley
4 tablespoons olive oil
8 flat, canned anchovy fillets, drained and chopped
4 cloves garlic, crushed
freshly ground black pepper
sugar

Cut a slice from the top of each tomato and set slices aside. Scoop out pulp with a sharp-edged spoon, leaving a shell about 1 cm (½ inch) thick, and place pulp in a sieve set over a bowl. Sprinkle inside shells with salt and stand upside down on paper towels to drain. Rub the pulp through the sieve and discard the seeds.

Place rice, parsley, basil, oil, anchovies, garlic and 120 ml (4 fl oz) of the tomato pulp in a bowl and mix lightly together. Season to taste with salt and pepper and a dash of sugar.

Stand tomato shells upright in an oiled, shallow baking dish just large enough to hold them (prop them up with crumpled aluminium foil if necessary). Spoon the rice mixture into each shell and cover tops with reserved slices. Bake in a preheated moderately hot oven (190°C/375°F/Gas 5) for 10–15 minutes, until tomato shells are slightly softened. Serve hot or cold as a first course or as an accompaniment to grilled meat or fish. SERVES 4.

Insalata di Crescione
❧ *Watercress Salad*

A dream shared by many travellers is to spend a long time in the beautiful Tuscany area of Italy. Everything there seems perfect—the climate, the landscape, the friendly people and, of course, the food! In summertime, the salads are especially inventive and colourful. This example is from a family-run restaurant in the small town of Arezzo.

❧ Mustard and Garlic Vinaigrette

Beat together 2 tablespoons wine vinegar, 1 crushed clove garlic, ¼ teaspoon salt, a good grinding of black pepper and 2 teaspoons Dijon mustard. Gradually beat in 4–6 tablespoons olive oil, tasting until the dressing is to your liking.

1 bunch of watercress
50 g (2 oz) Gruyère cheese, cut into small dice
1 large red eating apple, cored and diced (do not peel)
125 g (4 oz) coarsely chopped walnuts
1 small onion, finely chopped
4 hard-boiled eggs, cut into quarters
Walnut Dressing (see below)

Wash and dry the watercress and pick off the tough stems. Place the sprigs in a bowl with the remaining ingredients, toss with dressing and serve at once. SERVES 6 as a first course, 4 as a main course.

Walnut Dressing

Place 120 ml (4 fl oz) walnut oil, 1 tablespoon wine vinegar, ¾ teaspoon salt, ¼ teaspoon freshly ground white pepper in a screw-top jar and shake well. *Note:* If watercress is unavailable, use sliced, tender lettuce or young spinach leaves.

Peperoni Dolci all'Olio
❧ *Sweet Pepper Salad*

Sweet peppers (capsicums) are a favourite vegetable in Italy. They are usually on the *antipasti* table in one form or another as well as accompanying main dishes or going into stews and casseroles. I enjoyed a marvellous pepper salad—served from a silver chariot!—as part of an *antipasti* at the *Ristorante Sabatini* in Florence.

4 medium red or green peppers or a mixture
Mustard and Garlic Vinaigrette (see left)
2 large, ripe tomatoes, skinned and thinly sliced
2 medium onions, sliced
parsley or fresh basil, to garnish

Preheat the grill to very hot. Grill the peppers about 2.5 cm (1 inch) from the heat until the skin blackens and blisters, then turn and grill the other side. Turn as needed until all the skin is blistered. Cut the peppers in half lengthwise, remove ribs and seeds and rub off the skin. Cut into lengthwise strips about 1 cm (½ inch) wide.

Place peppers in a bowl, cover with mustard vinaigrette and leave for 20 minutes. Arrange peppers, tomatoes and onions on a serving platter and sprinkle with chopped parsley, or fresh basil cut into tiny ribbons. Serve as a first course with crusty bread. SERVES 4.

Pomodori alla Romana; Peperoni Dolci all'Olio;
Insalata di Crescione

Carciofi Ripieni alla Siciliana
❧ Stuffed Artichokes Braised in Olive Oil

The Italians have made a fine art of preparing vegetables . . . as you will agree when you taste this Sicilian specialty. Large globe artichokes (in Sicily, about the size of an orange) are stuffed with breadcrumbs, cheese and parsley, then cooked slowly in olive oil and garlic.

6 globe artichokes
lemon juice
6 cloves garlic, roughly chopped
170 ml (6 fl oz) olive oil
STUFFING
75 g (3 oz) fine, soft breadcrumbs
75 g (3 oz) freshly grated Parmesan cheese
25 g (1 oz) finely chopped parsley
salt and freshly ground pepper
2–3 tablespoons melted butter

Cut the stems from the artichokes and with scissors trim 1 cm (½ inch) from the tip of each leaf. Brush cut surfaces with lemon juice as you work to prevent them discolouring.

Bring a large saucepan of salted water to the boil, add artichokes (in 2 batches if necessary) and parboil for 10 minutes. Drain and press the leaf ends down against a board to open them slightly.

Mix stuffing ingredients together, adding just enough melted butter to bind them into a workable mixture. With your fingers, press stuffing between the leaves so there is some at the base of each leaf. Sprinkle garlic on the bottom of a heavy casserole dish and arrange artichokes upright on top. Add

The Bologna region of Italy is rich in food legends. One of the most enchanting explains the invention of tortellini, the little dimpled parcels of pasta dough. It is said that when Venus stayed overnight at a trattoria with Mars and Bacchus, the cook caught a glimpse of her naked beauty the morning after. Inspired, he created tortellini in the shape of her perfect navel!

enough water to give a depth of about 1 cm (½ inch) and pour the oil over the artichokes. Cover the casserole tightly and bake in a preheated moderate oven (180°C/350°F/Gas 4) for 45 minutes or until a leaf pulls out easily. (During this time, baste artichokes once or twice with liquid in the dish.) If using a flameproof casserole, cook over gentle heat for about 30–40 minutes.

Serve 1 artichoke to each diner, with a little of the pan juices spooned over. A leaf at a time is pulled out and the tender base eaten with its stuffing. Then the hairy choke—not always present in young artichokes—is removed with a spoon and the tender heart eaten. Don't forget to provide finger bowls and an extra plate for the discarded leaves. SERVES 6.

Veal Piccata
❧ Veal with Lemon

Visitors to Italy should not make a trip from Florence to Venice without a stop in the ancient walled city of Verona—setting for Shakespeare's *Romeo and Juliet*. If you visit the *Ristorante delle-Tre Corone* (Restaurant of the Three Crowns), you will find many simple but subtle veal dishes on the menu. I suggest you try this one with another house specialty, home-made *fettucine* noodles.

6 veal steaks
flour for dusting
salt and freshly ground pepper
75 g (3 oz) plus 2 teaspoons butter
juice of 2 lemons
2 tablespoons finely chopped parsley
thin slices of lemon, to garnish

Place the veal between 2 sheets of plastic film and pound with a steak mallet or rolling pin to make it as thin as possible without breaking through. Trim ragged edges and cut each in two, then dust with flour and season well with salt and pepper.

Heat the 75 g (3 oz) butter in a large, heavy frying pan over fairly high heat. When foam subsides, add veal pieces a few at a time and brown on both sides (this will only take about 1 minute each side). Transfer each batch to a heated serving platter and keep warm.

Add lemon juice and parsley to the pan and stir well to scrape up the brown crusty bits from the bottom. Remove the pan from the heat and stir in the 2 teaspoons butter in small pieces. Taste for seasoning, spoon over the veal and serve at once garnished with lemon slices. SERVES 6.

Involtini di Vitello
🐦 *Stuffed Veal Rolls*

Guests at the *Grand Hotel* in Venice always choose to have at least one meal on the terrace at the water's edge. It is a memorable experience. Delicate veal, stuffed with cheese and rolled into little 'birds', is a house specialty.

4 thin veal steaks
175 g (6 oz) ricotta cheese
125 g (4 oz) minced or very finely chopped ham
salt and freshly ground pepper
2 tablespoons oil
40 g (1½ oz) butter
4 tablespoons Marsala

Place the steaks between 2 sheets of plastic film, and beat with a steak mallet or rolling pin until very thin. Trim any ragged edges; if large, cut the steaks in two.

Blend ricotta and ham and spread on the steaks. Roll up, tie with white thread, and season with salt and pepper. Heat oil and butter in a heavy frying pan and cook the rolls slowly until browned on all sides and tender, about 20 minutes. Remove the rolls, cut away threads, and arrange on a heated serving platter.

Add Marsala to the pan juices and boil over high heat for 1 minute or until syrupy, scraping up the brown bits from the bottom. Taste for seasoning, spoon over the rolls and serve at once with creamy mashed potatoes. SERVES 4.

Tortellini Alfredo
🐦 *Pasta with Prosciutto, Cream and Cheese*

The *Trattoria da Alfredo* in Rome specializes in pasta. Luckily, we can now buy frozen or dried *tortellini* (little pasta 'dumplings' stuffed with meat or spinach) from Italian groceries and many supermarkets, making it easy to enjoy this creamy, colourful dish at home.

500 g (1 lb) tortellini
125 g (4 oz) butter
150 ml (¼ pint) double cream
5 thin slices of prosciutto (raw ham), cut into ribbons
50 g (2 oz) cooked green peas
125 g (4 oz) freshly grated Parmesan cheese
salt and freshly ground pepper
extra grated Parmesan, to serve

Drop the tortellini (do not thaw if using frozen) into

a large saucepan of boiling, salted water and cook for 15–25 minutes until tender. Drain in a colander.

Melt the butter in a heavy frying pan over moderate heat, add tortellini and stir gently until coated with butter. Add cream, prosciutto and peas and cook gently until the cream thickens slightly. Stir in grated Parmesan and season with salt and pepper to taste. Serve with extra Parmesan and a peppermill for diners to grind extra pepper on top. SERVES 6–8.

Abbacchio alla Cacciatora
🐦 *Spring Lamb with Wine and Anchovy Sauce*

The true *abbacchio* appears on Italian menus only in spring. It is baby, milk-fed lamb, with meat almost white and meltingly tender. Our nearest equivalent is young spring lamb.

1 kg (2 lb) boneless lamb from leg, shoulder or loin, cut into large cubes
2 tablespoons olive oil
40 g (1½ oz) butter
salt and freshly ground pepper
1 tablespoon flour
1 clove garlic, crushed
½ teaspoon each chopped, fresh rosemary and sage (or a good pinch of each, dried)
1 small green pepper, seeded and coarsely chopped
250 ml (8 fl oz) dry white wine
120 ml (4 fl oz) wine vinegar
250 ml (8 fl oz) hot Chicken Stock (page 90) or water
6 drained, canned anchovy fillets, finely chopped
chopped parsley, to garnish

Dry the lamb with paper towels. Heat the oil and butter in a large heavy saucepan or flameproof casserole and brown the lamb on all sides over medium heat. Season well with salt and pepper, sprinkle the flour over the top and stir into the fat. Add garlic, herbs, pepper, wine and vinegar to the pan and stir until boiling and slightly thickened. Add stock or water, cover, and cook very gently for 30 minutes or until lamb is tender. Stir anchovies into the sauce and cook a few minutes longer. Taste for seasoning, and sprinkle with chopped parsley to serve. SERVES 6.

🐦 Court Bouillon
This is the liquid often called for to poach fish. Place in a saucepan 220 ml (8 fl oz) each water and dry white wine, 1 bay leaf, 2 parsley stalks, 4 peppercorns, 1 sliced onion, 1 small sliced carrot, 1 small stick of celery and ½ teaspoon salt. Bring to the boil, then simmer covered for 20 minutes. Strain and use as recipe directs. Makes about 450 ml (¾ pint).

One of the most unforgettable eating experiences in the world is to enjoy a meal on the inviting waterside terrace of the *Gritti Palace Hotel* in Venice, overlooking the Grand Canal. The gondolas glide past, the work barges bustle along, there is a wedding party, the postal boats, and the rest of the amazing, never-ending water traffic. The food, the wine and the landscape are irreproachable.

Risotto con Scampi
Braised Rice with Prawns

If you love seafood, and if you are lucky enough to be in Venice, you are sure to hear about the restaurant called *La Colomba* (the Dove). To greet you as you enter is a magnificent still-life of lobsters, crabs, scampi, oysters, mussels, clams and other treasures of the Adriatic. You can choose from seven dining-rooms, or eat outdoors on the terrace on warm summer nights.

A beautifully flavoured risotto like this is not difficult to duplicate in your own kitchen.

500 g (1 lb) green prawns
1.1 litres (2 pints) water
1 fish head or small, whole fish
1 stick of celery, sliced
1 small onion, sliced
1 small carrot, sliced
1 bay leaf
salt and freshly ground pepper
75 g (3 oz) butter
2 tablespoons olive oil
1 clove garlic, crushed
200 g (7 oz) raw, short-grain rice
good pinch each of ground cinnamon, nutmeg
*   and cloves*
1 tablespoon finely chopped parsley
3 tablespoons freshly grated Parmesan cheese

If the prawns are still in their shells, peel, devein and place the shells and heads in a large saucepan with the water, fish head or whole fish, celery, onion, carrot, bay leaf and salt and pepper to taste. Bring to the boil, simmer for 30 minutes, then strain into a measuring jug.

Heat 50 g (2 oz) butter and the oil in a wide, heavy saucepan or deep frying pan. Fry the garlic over medium heat for 1–2 minutes, then add the rice and stir until golden. Add 250 ml (8 fl oz) reserved fish stock, cover the pot, and simmer for 10 minutes or until liquid is absorbed. Add another 600 ml (1 pint) stock and simmer, covered, for a further 10 minutes. Add the raw prawns and continue cooking, covered, for 5–6 minutes longer or until prawns are pink and stock absorbed. Gently stir in the spices, remaining butter, parsley and cheese. Taste for seasoning and serve at once on heated plates. SERVES 4.

Risotto con Scampi

Trota al Burro
Trout with Browned Butter

The Italian lakes provide Northern Italy with hand-some salmon trout, perch and carp, which are shown particular deference in surrounding restaurant kitch-ens. I think this combination of tender pink trout with crunchy croûtons is especially good.

Court Bouillon (page 29)
4 trout, about 225 g (8 oz) each, cleaned
75 g (3 oz) butter
2 thick slices of white bread, crusts removed and
*   cut into small cubes*
lemon wedges, to garnish

Bring the court bouillon to simmering point in a baking dish or other flameproof dish large enough to hold the fish in a single layer. Place trout in the liquid, cover the pan, and poach over very low heat for 10 minutes or until flesh is tender and flakes easily when tested with a toothpick. (Be careful not to let the liquid boil while trout is cooking—it should barely quiver.) Lift fish from the liquid with a slotted fish or egg slice and arrange on a heated serving dish.

Heat the butter until foaming, and fry the bread cubes until they are crisp and golden and the butter is lightly browned. Spoon hot butter and croûtons over trout and serve at once with lemon. SERVES 4.

Calamaretti con Aglio
Baby Squid with Garlic

The region of Italy known as Marche (the Marches) lies between the Apennine ranges and the Adriatic. The fishermen of the area are famous for their skill and the seafood dishes are memorable. Among the dishes you will enjoy is this great way with squid.

1 kg (2 lb) prepared baby squid (see right)
4 tablespoons olive oil
2 cloves garlic, peeled and smashed but not crushed
salt and freshly ground pepper
4 tablespoons finely chopped parsley
juice of ½ lemon

Cut the prepared squid into circles, or lengthwise into 4. If liked, the tentacles may also be cooked.

Heat the olive oil gently with the smashed garlic cloves until they begin to brown, then discard garlic. Add pieces of squid, season with salt and pepper and cook over brisk heat for 1 minute. Sprinkle with parsley and lemon juice and serve very hot with triangles of fried bread. SERVES 4.

Cleaning Squid
Pull the head and body of the squid apart—the intestines will pull out with the head. Discard head and intestines. Cut off tentacles just below the eyes and remove the transparent quill from inside the body sac. Rinse the sac well, peel off the purple outside membrane and pull off the back fins. Reserve tentacles, sac and fins and use as recipe directs. Octopus is cleaned in the same way.

Gnocchi Verdi
Spinach Gnocchi

This dish is one of Tuscany's many contributions to good food. It is served everywhere you travel in the province, from small family eating-houses to the restaurants of 4-star hotels. Sometimes, the pretty little green pasta dumplings are served as a first-course; other times I've enjoyed them with a tomato and basil salad as a main course. Always, they have been absolutely delicious. (Illustrated on page 22.)

750 g (1½ lb) spinach
125 g (4 oz) butter, softened
350 g (12 oz) ricotta cheese
salt and freshly ground pepper
freshly grated nutmeg
3 eggs
3 tablespoons flour
75 g (3 oz) grated Parmesan cheese
extra grated Parmesan, to serve

Remove white stalks from the spinach and wash the leaves well. Place in a saucepan with only the water clinging to the leaves and cook, covered, until tender. Drain thoroughly and chop finely in a food processor fitted with the steel blade, or very finely by hand. Place in a large saucepan with one-third of the butter and the ricotta cheese. Beat well together, then place over low heat and stir constantly until butter has melted and the mixture is smooth, about 4 minutes. Remove from heat, and season with salt, pepper and nutmeg to taste.

Beat in the eggs one at a time, then beat in the flour and one-third of the Parmesan cheese. Spread out on a flat dish and chill until firm.

Using floured hands, form tablespoons of the mixture into cork-shaped dumplings.

Fill a large pan half-full of lightly salted water and bring to the boil. Lower 4 or 5 dumplings into the water at once and keep them at a steady simmer until they bob to the surface of the water and look puffy. (Be careful not to let the water boil too hard while they are cooking or they may disintegrate.)

Drain the cooked gnocchi on paper towels, then repeat with the remaining mixture. When all are cooked, butter a shallow baking dish with half the remaining butter and arrange gnocchi on top in a single layer. Sprinkle the remaining Parmesan cheese over and dot with the rest of the butter. Place the dish under a preheated hot grill for 1–2 minutes to brown cheese and melt butter. Serve at once with extra grated Parmesan cheese. SERVES 6 as a first course, 4 as a main course with salad and bread.

The wine synonymous with Italy is *Chianti*, in its romantic straw-covered bottle. Watch for the bottle labelled *Chianti Classico*, with its symbol of a black cockerel on a gold ground. This is the registered trademark of a group of growers who still raise their grapes on the beautiful slopes of the Chianti Hills, between the ancient cities of Florence and Siena in Tuscany, and is a good guide to quality.

Pollo Grillettato alla Siciliana
Chicken with Onions and Marsala

Lord Nelson victualled his fleet in Marsala, Sicily, and is said to have been one of the early customers of the now famous fortified wine of the area. Today, it often appears in delicious sauces for veal and chicken, adding an intriguing touch of sweetness. You will find this dish on menus throughout Italy.

1.5 kg (3½ lb) chicken, or 1.5 kg chicken pieces
   (breasts and thighs)
225 g (8 oz) tiny onions
4 tablespoons olive oil
50 g (2 oz) butter
salt and freshly ground pepper
120 ml (4 fl oz) Marsala
2 ripe tomatoes, skinned, seeded and chopped
1 tablespoon chopped parsley
120 ml (4 fl oz) hot Chicken Stock (page 90)
extra chopped parsley, to garnish

If using a whole chicken, cut it into serving pieces. Wash the chicken pieces and pat dry with paper towels. Peel onions and parboil for 5 minutes in salted water. Drain and pat dry.

Heat the oil and butter in a frying pan or flameproof dish large enough to take the chicken in one layer. Add chicken and onions and sauté over moderately high heat until lightly browned, turning to brown evenly. Season with salt and pepper, add Marsala to the pan and simmer until it is reduced by half. Add the remaining ingredients and cover the pan.

Cook gently until chicken is tender and juices run clear when tested with a skewer—about 20 minutes. (Check from time to time and add a little extra stock if liquid is drying out.) Arrange chicken on a heated serving dish, spoon sauce over and sprinkle with chopped parsley. SERVES 4.

Cenci Fiorentina
Fried Sweet Pastry Strips

The word *cenci* means 'rags', and is an affectionate way of referring to the rather tattered appearance of these crisp, light pastry strips! You will find them one of the irresistible delights of eating in Italy, and luckily they are available everywhere—from street stalls and carnivals to smart little pâtisseries.

225 g (8 oz) flour
25 g (1 oz) butter, softened
2 egg yolks, lightly beaten
1 egg white, lightly beaten
pinch of salt
1 tablespoon caster sugar
2 tablespoons white wine
oil for deep frying
icing sugar for dusting

Sift the flour into a bowl and work in the butter with the fingertips. Make a well in the centre and add egg yolks, egg white, salt, sugar and wine. Gradually stir from the centre out with a wooden spoon, until all the flour is incorporated. (If necessary, add a little extra wine to make a pliable, fairly soft dough.) Form dough into a ball, wrap in plastic and chill for 1 hour.

Divide dough in two. Roll each part out very thin on a floured surface (as thin as possible without tearing) and then cut into strips about 1 cm (½ inch) wide and 20 cm (8 inches) long.

Tie each strip into a loose knot and deep fry in hot oil, a few at a time, until crisp and golden. Remove each batch with a slotted spoon and drain on paper towels. When all are cooked, pile on to a large, heated platter and dust generously with icing sugar. Serve with coffee as a snack, or for dessert. SERVES 6.
<u>Note</u>: Oil should be heated to 190°C/375°F, when a bread cube browns in 25–30 seconds.

Dolce Cavour
❧ *Chocolate-Orange Meringue Cake*

There is a delightful little family trattoria in Florence called *Camillo*, named after the 19th-century statesman, Count Camillo Cavour. Also in honour of this great statesman (twice Prime Minister of Italy), the *Camillo* proudly serves *Dolce Cavour*, a delectable meringue dessert.

5 egg whites
pinch of cream of tartar
275 g (10 oz) caster sugar
1 teaspoon vanilla
450 ml (¾ pint) double cream
4 tablespoons Grand Marnier or Orange Curaçao
2 tablespoons icing sugar
175 g (6 oz) dark chocolate, coarsely grated

Whisk the egg whites with cream of tartar until they hold soft peaks. Add the sugar, 50 g (2 oz) at a time, beating well after each addition. Add vanilla and continue to beat until the meringue holds stiff peaks.

Using a 23 cm (9 inch) round cake tin as a guide, trace 2 circles on to sheets of parchment cooking paper placed on baking trays.

Transfer the meringue to a piping bag, fitted with a 1 cm (½ inch) tube, and pipe circles of meringue on to the traced circles, filling them completely.

Also make 10 small rosettes of meringue with the piping bag on to the parchment paper, or use a teaspoon to shape 10 small balls. (These will be used as decoration.)

Bake the meringues in a preheated very slow oven (120°C/250°F/Gas ¼) for 20 minutes. Turn the oven off and leave the meringues in the oven for 6 hours or until dry. Whip the cream until it holds stiff peaks, then fold in the liqueur, icing sugar and chocolate.

Place 1 meringue on a serving plate, spread half the chocolate cream on top and cover with the second meringue. Spread the remaining cream over and decorate with a circle of meringue rosettes. Chill, loosely covered, for 24 hours before serving. SERVES 6–8.

Gelato Albichocche
❧ *Apricot Icecream*

Fresh fruit icecreams are favourites throughout Italy, but when it comes to apricots they often use the dried variety because the flavour is more concentrated. Here is a Florentine recipe for apricot icecream that is superb.

175 g (6 oz) dried apricots
450 ml (¾ pint) double cream
6 egg yolks
50 g (2 oz) sugar

Soak the apricots overnight in just enough cold water to cover. Next day, place apricots and soaking liquid in a saucepan and cook for 20 minutes, or until apricots are tender and liquid has evaporated. Put in a blender or rub through a sieve to make a purée.

Beat cream and egg yolks together in the top of a double boiler and place over gently simmering water. Stir constantly until the custard coats the back of a metal spoon, then remove from heat and stir in sugar until sugar dissolves. Allow to cool, then combine with apricot purée.

Process in an electric icecream-maker (*sorbetière*) or pour into a round cake tin and place in freezer. When the mixture starts to set around edges, stir vigorously and continue to stir every 10 minutes until firm, about 2 hours. (Constant stirring helps to give a creamy texture.) SERVES 6–8.

❧ Ricotta Dessert
Creamy ricotta cheese is the basis of many delicious Italian desserts. Serve this with stewed fruit. Beat together 350 g (12 oz) ricotta, 50 g (2 oz) caster sugar, 1 tablespoon chopped, candied peel, 2 tablespoons chopped nuts, 120 ml (4 fl oz) double cream and 2 teaspoons grated lemon rind. Fold in 6 tablespoons grated dark chocolate. Bellissima!

ASIA AND THE ORIENT

In many Western countries, Chinese restaurants head the popularity lists when people are asked where they like to eat out. Indian restaurants are favourites, too—everyone loves a curry, or chicken spiced and seasoned in a myriad different ways. And as more and more cooks from the East settle in Western countries, our big cities offer food from Japan, Indonesia, Vietnam, Thailand, Malaysia and more.

Luckily, now that travel to Asia and the Orient is within the reach of so many people, we also have the added interest of trying favourite and new dishes in their home countries.

I have been devoted to Asian and Oriental food as long as I can remember, and have had the chance to visit most Eastern countries. In many of them, including India, Japan, Hong Kong, Taiwan and the People's Republic of China, I have worked beside chefs in restaurant kitchens, learning invaluable on-the-spot 'tricks of the trade'.

Luckily, cooking Eastern dishes at home is easier than ever with so many Asian grocery shops importing authentic ingredients. Even the local supermarket and delicatessen can now supply all that's required for many dishes.

That doesn't mean you have to cook a complete traditional meal to enjoy the exciting flavours and textures of Asian and Oriental food. You can choose just one course from these restaurant dishes, and add your own ideas to round out the meal. For example, the Chinese Smoked Meatballs make a marvellous opening course for a dinner party, or can be made smaller to serve with drinks. The Indian dish of Baked Chicken in Yogurt is a splendid buffet idea, served with rice and your favourite salads.

As a talking point for any luncheon, try Sashimi, the delicate Japanese way with raw fish. Add a platter of fresh fruit and lunch is complete! And for a cool dessert that can follow any main course, I recommend the Malaysian combination of Almond Jelly with Lychees.

I think you will find the recipes in this chapter will help you to plan menus that are flexible as well as intriguing. You will certainly be sharing many of my happiest working and eating experiences when you try them.

Every visitor to Peking wants to try authentic Peking Duck. Oddly enough, Peking Duck isn't really Chinese in origin! The legendary dish had its modest beginning when Mongol invaders insisted on roasting duck and other poultry, in the face of Chinese tradition, which considered roasting a wasteful use of precious fuel.

Suan Ni Bai Jou
❧ Cold Pork Slices with Garlic Sauce

The Chinese Western provinces of Szechwan and Hunan make great use of garlic, the famous Szechwan peppercorns, and hot pepper oil. The pepper oil used in this dish is not intended to overpower other flavours, but to sensitize the taste buds so they appreciate the pungency of garlic and the lemony tartness of fresh coriander—often bought as Chinese parsley. It is an easy and delicious beginning to a Chinese meal, or part of an *hors d'oeuvre* platter.

750 g (1½ lb) boneless pork, fillet or loin
3 spring onions, chopped
1 teaspoon salt
2 slices of fresh ginger, chopped
3 tablespoons rice wine
water, to cover
2 tablespoons finely chopped fresh coriander, to garnish
SAUCE
3 cloves garlic, crushed
2 tablespoons soy sauce
1–2 teaspoons Chinese hot pepper oil (see Note)
1 teaspoon wine vinegar
1 teaspoon sugar

Place the pork in a saucepan with onions, salt, ginger, wine and water to cover. Bring the liquid to the boil, cover the pan, and simmer for 30 minutes or until meat is tender. Transfer to a cutting board and allow to cool (but do not chill). Trim meat of any fat, slice across the grain into paper-thin slices and arrange on a serving platter.

Combine all the sauce ingredients, adding the smaller amount of pepper oil first, then adding more as necessary to suit your own taste. Pour the sauce over the pork slices and sprinkle with chopped coriander. SERVES 6 as a first course.
Note: Chinese hot pepper oil is available from Asian grocery shops. However, it is easy to make your own: crush enough dried, red chillies in a mortar to make 4 tablespoons. Heat 4 tablespoons peanut oil until smoking, remove from the heat and add crushed chillies. Allow to stand for 30 minutes, then strain through a fine sieve into a jar and store tightly covered.

Rathu Isso Curry
🐟 *Prawn Curry*

Every South-East Asian country has its version of prawn curry. I enjoyed this one when I tasted it many years ago in Sri Lanka—and now this beautiful island is once more becoming a top tourist attraction, its cuisine will be appreciated by more and more people.

500 g (1 lb) green prawns, shelled and deveined
juice of 1 lime or 1/2 lemon
1/4 teaspoon saffron threads, soaked in 1
*   tablespoon hot water*
5 garlic cloves, crushed
3 curry leaves or 1 small bay leaf
2 teaspoons grated fresh ginger
2 cloves
1 teaspoon ground cinnamon
1/2 teaspoon ground fenugreek
1/2 teaspoon crushed cardamom
1/4 teaspoon cayenne pepper or to taste
2 tablespoons peanut oil
2 large, ripe tomatoes, skinned, seeded and chopped
250 ml (8 fl oz) Coconut Milk (page 38)
salt

Mix the prawns with the lime or lemon juice and the saffron and water in a large bowl. Add garlic, curry leaves or bay leaf, ginger and spices; then cover and stand at room temperature for 1 hour.

Heat oil in a wok or heavy frying pan, add prawn mixture and sauté briskly for 2 minutes or until prawns turn pink. Remove prawns with a slotted spoon and set aside. Add tomato to the pan and fry gently for 3 minutes, then add coconut milk and simmer until mixture thickens a little. Stir in salt to taste. Return prawns to pan, heat through and serve at once. SERVES 2–3 with rice.
Note: If saffron is unobtainable or too expensive, substitute 1 teaspoon turmeric.

Lassi
🐟 *Yogurt Drink*

An iced drink that is Indian in origin, but also popular in South-East Asia.

2 tablespoons plain yogurt
170 ml (6 fl oz) iced water
pinch of salt

Blend the yogurt, water and salt in a blender or with a rotary beater. Pour over ice cubes in a tall glass. SERVES 1.

Kao Yang Jou Ch'uan
🐟 *Oriental Lamb Kebabs*

Lamb is popular in Northern China, and a beautifully seasoned dish of skewered lamb is featured at the famous *Peking Duck* restaurant in Peking. There, it is served with steamed lotus buns, but at home you can enjoy it with boiled rice and sweet bean paste for dipping.

1 teaspoon Szechwan peppercorns (from Asian
*   food stores) or black peppercorns*
4 tablespoons light soy sauce
2 tablespoons Chinese rice wine or dry vermouth
1 tablespoon finely chopped garlic
1 tablespoon finely chopped fresh ginger
2 teaspoons Chinese sesame oil
1 teaspoon five-spice powder
1/4 teaspoon freshly ground white pepper
1 kg (2 lb) boneless lamb shoulder, trimmed and
*   cut into bite-size cubes*
6 long bamboo skewers
sweet bean paste (from Asian food stores), to
*   serve*

Place the peppercorns in a small, heavy frying pan and stir over moderate heat for 3 minutes or until fragrant. Pulverize in a blender, or by hand with a mortar and pestle, and place in a large bowl. Add soy sauce, wine, garlic, ginger, sesame oil, five-spice powder and pepper and stir to combine. Add the lamb to the marinade, tossing to coat each piece, and leave covered for 3 hours at room temperature or overnight in the refrigerator.

Soak the skewers in water for 1 hour (to prevent charring). Then thread drained pieces of lamb on to skewers, leaving a little space between each piece. Reserve the marinade.

Arrange skewers on a rack placed over a grill pan and grill about 10 cm (4 inches) from the heat for 8–10 minutes. While lamb is cooking, turn skewers to cook evenly and baste several times with reserved marinade. Serve with rice and sweet bean paste. SERVES 6.

🐟 Chinese Chicken Stock
Place in a large saucepan 500 g (1 lb) chicken bones or pieces (backs, necks, wings), 8 peppercorns, 1 stick of celery, 2 slices of onion, 2 slices of fresh ginger, 4 fresh coriander or parsley stalks. Cover with cold water, bring to simmering point and simmer, covered, for 1 hour. Strain, cool, chill, and lift off fat before using.

Murgh Mussallam
🐟 *Chicken Baked in Yogurt*

The Moguls who settled in Northern India in the 16th century brought with them a love of delicately spiced meat cooked in yogurt. Many dishes have survived unchanged—this one from a New Delhi restaurant is said to be an authentic Mogul recipe. We can now buy a mixture of spices already blended under the name *garam masala*—a marvellous shortcut for the home cook.

10 meaty chicken pieces (legs, thighs, breasts),
  skinned
4 tablespoons lemon juice
3 teaspoons salt
MARINADE
1 large onion, coarsely chopped
pinch of saffron soaked in 1 tablespoon hot
  water or 2 teaspoons turmeric
1 clove garlic, peeled
1 small fresh chilli, seeded, or to taste
4 slices of fresh ginger, coarsely chopped
1 tablespoon garam masala
220 ml (8 fl oz) natural yogurt
TO GARNISH
lemon wedges
sprigs of fresh coriander or parsley
TO SERVE
pappadams

Make 3 or 4 deep diagonal slashes in the chicken flesh so the marinade can penetrate. Place chicken in one layer in a shallow glass or pottery dish, sprinkle with half the lemon juice and salt and rub well in. Turn pieces over and repeat with the remaining juice and salt. Cover and leave at room temperature for 20 minutes.

Place all marinade ingredients in a blender or food processor fitted with the steel blade and process until smooth. (By hand, chop onion, garlic, chilli and ginger as finely as possible before mixing with other ingredients.) Pour marinade over chicken and rub well into each piece. Cover and refrigerate overnight, turning pieces once or twice.

Next day, drain chicken pieces, reserving marinade. Arrange in one layer in a baking dish, bony side up, and bake in a preheated hot oven (200°C/400°F/Gas 6) for 8 minutes. Remove from oven, turn chicken pieces over and brush with reserved marinade. Bake for another 5 minutes and brush again with marinade. Continue baking until chicken is done, about another 15 minutes. (To test if chicken is cooked, insert a fine skewer in the thickest part of the flesh—juices should run clear.) Serve the chicken hot or at room temperature, garnished with lemon wedges and coriander or parsley. Serve crisp, fried pappadams separately. SERVES 5–6.

Gimbal Udang
🐟 *Prawn and Coconut Fritters*

Visitors to Indonesia will recall delicious tid-bits as part of a buffet spread. At home, serve these intriguing, lacy fritters as a first course before a spicy chicken dish or beef or pork satays.

225 g (8 oz) cooked prawns, shelled, deveined
  and finely chopped
75 g (3 oz) fresh bean sprouts
120 ml (4 fl oz) Coconut Cream (see Note)
1 egg, lightly beaten
5 tablespoons flour, or a little more
4 spring onions, finely chopped
2 teaspoons ground coriander
1 teaspoon ground cumin
salt and freshly ground pepper
small piece lemon grass, crumbled
oil for frying
sprays of fresh coriander and ketjap manis
  (sweet soy sauce), to serve (see Note)

Place the prawns in a bowl with all ingredients, except the oil and *ketjap manis*, and mix well. Heat enough oil in a wok or heavy frying pan to give a depth of about 5 cm (2 inches). Drop a heaped tablespoon of the mixture into the hot oil to test its consistency. The fritter should hold together, but spread out into a lacy circle about 6 cm (2½ inches) across. If fritter breaks up, remove with a slotted spoon and add more flour (a tablespoon at a time) until the mixture is firm enough to fry without breaking.

Fry fritters in batches, 2 or 3 at a time, for 1–2 minutes or until golden-brown and crisp. As they cook, transfer them with a slotted spoon to paper towels to drain. Arrange fritters on a heated platter, garnish with sprays of fresh coriander and serve with a bowl of *ketjap manis* for dipping. SERVES 6 as a first course.

Note: Ketjap manis, lemon grass, fresh bean sprouts and coconut cream should all be available at Asian grocery stores and some supermarkets. Or you can make your own coconut cream (see far left).

Murgh Mussallam

🐟 Coconut Cream
Indispensable in Asian cooking, and easy to make in a blender. Heat 75 g (3 oz) desiccated coconut and 350 ml (12 fl oz) milk just to boiling point. Blend for 30 seconds, then strain through a fine sieve, pressing hard to extract liquid. This gives a thick coconut cream. For coconut milk, repeat the process with the same coconut and another 350 ml (12 fl oz) milk. Use cream or milk as recipe specifies.

Sawsawang Kamatis
❧ Tomato-Ginger Salad

This dish shows the Filipino love of sharp flavours, so refreshing in a humid climate.

4 large, ripe tomatoes
3 spring onions, including some green tops, finely chopped
1 tablespoon lime juice
3/4 teaspoon grated fresh ginger
salt and freshly ground pepper

Cut the tomatoes crosswise into thin slices and arrange in overlapping circles on a platter. Sprinkle with the remaining ingredients, adding salt and pepper to taste. Serve at once. SERVES 4.

Hai Yung Shok Mai Gung
❧ Velvet Crab Corn Soup

The Guangzhou is one of the most famous Cantonese restaurants for foreigners. It serves this traditional soup, better known in the western world made with shredded breast of chicken in place of the crab meat. Both versions are excellent. It is at its best made with fresh, young corn; out of season it is still delicious with canned creamed corn.

75 g (3 oz) crab meat (see Note)
1 litre (1 3/4 pints) Chinese Chicken Stock (page 37)
125 g (4 oz) corn kernels, scraped from the cob
    (or same amount of canned, creamed corn)
salt
1 tablespoon cornflour dissolved in 2 tablespoons
    chicken stock
2 egg whites
2 tablespoons milk
1/4 teaspoon Chinese sesame oil
few drops of Chinese hot pepper oil or hot pepper sauce

Remove any cartilage from crab meat and separate into flakes. Bring chicken stock to the boil and add crab meat, corn and salt to taste. Bring to the boil again, stir in cornflour mixture and continue stirring for a minute or two until mixture thickens.

Beat egg whites and milk lightly together. Remove pan from heat and add the egg whites, stirring constantly. Season with sesame oil and hot pepper oil or sauce. Serve the soup immediately in heated bowls. SERVES 6.
Note: You should get this amount of crab meat from 1 small, cooked crab. Good frozen crab is also widely available from supermarkets and food sections of department stores. Otherwise, use canned crab.

❧ Sesame Noodles
A superb accompaniment to Oriental dishes. Cook 500 g (1 lb) fine egg noodles according to packet directions. While they cook, sauté 2 tablespoons sesame seeds in 75 g (3 oz) butter over moderate heat for 2–3 minutes or until seeds are golden. Stir in 1 tablespoon Chinese sesame oil. Drain noodles, toss with sesame butter and serve at once. Serves 6–8.

Wu Hsiang Cha Chi
❧ Five-Spice Fried Chicken

The Chinese formal banquet usually begins with cold hors d'oeuvre, then an assortment of spicy, crispy dishes that go so well with rice wine. This is one of the dishes I enjoyed at a banquet in Peking. It demonstrates the Chinese method of double-frying, the secret of juicy meat with a deliciously crispy coating.

4 half-breasts of chicken
2 spring onions, flattened with a knife or
    Chinese chopper to release the flavour
1 tablespoon soy sauce
1 tablespoon Chinese rice wine
1 teaspoon finely chopped fresh ginger
1 teaspoon five-spice powder
1 teaspoon Chinese sesame oil
1 teaspoon sugar
1 teaspoon salt
1 egg, lightly beaten
125 g (4 oz) cornflour
peanut oil, for frying

Rinse the chicken breasts in cold water and pat dry. Using a Chinese chopper or heavy knife, cut breasts through the bone into bite-size pieces.

Place remaining ingredients, except egg, cornflour and peanut oil, in a deep bowl and combine well. Add chicken pieces, stirring to coat with the mixture, and marinate, covered, for at least 1 hour in the refrigerator. (The chicken may be left overnight.)

Remove and discard the spring onions and add the egg to the bowl, stirring well. Spread the cornflour out on a sheet of greaseproof paper and roll each piece of chicken in flour, shaking off excess.

Heat the oil in a wok or deep-fryer to medium hot (190°C/375°F) and fry the chicken pieces for 9 minutes. It may be necessary to do this in batches to avoid crowding the pan. As each batch is cooked, remove with a slotted spoon and transfer to paper towels to drain.

Heat the oil to very hot (210°C/425°F) and re-fry the chicken in batches for 1 minute, or until golden-brown and very crisp. Drain each batch on paper towels and serve as soon as all the chicken is cooked. SERVES 6 as a first course.
Note: This recipe is easy if you have a deep-fryer with temperature control, or are familiar with judging the temperatures for deep frying. Otherwise, watch chicken carefully while cooking; you will soon learn to judge temperatures.

I love some of the names given to Chinese dishes. For instance a dish of noodles and minced pork translates as 'Ants Climbing Trees'. A dessert of custard, apples and meringue is called 'Plum Blossom and Snow competing for Spring', while 'Golden Flower and Jade Tree Chicken' describes a recipe with ham, chicken and broccoli. How different in imagination to the American restaurateur who described a Chinese dish on his menu as 'Miscellaneous, with Fried Rice'!

Saté Kuta-Kacang Tanah
🍂 *Chicken Satés with Peanut Sauce*

The sunset hour is a magic time on Kuta Beach, Bali. Balinese and tourists alike gather to watch the golden sunset, and not surprisingly, enterprising local *saté* vendors do brisk business selling hot, spicy morsels on bamboo skewers.

3 boneless chicken breasts, skinned and cut into
   bite-size pieces
10–12 bamboo skewers
Peanut Sauce (see right)
MARINADE
2 cloves garlic
¼ teaspoon salt
2 tablespoons light soy sauce
½ teaspoon brown sugar
1 tablespoon oil

Place the chicken cubes in a bowl. Soak skewers in water to prevent them charring as the chicken cooks.

Crush garlic with salt and mix with remaining marinade ingredients. Pour over chicken, cover, and allow to stand at room temperature for 30 minutes, tossing once or twice.

Remove skewers from water and thread 4–5 pieces of chicken on each one, leaving a little space between the chicken so it will cook evenly. Grill under a preheated grill or over hot coals, turning to brown evenly and brushing several times with the marinade. Cooking time will be about 8 minutes altogether. Serve with peanut sauce poured over, or in a separate bowl. SERVES 4.

<u>Note:</u> Tender steak or boneless pork may be cooked this way. Allow extra cooking time for pork.

<u>Peanut Sauce</u>
1–2 fresh or dried red chillies (or to taste)
3 tablespoons peanut oil
3 cloves garlic, split in half
3 spring onions, including some green tops,
   finely chopped
1 teaspoon trassi (fish paste available at Asian
   food shops)
1 tablespoon light soy sauce
1 tablespoon lemon juice
225 g (8 oz) crunchy peanut butter
1 tablespoon sugar
Coconut Milk as required (page 38)

If using fresh chillies, slit and remove seeds under running water. If using dried chillies, soak in hot water for 5 minutes, then slit and remove seeds.

Heat oil and gently fry garlic and spring onions until crisp. Remove with a slotted spoon and drain on paper towels. Add chillies and fry for 30 seconds, then remove.

Stir *trassi*, soy sauce and lemon juice into the pan and blend well. Turn into a bowl, add peanut butter and sugar, and mix thoroughly together. Allow to cool.

Crumble the garlic, spring onions and chillies into small pieces. Blend into the peanut butter mixture and store in a screw-top jar in the refrigerator. When required, add 2 parts coconut milk to 1 part peanut mixture and stir together over gentle heat until well blended and piping hot.

The basic peanut mixture keeps for weeks, and can also be used as a spread for crisp biscuits or raw salad vegetables.

Hsun Niu Jou Wan
🐟 Smoked Meatballs

The famous *Chang Sing Sik* restaurant in Guangzhou (Canton) is best known for its *dim sum*, and all five floors off the rickety staircase are packed to capacity from dawn to closing time. Like many foreign visitors to the People's Republic of China, I included the *Chang Sing Sik* on my itinerary.

The *dim sum* are served from trolleys stacked with little bamboo steamers containing a seemingly endless variety of delicate and fragrant morsels. Delicious little smoked meatballs are a favourite!

4 dried Chinese mushrooms
1 small can water chestnuts, drained, rinsed and
    finely chopped
500 g (1 lb) lean minced beef
2 tablespoons soy sauce
2 tablespoons cornflour
1 tablespoon finely chopped spring onion
1 tablespoon finely chopped fresh ginger
1 medium carrot, grated
1 tablespoon rice wine or dry sherry
1 teaspoon Chinese sesame oil
FOR SMOKING
2 tablespoons brown sugar
2 tablespoons black tea leaves
2 tablespoons fennel seeds
TO SERVE
2 teaspoons sesame oil mixed with 2 tablespoons
    soy sauce
2 spring onions, finely chopped or shredded

Soak the mushrooms in hot water to cover for 15 minutes or until soft. Drain, remove stems and chop caps finely. Place them with the chestnuts in a large bowl, add the remaining ingredients and mix very well by hand until the mixture is firm and compact. Shape into walnut-size balls and arrange in one layer on a greased wire rack or Chinese bamboo steamer. Cover and steam over boiling water in a wok or deep frying pan for 15 minutes.

To smoke the meatballs, you need an old frying pan, wok or other metal container, lined with foil. Combine brown sugar, tea leaves and fennel seeds and place in the bottom. Set over high heat and when the mixture starts to smoke, put the rack containing the meatballs over the smoke. Cover tightly with a lid or foil and leave for another 5 minutes, then turn heat off and leave meatballs for a further 10 minutes, still covered.

Hsun Niu Jou Wan

To serve, brush the meatballs with a little of the sesame-soy mixture and sprinkle with spring onions. Serve remaining soy-sesame mixture separately, for dipping. SERVES 6–8 as a first course, or 4 as a main course, with rice.
Note: The burnt sugar mixture used for smoking will lift off the wok if you soak it for several hours in water and scrub with a stiff brush. Bamboo steamers are available from Chinese grocery shops.

Huo Tuei Tung Ku Cheng Yu
🐟 Steamed Fish with Ham and Mushrooms

I learned how to cook many superbly flavoured fish dishes at the *Grand Hotel* in Taipei, capital of Taiwan. If your Asian grocery shop can't supply Chinese ham for this recipe, use *prosciutto* (raw, cured ham available from Continental delicatessens).

1 whole white-fleshed fish, weighing about 1.5 kg (3½ lb)
2 thin slices of fresh ginger
1 tablespoon Chinese rice wine, sherry or vermouth
2 teaspoons salt
6 dried Chinese mushrooms, soaked in hot water
    for 20 minutes
75 g (3 oz) thinly sliced Chinese ham or prosciutto, cut
    into 2.5 cm (1 inch) squares
1 tablespoon soy sauce
2 tablespoons finely chopped spring onions,
    including some green tops
1 tablespoon finely chopped fresh ginger
2 tablespoons Chinese sesame oil

Have fish cleaned and scaled, but leave head on. With a sharp knife, make 8 diagonal slashes on one side of the fish, cutting through to the backbone.

Mix sliced ginger, wine and salt in a flat dish and turn fish around in the mixture, rubbing it well into the slashes. Leave for 20 minutes, covered, then discard the ginger.

Drain mushrooms, remove stems and cut the caps in half. Insert a slice or two of ham and a piece of mushroom in each gash on the fish and sprinkle both sides with soy sauce. Place fish on a heatproof serving dish in a steamer (or on a rack) wide enough to hold it flat. *Steam tightly covered for 15–20 minutes or until flesh flakes when tested with a fork.

Remove fish to a heated serving platter and sprinkle with spring onions and chopped fresh ginger. Heat the sesame oil in a small saucepan until smoking hot and pour over the fish. Serve at once. SERVES 2 as a main course, 4 as part of a Chinese meal.
Note: See special note on steaming in this chapter.

🐟 Oriental Fruit Salad

Fresh or stewed fruits make a perfect ending to a spicy Oriental meal. For a fruit salad with an exotic flavour, combine 1 small can lychees with their juice, 1 can mangoes with their juice and 2 tablespoons finely chopped, preserved ginger. Chill until serving time and serve with vanilla icecream with a little ginger syrup poured over.

Hung Shao Niu Jou

Braised Beef in Soy Sauce

The *Hong Bin Lou* restaurant in Peking, in existence for over a century, serves northern, Mongolian food. This combination of flavourings and the slow cooking certainly make something very special from a piece of stewing beef. Serve the beef hot with rice as a main course, or cold, in small portions, as a first course.

1 cup water
4 spring onions, flattened with a knife or
    Chinese chopper to release the flavour
3 slices of fresh ginger, flattened as above
4 tablespoons soy sauce
4 tablespoons Chinese rice wine
3 pieces of star anise (from Asian foodstores and
    some supermarkets)
1 tablespoon sugar
2 tablespoons peanut oil
1 kg (2 lb) stewing beef, trimmed and cut into
    5 cm (2 inch) cubes

Combine all ingredients, except the oil and beef, in a small bowl.

Heat 1 tablespoon of the oil in a wok or large, heavy frying pan. Add half the meat and stir-fry over high heat for 3 minutes or until brown. Transfer to a dish, add remaining oil to the pan and brown the rest of the meat.

Return first batch of meat to pan with soy sauce mixture, stir to combine and bring to the boil. Cover the pan, reduce heat and simmer until meat is very tender—about 1½ hours. Remove the spring onions, ginger and star anise from the sauce and discard. There should only be about 170 ml (6 fl oz) of sauce left; if necessary, reduce to this amount by rapid boiling. SERVES 6 as a main course, 10 as a first course.

Sesame-Soy Dipping Sauce

For spring rolls, kebabs, grilled prawns, chicken wings, etc. Place in a bowl 120 ml (4 fl oz) soy sauce, 4 tablespoons Chinese rice wine or medium-dry sherry, 2 teaspoons Chinese sesame oil, 1 clove crushed garlic, 2 slices of minced fresh ginger and 1 tablespoon sugar. Combine well and sprinkle with chopped spring onions to serve. Makes about 170 ml (6 fl oz).

Som Tum

Thai Salad

Vegetables and fruits flavoured with peanuts and the fish-based sauce called *nam pla* are combined in many salads you will be served in Thailand. This one is an interesting accompaniment to fried chicken or pork.

50 g (2 oz) finely shredded cabbage
1 large carrot, shredded
40 g (1½ oz) crushed, roasted peanuts
½ small paw paw, peeled and cut into bite-size
    cubes
pinch of dried, ground prawns (optional)

DRESSING
1 tablespoon nam pla (see Note)
2 teaspoons sugar
1 clove garlic, crushed
2 tablespoons lemon or lime juice
3 tablespoons oil
freshly ground pepper

Place cabbage, carrot, peanuts, paw paw and ground prawns in a bowl and toss to combine. Mix dressing ingredients together, adding freshly ground pepper to taste. Pour over salad and toss well; chill. SERVES 4.
Note: *Nam pla* and dried prawns are available at Asian food stores.

Ca Kno Thom

Fish with Pineapple

The Vietnamese have taken their cooking skills all over the world, settling in the USA, Britain, Australia and other countries. This recipe is from a Sydney Vietnamese restaurant, using fresh local snapper and golden Queensland pineapple.

3 tablespoons oil
4 snapper steaks, each weighing about 175 g (6 oz)
6 spring onions, coarsely chopped
½ small ripe pineapple, peeled, cored, and cut
    into bite-size cubes
4 tablespoons nuoc cham (fish sauce)—see Note
4 tablespoons sugar
1 tablespoon Caramel (see below)
shredded spring onions, to garnish

Heat 2 tablespoons of the oil in a heavy frying pan and quickly brown fish steaks on both sides, turning once. Heat remaining oil in a separate small frying pan and toss spring onions and pineapple over moderately high heat until pineapple starts to brown, about 3 minutes.

Put half the pineapple mixture in a shallow casserole dish, arrange fish on top and cover with remaining pineapple. Mix together *nuoc cham*, sugar and caramel, pour into the casserole and cover tightly. Bake in a preheated oven (200°C/400°F/Gas 6) for 15 minutes or until fish flakes easily. Garnish with spring onions and serve with boiled rice. SERVES 4.
Caramel
Stir together 1 tablespoon sugar and 4 tablespoons water over high heat until the mixture turns brown. Remove from heat and add a squeeze of lemon juice. Store in a screw-top jar in the refrigerator.
Note: *Nuoc cham* is the Vietnamese name for the fish sauce known as *nam pla* in Thailand.

Yan Ts'ai Pan Chi Szu

🖎 *Spicy Chicken, Cucumber and Agar Salad*

This main course Chinese salad is particularly interesting, with its unusual combination of textures and flavours. The chef in the Peking restaurant kindly showed me the main points of its preparation.

AGAR
25 g (1 oz) agar strips (see Note)
1 tablespoon Chinese sesame oil
CHICKEN
750 ml (1¼ pints) water
2 slices of fresh ginger
1 tablespoon rice wine or dry sherry
4 half-breasts of chicken
OMELETTE
4 eggs
1 tablespoon water
½ teaspoon salt
peanut oil for cooking
SAUCE
4 tablespoons light soy sauce
3 tablespoons rice vinegar or white wine vinegar
2 tablespoons Chinese sesame oil
1 tablespoon rice wine or dry sherry
2 teaspoons sugar
1 teaspoon salt
CUCUMBER
1 large, peeled cucumber, cut into lengthwise ribbons with a potato peeler (stop before you get to seeds)

Soak the agar in warm water to cover for 2 hours, then drain and pat dry with paper towels. Place in a bowl and toss with sesame oil.

To prepare the chicken: bring water, ginger and wine to the boil, add chicken and poach gently for 10 minutes. Allow chicken to cool in the broth, then remove skin and bones and cut meat into fine strips.

To make the omelette: beat eggs lightly with water and salt. Heat an omelette pan or small frying pan with just enough oil to grease the bottom. Pour in enough egg mixture to make a thin layer, cook until set (this will only take 10 seconds or so), then turn over with an egg slice and cook the other side. Repeat until all egg is used up, being careful to cook it only until firm—not brown. Roll omelettes up tightly, then slice into fine strips. Set aside.

Mix all the sauce ingredients together.

To assemble the salad: choose a large platter and place agar down the centre. Arrange cucumber ribbons on top of agar and chicken on top of cucumber. Place shredded omelette in a border around the edge. Pour sauce over all and serve immediately. SERVES 6–8.

Note: Agar is made from seaweed and looks like transparent Cellophane noodles. It is obtainable from Asian food shops.

Almond Jelly with Lychees

Many eating houses in Kuala Lumpur and Penang in Malaysia serve versions of this popular dessert. Canned mandarins or pineapple chunks may replace the lychees.

600 ml (1 pint) water
3 teaspoons agar agar powder (see Note)
125 g (4 oz) sugar
250 ml (8 fl oz) evaporated milk
½ teaspoon almond essence or to taste
1 × 500 g (1 lb) can lychees in syrup, chilled
6 maraschino cherries, to decorate

Place water in a saucepan and sprinkle agar agar powder over the top. Bring slowly to the boil, then simmer for 5 minutes. Add sugar and milk and heat gently, stirring all the time, until sugar dissolves. Add almond essence drop by drop, to suit your taste. Pour into a cake tin or mould, and chill for 1 hour or until set.

To serve, cut jelly into squares or diamond shapes. Drain lychees and reserve 1 cup of syrup. Arrange jelly pieces and lychees in 6 individual bowls, pour a little syrup over and decorate each serving with a cherry. SERVES 6.

Note: Agar agar powder is a setting agent, like gelatine (from Asian and Oriental food stores). If not available use 1 sachet of gelatine.

What do you drink with a Chinese meal? In China, rice wine is served first with assorted savoury dishes. Then there is a choice of wine, Chinese tea or beer with the rest of the meal. Chinese beer is excellent, by the way, with exotic names such as Dragon Flee Tonic, Crab Apple, Bubble and Chrysanthemum and Double Evaporated!

Mu Sui Pork

🍢 *Spicy Sliced Pork in Pancakes*

The *Pleasure* restaurant in Hong Kong serves a special sliced pork dish, which is eaten in the same fashion as Peking Duck—rolled inside tender little 'doyleys' or pancakes. It is easy to make this version at home.

120 ml (4 fl oz) peanut oil
1 teaspoon grated fresh ginger
2 cloves garlic, crushed
750 g (1½ lb) pork fillet, trimmed of fat and cut into fine shreds
2 tablespoons Chinese rice wine or dry sherry
2 teaspoons sugar
120 ml (4 fl oz) light soy sauce
1 teaspoon pepper
Chinese Pancakes (see below)
sliced spring onions and Chinese bean paste, to serve

Heat the oil in a wok or heavy frying pan and fry ginger and garlic over moderate heat until softened, about 2 minutes. Add pork, increase heat to high, and stir mixture until pork is brown. Add wine, sugar, soy sauce and pepper and continue cooking over moderate heat until liquid is absorbed and pork is dark brown and tender. Serve in pancakes (see below) with spring onions and bean paste. SERVES 8 as a first course, or part of a Chinese meal.

Chinese Pancakes

225 g (8 oz) flour
120–170 ml (4–6 fl oz) boiling water
1½ tablespoons Chinese sesame oil

Sift flour into a mixing bowl and make a well in the centre. Pour in boiling water a little at a time, gradually stirring in the flour. (Use just enough water to make a soft dough.) Knead dough for 10 minutes or until it feels pliable and elastic, then wrap in plastic film and allow to rest for 15 minutes.

Roll out dough to 6 mm (¼ inch) thickness on a lightly floured surface and cut into 5 cm (2 inch) circles. Brush tops of circles with sesame oil and press oiled surfaces together in pairs, sandwich fashion. Roll out each 'sandwich' again into a slightly bigger circle, about 8 cm (3 inches) across.

Lightly grease a heavy frying pan. Cook the pancakes over moderate heat for 1 minute each side. As they are cooked, peel apart and stack on a warm plate until ready to serve. A dab of bean paste is spread on each pancake, then a slice or two of spring onion and a spoonful of pork. The pancake is rolled up and eaten in the hand.

On my visits to the People's Republic of China, I have been intrigued by the number of cold dishes served—something we don't tend to associate with Chinese restaurants in other countries. A banquet will begin with a selection of cold *hors d'oeuvre*, and main courses are sometimes cold. Chinese cooks also buy many foods ready prepared—they appreciate the convenience just as we do in the West!

Sashimi

Sashimi is perhaps the queen of Japanese delicacies. This dish of beautifully sliced fresh, raw fish can be an artistic triumph: the red or white gauzy tints of the fish flesh, arranged on a long narrow dish—it may also be round—with a mound of shredded white Japanese radish (*daikon*), a tiny bowl or mound of the green and pungent horseradish *wasabi* and a little bowl of soy. The beauty of *sashimi* is that it lacks, oddly enough, both the fishy taste and smell. The taste is delicate, but enchanting. Formerly a restaurant dish, it is now easy to prepare at home, with fresh fish so readily available.

500 g (1 lb) fresh white fish fillets (including squid, prawns)
1 piece of daikon (white radish), shredded and soaked in iced water (see Note)
1 stick of celery, shredded and soaked in iced water
1 small carrot, shredded and soaked in iced water
3–5 tablespoons Japanese soy sauce
2 teaspoons wasabi (green horseradish)—see Note

Cut fish into very thin, flat slices, or thicker, oblong slices or strips. (Squid may be cut in ribbons.) Arrange fish decoratively on a chilled plate or 4 individual plates. Decorate with strips of *daikon*, celery and carrot. Cover with a sheet of plastic film and refrigerate for 1 hour. Serve with a tiny bowl of soy sauce and *wasabi* which has been mixed to a paste with water. The fish is dipped in the *wasabi* and then the soy. SERVES 4.

Note: Wasabi comes in powdered form, from Oriental food stores. *Daikon* is a fresh, long white radish, now available from many greengrocers.

Sashimi

Hsieh Jou P'a Tou Fu

Stir-fried Bean Curd with Crab

This light, delicate dish was served to me in a Shanghai restaurant, the *Yangchow*, acclaimed for its superb bean curd dishes.

225 g (8 oz) fresh bean curd
4 spring onions, including some green tops,
    finely chopped
1 teaspoon grated fresh ginger
225 g (8 oz) crab meat, preferably fresh or
    frozen (not canned)
2 tablespoons rice wine or dry sherry
450 ml (¾ pint) Chinese Chicken Stock (page 37)
2 teaspoons salt
1 teaspoon Chinese sesame oil
¼ teaspoon freshly ground white pepper
2 tablespoons water
1 tablespoon cornflour
1 tablespoon peanut oil
2 egg whites, lightly beaten
2 shredded spring onions, to garnish

Rinse bean curd under gently running water, drain, and cut off any hard edges. Cut into 2.5 cm (1 inch) squares. Using separate dishes, mix the chopped spring onions and ginger together, then toss the crab meat with the wine. Mix chicken stock, salt, sesame oil and pepper in another dish. Combine the water and cornflour.

Heat peanut oil in a wok or heavy frying pan over high heat. Add spring onion mixture and stir-fry for 30 seconds. Add stock mixture and bean curd, bring to the boil, add the crab meat and wine then turn heat down and cook for 5 minutes.

Add cornflour mixture to the pan, stirring carefully to avoid breaking the bean curd. Simmer for 1 minute. Add lightly beaten egg whites in a stream, rotating the pan to combine the ingredients. Turn into a heated serving bowl and sprinkle with shredded spring onion. SERVES 6.

Doh Peeazah

Lamb Curry

Many curries in India are merely fragrant, not 'hot'—the heat is controlled by the amount of chilli used, and this is entirely up to the cook! You may certainly decrease the amount of chilli in this dish to suit your own taste—though, for me, it was just right when I enjoyed it at the magnificent *Rambagh Palace Hotel* in the pink city of Jaipur.

175 g (6 oz) ghee (clarified butter)
500 g (1 lb) onions, finely chopped
1 kg (2 lb) boneless lamb shoulder, cut into bite-size cubes
1 teaspoon chilli powder
6 cardamom pods, crushed
1 teaspoon finely chopped fresh ginger
2 tablespoons coriander seeds
250 ml (8 fl oz) water
300 ml (½ pint) natural yogurt
6 cloves garlic, crushed with 2 teaspoons salt
1 teaspoon black cumin seeds
½ teaspoon garam masala
2 tablespoons chopped, fresh coriander

Heat ghee in a large, heavy saucepan and fry onions over moderate heat until softened, about 4 minutes. Remove to a plate with a slotted spoon.

In the semi-tropical southern zone of the People's Republic of China, summer brings an abundance of wonderful fruits. They herald a season that poets and artists have celebrated for centuries as a time to relax and enjoy the gifts of nature. As one poet says: 'On a hot summer's day, you sit in a rattan chair, with a bowl of cold plum juice beside you, and fan yourself lazily.'

A note on steaming

Steaming is a popular method of cooking in China and other Oriental countries, and the stacking bamboo steamers sold in Chinese grocery shops are ideal for both cooking and serving. If you haven't used one before, here is the method:

☐ Line the latticework base of the steamer tray with cheesecloth or other thin, porous fabric rinsed in hot water and squeezed dry. (A plain white, porous tea-towel can be kept for the purpose.)

☐ Arrange the food on top of the cheesecloth. If using more than one steamer at a time, line all the trays and stack them so they interlock. Cover firmly with the steamer lid.

☐ Bring 5 cm (2 inches) of water to the boil in a wok. Place the bamboo steamer over the water so the bottom of the rim touches the water, but the water doesn't touch the food itself. The tray is constructed to permit this.

☐ Steam the food over moderate heat for the length of time the recipe suggests, adding more boiling water, if necessary, to keep the water level constant. Turn off the heat, take off the lid so steam can escape, then remove the steamer.

If you don't have a wok, the steamer can be placed in a frying pan or large saucepan. Adjust the water level as above, so the water touches the base of the rim but not the food.

It is also possible to steam without a bamboo steamer. Line a wire rack with cheesecloth and place food directly on it, or in a heatproof dish. Bring 5 cm (2 inches) of water to the boil in a deep frying pan, wok or wide saucepan, and set the rack or dish in the pan so it is at least 1 cm (½ inch) above water level. (You may need to set the rack on heatproof egg cups or custard cups to elevate it sufficiently.) Cover and steam over moderate heat for the required time, then turn off the heat and remove the lid for steam to escape before lifting the rack or dish from the pan.

Fry the lamb in the same pan until golden—this may need to be done in 2 batches. Remove to the plate of onions.

Add chilli powder, cardamom, ginger and coriander to pan and cook for 2 minutes, stirring constantly. Stir in water and yogurt and bring to simmering point, then add reserved lamb and onions. Cover the pan and cook over gentle heat for 1 hour. Add crushed garlic and salt and cook for a further 30 minutes or until lamb is very tender. Taste for seasoning, spoon into a heated serving bowl and sprinkle with black cumin seeds, garam masala and chopped coriander. SERVES 6.

Raffles Singapore Sling

Raffles hotel in Singapore is one of the great and romantic names of the world. Happily unchanged in a world of change, it still offers the same long, cool drinks at the Long Bar, the ceiling fans, the travellers' palms, the ambience of a more leisurely age. This is the drink no visitor to Raffles would miss—created in 1915 by head barman Ngiam Tong Boon.

2 measures gin
1 measure cherry brandy
1 measure each of fresh orange, lemon and
*   pineapple juice*
1 drop each of Angostura bitters and Cointreau
ice
1 pineapple slice and maraschino cherry, to
*   decorate*

Shake all ingredients well with ice, strain into a tall, chilled glass and decorate with pineapple slice and cherry. MAKES 1 tall drink.

In Thailand, one of the most honoured roles in the restaurant kitchen is that of the fruit carver. With the eye of an artist—and years of meticulous training behind him—he carves jewel-like tropical fruits into flowers and fantasies. Massed together, they are used as table decorations. Arranged on individual plates, they make a still-life dessert almost too beautiful to eat.

THE MIDDLE EAST
AND THE
MEDITERRANEAN

Along Europe's Mediterranean coastline the food seems to have an extra dimension of flavour, colour and freshness. Olive oil, lemons, garlic, olives, herbs, baby vegetables, luscious fruits and magnificent seafood are just some of the local products that contribute to a cuisine honoured with its own name—'Mediterranean Cuisine'. It is a fascinating fact that as you move from inland Europe towards the sea there is a noticeable change in the style of food, culminating in the exuberant, robust cooking of the coastal towns and villages.

Middle Eastern countries bordering the Mediterranean share the same love of fresh fruits and vegetables as their European neighbours. In many cases, dishes have travelled backwards and forwards across the sea, so you can enjoy some of the same things in Turkey and Lebanon that you might in Spain and Greece.

What you may notice, especially in the Middle East, is the emphasis on grains and legumes. Cracked wheat, rice, barley, lentils and chick peas turn up in a myriad different forms, helping to make the Middle Eastern diet one of the healthiest in the world.

There is also the allure of the exotic! Ginger, mint, cumin, coriander, honey, rosewater, cardamom and cinnamon are everyday flavourings; fresh dates come in 10 or more varieties; rich, brightly coloured jams are eaten with tiny spoons as an accompaniment to coffee.

On both sides of the Mediterranean, there is a warm and lavish approach to the serving of food in restaurants. Portions are huge, the welcome genuine, you are encouraged to linger and to come again. There is something about the Mediterranean sun that encourages hospitality as well as beautiful food—whether in Europe or the Middle East.

The *Fujairah Hilton* is a modern architectural interpretation of an ancient *caravanserai*—Fujairah having always been a resting place for ships and caravans. The hotel is built around a shady garden, and has a swimming-pool which—in contrast to the heated pools of cooler countries—is refrigerated to a refreshing temperature!

Gazpacho Andalusia

There are many versions of the refreshing cold soup called *Gazpacho*. In Andalusia in southern Spain it is often highly seasoned and served with separate accompaniments. This soup-cum-salad will be found in many of the small restaurants in Málaga, on the Mediterranean coast looking across at North Africa.

2 slices of white bread, crusts removed
2 cloves garlic, crushed with a little salt
120 ml (4 fl oz) olive oil
3 large ripe tomatoes, skinned, seeded and chopped
1 large cucumber, peeled, seeded and coarsely chopped
1 large pepper, seeded and chopped
1 large onion, chopped
450 ml (¾ pint) tomato juice
250 ml (8 fl oz) white wine or water
4 tablespoons chopped parsley
good pinch each of ground cumin, cinnamon and sugar
salt and freshly ground black pepper
TO SERVE
icecubes and bowls of finely chopped cucumber, onion,
    pepper, parsley, snipped chives and croûtons (page 89)

Using a blender or food processor fitted with the steel blade, purée first the bread, garlic and oil, then add tomatoes, cucumber, pepper and onion and whirl until roughly processed.

Place the mixture in a large bowl and stir in tomato juice, wine or water, parsley, spices, sugar and salt and pepper to taste. Cover soup and chill.

Place a couple of icecubes in each bowl, ladle the chilled soup over and pass accompaniments so each diner can sprinkle his own choice on top. SERVES 6–8.

Chilled Yogurt and Cucumber Soup

Yogurt is used lavishly throughout the Middle East in soups, dips, main courses, desserts and drinks. This soup recipe from Iran has some interesting additions.

50 g (2 oz) sultanas
450 ml (¾ pint) cold water
450 ml (¾ pint) natural yogurt
250 ml (8 fl oz) double cream
1 cucumber, peeled, seeded and finely chopped
125 g (4 oz) finely chopped walnuts
1 hard-boiled egg, finely chopped
2 teaspoons salt
½ teaspoon freshly ground pepper
finely chopped parsley or fresh dill, to garnish

Soak the sultanas in cold water for 30 minutes. Combine the sultanas and water with remaining ingredients except the parsley or dill, and chill, covered, for 3–4 hours. Taste for seasoning and serve in bowls, sprinkled with chopped parsley or dill. SERVES 4–6.

Ashe Reshte
❧ *Persian Noodle Soup*

This soup is typical of the home-style cooking offered at many eating houses in Iran (formerly Persia).

MEATBALLS
225 g (8 oz) finely minced beef
1 small onion, grated
¼ teaspoon ground cinnamon
¼ teaspoon freshly ground black pepper
½ teaspoon salt
SOUP
1.2 litres (2 pints) water
1½ teaspoons salt
50 g (2 oz) black-eyed peas
50 g (2 oz) lentils
125 g (4 oz) fine noodles
½ teaspoon freshly ground pepper
4–6 tablespoons chopped parsley
SPICING
2 tablespoons chopped fresh mint, or 1 tablespoon dried
½ teaspoon ground cinnamon
½ teaspoon freshly ground pepper

Mix the meatball ingredients thoroughly with your hands until they form a paste, then mould into walnut-size balls.

Put water, salt and black-eyed peas in a large saucepan and simmer for 15 minutes. Add meatballs, lentils, noodles, pepper and parsley and simmer for 35 minutes or until lentils and peas are tender.

Combine mint, cinnamon and pepper and stir into the soup just before removing it from the heat. Serve immediately. SERVES 6.

Kabab Halla
❧ *Lamb and Vegetables in Spicy Sauce*

The *Hilton International Fujairah* in the United Arab Emirates is a magnificent resort hotel, backed by marble mountains and looking on to its own beach on the Gulf of Oman. Guests dining in the *Siji* restaurant or the poolside terrace can feast on international cuisine or Middle Eastern specialties. *Kabab Halla* is a typical Gulf Arabic dish. (Illustrated on pages 50 and 51.)

4 tablespoons oil
3 medium onions, thinly sliced
2 cloves garlic, crushed
3 cloves
1 bay leaf
600 g (1¼ lb) lean, boneless lamb, cut into cubes
4 tablespoons tomato purée
1½ tablespoons mixed Arabic spices (see Note)
450 ml (¾ pint) Lamb or Beef Stock (page 77)
salt and freshly ground pepper
10 button onions
4 small carrots
2 medium potatoes
TO SERVE
575 g (1¼ lb) hot, cooked long-grain rice (200 g/7 oz raw)
125 g (4 oz) hot, cooked vermicelli (50 g/2 oz raw)

Heat the oil and fry the onions, garlic, cloves and bay leaf on medium heat until onion is lightly browned. Push the contents of the pan to one side, turn the heat up and fry the lamb until well browned all over. (Do this in 2 batches if necessary to avoid crowding the pan.) Add the tomato purée and Arabic spices and cook for 1 minute. Stir in the stock, bring to simmering point and season to taste. Cook, covered, over very low heat for 45 minutes.

Meanwhile, peel the button onions, leaving the root end on, and cut a cross in the root end of each. Scrape carrots, cut across in halves and trim each piece to a tapered cork shape. Peel potatoes, cut into quarters and trim each piece to a barrel shape.

Add the vegetables to the lamb mixture and continue to cook gently, covered, until lamb and vegetables are tender—about 20 minutes more.

Have the hot, cooked rice and vermicelli ready. Mix them lightly together, pile on a heated serving dish and top with lamb mixture. SERVES 4.
<u>Note:</u> If mixed Arabic spices are not available, you can mix your own by combining crushed black peppercorns, ground coriander, cassia, cloves, cumin, cardamom, nutmeg and paprika.

❧ <u>Watermelon Punch</u>

A pretty punch that makes the most of the melon season. Remove rind and seeds from 1.5 kg (3½ lb) watermelon and purée flesh in a blender. Rub purée through a fine sieve into a bowl and stir in 450 ml (¾ pint) pineapple juice, 120 ml (4 fl oz) lemon juice, 250 ml (8 fl oz) vodka and caster sugar to taste. Serve over icecubes, garnished with lemon slices. Serves 8–10.

Alcohol is forbidden in some Arab countries, and even in those where it is permitted, it is more common to see groups laughing and chatting over coffee, mint tea or fruit juices than alcoholic beverages. In Iran, a sparkling yogurt drink called *Doogh* is popular, and easy to make: combine 5 tablespoons natural yogurt and ½ teaspoon salt in a tall glass and stir in 150 ml (¼ pint) chilled soda water. Add a few icecubes and garnish with a sprig of mint.

I think one of the unsung beauty spots of the Aegean Sea is the western seaport of Izmir (once called Smyrna) in Turkey. With a harbour sheltered by hills, the setting is magical. There are wonderful restaurants, one of the most beautiful bazaars in the Middle East and an overall atmosphere of gentleness and casualness— so relaxing after the bustle of bigger, more tourist-orientated cities.

Green Beans Corfu Style

On the lovely Greek island of Corfu, this is known as fasoulakia. Cook 2 chopped onions and 2 chopped cloves garlic in 120 ml (4 fl oz) olive oil until soft. Add a 500 g (1 lb) can of chopped tomatoes with their juice, 4 tablespoons chopped parsley, 2 teaspoons chopped oregano and 1 kg (2 lb) trimmed green beans. Season with salt and pepper and pour in enough boiling water to come half-way up vegetables. Simmer until beans are tender, about 30 minutes. Serves 6–8.

Pescado con Salsa Calde
Cold Fish with Pepper Sauce

A favourite restaurant of many visitors to the Spanish city of Cordoba is *El Caballo Rojo*, set in an 18th-century house. Like other restaurants in Cordoba, it makes excellent use of the local products. For example, the Mediterranean fish called *rape* (very firm and white, and resembling lobster in flavour) often appears on the menu. You can substitute lobster, scallops or any firm white fish.

750 g (1½ lb) poached and cooled lobster, scallops, or firm white fish fillets (see page 60 for poaching instructions)
crisp lettuce leaves, to serve
SAUCE
350 ml (12 fl oz) Blender Mayonnaise (page 68)
1 tablespoon tomato paste
1 tablespoon dry sherry
1 tablespoon brandy
1 tablespoon lemon juice
few drops of Tabasco
salt
120 ml (4 fl oz) cream, lightly whipped

If using fish, remove any skin and bones after poaching and separate into large chunks. (Slice scallops in half if large, and cut lobster into chunks.) Arrange on a serving dish.

Combine mayonnaise, tomato paste, sherry, brandy and lemon juice. Season to taste with Tabasco and salt and fold in the lightly whipped cream. Spoon the sauce over the fish and serve on crisp lettuce leaves. SERVES 6 as a first course.

Salata me Feta
Salad with Feta Cheese

In Greece, and many parts of the Middle East, olives, feta cheese and herbs add interest to refreshing salads. I tasted this version on the lovely island of Spetsai. The lemon dressing is particularly good!

4 medium, ripe tomatoes, quartered
1 large cucumber, peeled and halved lengthwise
1 medium onion, thinly sliced
125 g (4 oz) feta cheese, broken into chunks
12–16 soft black olives
Lemon Dressing (see right)
finely chopped parsley and chopped fresh basil or oregano, to garnish

Place the tomatoes in a bowl. Cut the cucumbers across into 6 mm (¼ inch) slices and add to the bowl of tomatoes with the onion, cheese, olives and lemon dressing and toss to combine. Arrange on a platter and sprinkle generously with parsley and basil or oregano. SERVES 4–6.

Lemon Dressing
Place 4 tablespoons olive oil, 2 tablespoons lemon juice, 1 crushed garlic clove and salt and pepper to taste in a screw-top jar. Shake until mixture is pale and smooth.
Note: If fresh basil or oregano are not available, use ½ teaspoon dried herbs, but add to the dressing instead of sprinkling on top. Lettuce leaves may be added to the salad if desired.

Tabouleh
Cracked Wheat Salad

Go to a Lebanese restaurant anywhere in the world and you will find Tabouleh. This salad of humble peasant origins is sometimes called Parsley Salad because so much of the herb is used in it. Burghul (cracked wheat), called bulgur by Turks and Cypriots, gives a delicious nutty flavour, and the mint and lemon can be varied to suit your taste. It makes a lovely first course for lunch.

125 g (4 oz) burghul
3 ripe tomatoes, skinned and chopped
3 tablespoons finely chopped spring onion
salt and freshly ground pepper
50 g (2 oz) finely chopped fresh parsley
25 g (1 oz) finely chopped fresh mint
4 tablespoons olive oil
4 tablespoons lemon juice
vine leaves, lightly poached, and cos lettuce leaves or pitta bread, to serve

Soak burghul in water for about 2 hours. Drain and squeeze out as much water as possible with your hands, then spread out on a tea-towel to dry further.

Combine tomatoes and spring onions with burghul and season to taste with salt and pepper. Add parsley, mint, oil and lemon juice and mix well. Taste to see if more seasoning is required—the salad should taste lemony.

Serve in individual bowls lined with vine or lettuce leaves, and provide a dish of firm young cos lettuce leaves or pieces of flat pitta bread to scoop up the salad.

Salata me Feta

It's Easy to Skin a Fish!

Place the fillet on a board skin side down, tail towards you. Make a small cut between flesh and skin at the tail end. Dip the fingers of one hand in salt and hold the skin firmly. With the other hand, hold a heavy knife at right angles to the table and ease it between flesh and skin. Move the knife towards the head end of the fillet with a slight sawing motion. The idea is to pull the skin off the flesh, rather than cutting the flesh off the skin. It's easier than it sounds!

Ternera con Tomates
Veal with Tomatoes

The Santa Cruz quarter of Seville is everyone's romantic dream of Spain, with its narrow cobble-stoned streets, flowery window-boxes and smell of orange and jasmine in the air. It also houses some of the most interesting restaurants in Seville, like the vast, lively *Bodegon Torre del Oro*. Here is the type of highly seasoned veal dish you will find on the menu there . . . very much in the Mediterranean style.

1 kg (2 lb) veal steak, cut about 1 cm (½ inch) thick
salt and freshly ground pepper
flour for dusting
120 ml (4 fl oz) olive oil
1 large onion, finely chopped
500 g (1 lb) ripe tomatoes, skinned, seeded and chopped
8 blanched almonds
2 cloves garlic, peeled
1 small, dried red chilli (soaked for 5 minutes and seeds removed)
1 teaspoon salt
1 teaspoon ground cumin
1 tablespoon finely chopped parsley
pinch each of cayenne pepper and saffron
50 g (2 oz) butter
225 g (8 oz) mushrooms, thinly sliced

Cut the veal steak into 2.5 cm (1 inch) strips, season with salt and pepper and dust with flour. Heat the oil in a large, heavy frying pan and sauté the veal strips for 2 minutes each side or until lightly browned. Remove to a plate with a slotted spoon.

Add the onion to the oil remaining in the pan and stir for 1 minute, then add tomatoes and simmer for 3–4 minutes until softened. Place almonds, garlic, chilli, salt, cumin, parsley, cayenne pepper and saffron in a small bowl and mash to a paste with a pestle or the top of a rolling pin. Add to the tomato mixture and simmer for 1 minute.

Meanwhile, heat the butter in a small frying pan and cook the mushrooms until tender but still firm, about 4 minutes. Stir into the tomato mixture with the reserved veal strips. Simmer the mixture for 2 minutes or until veal is heated through, and, if necessary, add salt and pepper to taste. Serve with rice or boiled potatoes. SERVES 4.

Escabeche de Pescado con Naranja
Marinated Seafood with Oranges

Fishing is a way of life on Spain's Mediterranean coast. When there is a good catch, some of it is sure to be put into a spicy marinade for a delicious cold dish which will appear on luncheon menus next day in any of the little village restaurants.

500 g (1 lb) white fish fillets, skinned
225 g (8 oz) scallops, dark beards removed
4 tablespoons vegetable oil
1 small green pepper, seeded
2 large oranges, thinly peeled (reserve rind)
2 spring onions, finely chopped
4 tablespoons Vinaigrette (page 78)
chopped parsley, to garnish
MARINADE
5 tablespoons olive oil
4 tablespoons orange juice
1 tablespoon lime or lemon juice
1 tablespoon red wine vinegar
1½ teaspoons salt
freshly ground black pepper
2 cloves garlic, crushed
1 teaspoon grated fresh ginger
pinch of cayenne pepper

Cut the fish fillets into strips about 10 × 3 cm (4 × 1¼ inches) and remove any bones. Dry fish and scallops with paper towels.

Heat the vegetable oil until it gives off a slight haze and lightly brown the fish strips, about 2 minutes each side. Using a slotted fish slice, remove fish to a shallow serving dish. Add scallops to the pan and cook on one side while you count to 10, turn over and cook the other side while you count to 10. Remove and add to the fish.

Cut pepper and reserved orange rind into julienne (matchstick strips) and sprinkle over the seafood with the chopped spring onion. Mix together all the marinade ingredients and pour over. Cover the dish with plastic film and refrigerate overnight.

Next day, remove all white pith from the oranges and cut them into thick slices, removing any seeds. Drizzle vinaigrette over the slices and chill, covered, for 1 hour.

Arrange orange slices round the marinated seafood, then sprinkle the seafood with chopped parsley. Serve chilled, with plenty of crusty bread to mop up the delicious juice. SERVES 4.

Crusted Crêpes with Veal Filling

Visitors to Crete are enchanted by the waterfront city of Hania, with its background of hills and citrus groves and its fascinating Old City revealing a Venetian and Turkish past. The *Hotel Doma* is a good spot to stay and eat, serving a delicious home-cooked mixture of Greek and Middle Eastern dishes—and original recipes such as this one for savoury crêpes.

12 crêpes, about 20 cm (8 inches) across (page 84)
250 ml (8 fl oz) Béchamel Sauce (page 20)
50 g (2 oz) butter
1 large onion, finely chopped
500 g (1 lb) lean minced veal
2 ripe tomatoes, skinned, seeded and chopped
50 g (2 oz) freshly grated Parmesan cheese
½ teaspoon ground cinnamon
½ teaspoon freshly grated nutmeg
salt and freshly ground pepper
3 eggs, beaten
125 g (4 oz) fine, dry breadcrumbs, seasoned
  with salt and pepper
50 g (2 oz) butter for frying

Have the crêpes and béchamel sauce ready.

Heat 50 g (2 oz) butter in a large, heavy frying pan and cook the onion over moderate heat until soft and golden, about 5 minutes. Add the veal and stir until it loses its pink colour. Add tomatoes and cook a further 10 minutes. Cool slightly and stir in Parmesan, spices and salt and pepper to taste. Spread a crêpe with about 1 tablespoon of béchamel sauce. Spoon 3 tablespoons of filling down the centre of the crêpe, tuck in the sides and roll up into a cylinder. Repeat with remaining crêpes.

Dip the filled crêpes first into beaten egg, then into breadcrumbs, rolling them to coat evenly. Arrange on a flat dish, cover loosely with plastic film and chill for 1 hour.

Heat half the butter for frying in a large frying pan and fry 3 or 4 of the crêpes until crisp and brown on the underside, then turn and brown the other side. (This will take 3–5 minutes altogether.) Remove and keep warm while frying remaining crêpes, adding more butter as necessary. SERVES 6.

Lamb and Quince Stew

This Moroccan recipe is from a restaurant in Casablanca. The young chef—a pretty Berber girl—confided the secret of the wonderfully rich flavour was the 'second baking'.

50 g (2 oz) butter
2 large onions, finely chopped
1.5 kg (3½ lb) boneless lamb, cut into bite-size cubes
350 ml (12 fl oz) Chicken Stock (page 90)
salt and freshly ground pepper
3 large quinces
2 tablespoons honey
1 teaspoon ground cinnamon
½ teaspoon allspice
thinly peeled rind of ½ orange
finely chopped parsley, to garnish

Heat the butter in a large, heavy saucepan and gently fry the onions until soft, about 5 minutes. Transfer to a deep casserole dish with a slotted spoon. Add the meat to the butter remaining in the pan and brown over moderate heat—you may have to do this in 2 batches to avoid crowding the pan. Transfer to the casserole with the onions.

Add stock to pan and bring to the boil, scraping up any brown bits from the bottom. Pour over meat and onions and season generously with salt and pepper. Cover the casserole tightly and bake in a preheated moderately slow oven (160°C/325°F/Gas 3) for 1½ hours.

Peel the quinces, cut into quarters and remove cores. Slice each quarter in half lengthwise and add to the casserole with honey, spices and orange rind. Cover and bake for a further 1 hour or until quinces are soft.

Cool the mixture in the casserole, then chill overnight. Next day, remove any fat that has set on the surface and return casserole to a moderately slow oven (160°C/325°F/Gas 3) for 45 minutes to reheat. Sprinkle with parsley to serve. SERVES 8.

Note: For a special Moroccan touch, serve this with *couscous* (coarse semolina). There is a special pre-cooked couscous now available in many delicatessens and supermarkets.

Morocco is becoming more and more popular with travellers. I think the nicest way to get there is to take the four-hour ferry ride from Málaga in Spain to the port of Tangiers. You step straight from the ferry into an Arabian Nights' world of veiled women, men in the long caftans called *djellabas*, donkeys and camels in the streets, sights, sounds and smells as exotic as you've ever imagined.

Kalamaria Yemistes
Squid Stuffed with Rice and Pine Nuts

The Greek island of Spetsai has pine and olive trees growing down to meet the water, and entrancing little white houses with gardens full of oleander and bougainvillea. It is a favourite resort of Athenian families themselves. The many excellent restaurants, cafés and bars on Spetsai have superb seafood dishes on the menu; this recipe for stuffed squid is typical.

8 large squid, cleaned (page 31)
5 tablespoons olive oil
1 medium onion, finely chopped
1 clove garlic, crushed
50 g (2 oz) raw long-grain rice
1 ripe tomato, skinned, seeded and chopped
3 tablespoons toasted pine nuts
3 tablespoons currants
2 tablespoons finely chopped parsley
1 teaspoon dried oregano
salt and freshly ground pepper
250 ml (8 fl oz) water
250 ml (8 fl oz) dry white wine
2 tablespoons lemon juice
little extra olive oil

Place the body sacs of the squid between 2 sheets of plastic film and tap with a steak mallet or rolling pin to tenderize them, being careful not to split the sides. Chop the fins and tentacles into tiny pieces.

Heat the oil in a large, heavy saucepan and fry the onion and garlic over medium heat until softened, about 3 minutes. Add the chopped squid and rice and stir the mixture for 2 minutes. Add tomato, pine nuts, currants, parsley, oregano and salt and pepper to taste and cook for another 2 minutes, stirring. Add the water, bring the liquid to the boil and simmer, covered, for 20 minutes. Allow to cool.

Sprinkle the insides of the body sacs with salt and fill each sac with rice mixture, closing the openings with toothpicks. Arrange the squid in an oiled flameproof casserole just large enough to hold them in one layer. Add white wine and lemon juice to the casserole, brush the squid with olive oil and sprinkle with salt and pepper. Bring the liquid to the boil over medium heat, then transfer the casserole to a pre-heated moderately hot oven (190°C/375°F/Gas 5). Bake the squid for 15 minutes, then turn them over and bake for another 15 minutes. Transfer the squid with a slotted spoon to a heated serving dish and remove toothpicks. Strain the liquid into a small saucepan, and reduce it over high heat to 170 ml (6 fl oz). Pour the sauce over the squid. SERVES 8.

Hot Chocolate

One of Spain's favourite drinks—try it for supper on a cold night accompanied by golden churros. Melt 50 g (2 oz) chocolate and 2 tablespoons honey in a basin over a pan of simmering water. Add 1 tablespoon ground almonds, 1 teaspoon vanilla and 450 ml (¾ pint) hot milk and beat until frothy. Serve in hot mugs. Serves 2.

Churros
Spanish Fried Pastries

These strips of golden-fried choux pastry are a favourite snack in Spain. Even late at night, after a splendid meal, the Spanish seem to find space for a couple of *churros* and a mug of hot chocolate . . . and tourists find them irresistible, too. So if you look in the window of a restaurant and see people munching on crispy puffs of pastry—this is what they are.

oil for deep frying
1 quantity Choux Pastry (page 128) with 1 tablespoon
*   sugar added to the butter and water mixture*
icing sugar

Heat oil to 190°C/375°F (when a bread cube browns in 25–30 seconds). It should be deep enough for the pastries to float.

Using a piping bag fitted with a 1 cm (½ inch) star tube, pipe 13 cm (5 inch) lengths of choux pastry into the hot oil. Hold the pipe fairly high so that the pastry will fall in thin strips. Fry until golden-brown all over.

As churros are cooked, transfer to paper towels to drain and sprinkle generously with icing sugar while still warm. MAKES 24.
<u>Note:</u> For Spanish Hot Chocolate to enjoy with churros, see recipe far left.

Iced Figs and Oranges

Figs are one of the most popular fruits in the Middle East. My sister brought back the recipe for this simple, luscious dessert after a stay in Cairo, Egypt.

250 ml (8 fl oz) orange juice
4 tablespoons fresh lime or lemon juice
120 ml (4 fl oz) honey
8 ripe figs, peeled and sliced
4 oranges
ground cinnamon

Stir fruit juices and honey together until honey dissolves. Add the figs to the mixture and chill.

Peel the oranges, removing white pith and outer membrane, and cut into the centre on both sides of the dividing membranes to remove skinless segments. Remove any seeds, cover and chill.

To serve, place figs and syrup in a pretty glass bowl. Arrange orange segments around the sides, spoon some of the syrup over them and sprinkle with cinnamon. SERVES 6–8.

Churros

➦ The Art of Poaching Fish
Add only enough liquid to come to top of fish, not to cover it. Bring liquid to the gentlest simmer—where it quivers, but no bubbles rise. Cover fish with buttered greaseproof paper (with a small hole in it for steam to escape) and then a lid. Cook over low heat until flesh is white and flakes when tested with a toothpick.

Samak Sayadieh
➥ *Mould of Fish, Tomatoes and Savoury Rice*

Dubai on the Persian Gulf is the commercial centre of the United Arab Emirates, so naturally it has a Hilton Hotel. The *Al Fahidi Grill*, decorated to resemble a wealthy merchant's home, offers fascinating Arab dishes such as this.

1 kg (2 lb) fish fillets, skinned, bones removed, and cut into cubes
750 ml (1¼ pints) Fish or Chicken Stock (pages 81 and 90)
3 tablespoons Beurre Manié (page 113)
salt and freshly ground pepper
lemon juice
125 g (4 oz) butter
1 medium onion, sliced and separated into rings
2 medium tomatoes, skinned and cut into wedges
2 tablespoons chopped parsley
ORIENTAL RICE
225 g (8 oz) raw long-grain rice
50 g (2 oz) butter
1 large onion, chopped
175 g (6 oz) raw minced lamb
1 tablespoon ground cinnamon
1 teaspoon salt
600 ml (1 pint) hot water
2 tablespoons raisins
extra nut of butter
2 tablespoons pine nuts

Make oriental rice first. Wash rice in several changes of water, drain and set aside. Heat butter in a heavy saucepan, add onion and cook gently until soft. Turn heat up to medium, add lamb and cook, stirring and breaking up lumps with a fork, until lamb changes colour. Stir in cinnamon and salt, add water and bring to the boil. Sprinkle in rice and raisins and simmer gently until water evaporates and steam holes appear in the rice. Turn heat very low, cover and cook for a further 10 minutes or until rice is tender. Turn off heat, uncover and fluff up rice with a fork.

While rice is cooking, melt the extra nut of butter in a small pan, add pine nuts and toss over gentle heat until the nuts are lightly browned. Remove from heat and set aside until you are ready to use the rice.

Poach the fish gently in stock (the surface of the liquid should shiver without bubbling) until the fish turns white, 3–4 minutes. Remove fish with a slotted spoon and set aside. Boil stock down rapidly if necessary to make about 350 ml (12 fl oz) liquid and whisk *beurre manié*, a little at a time, into the boiling liquid to thicken it. Season sauce to taste with salt, pepper and lemon juice; cover and keep hot.

Heat half the butter and fry onion rings until brown and crisp. Remove onion with a slotted spoon, set aside and keep warm. Add remaining butter to the pan and when it is melted, add tomato wedges and heat gently without cooking. Remove tomato wedges with a slotted spoon and arrange them in a circular pattern in the bottom of a heatproof bowl. Season lightly with salt and pepper. Add poached fish to the butter left in the pan, turn the pieces gently to coat them with butter and arrange in a layer on top of tomatoes. Season lightly and sprinkle parsley over.

Fork pine nuts through the rice, top the bowl with the rice and press down gently. Place the bowl in a preheated moderate oven (180°C/350°F/Gas 4) for 7 minutes, then remove and unmould on to a heated serving plate. Garnish the mould with fried onions and serve with the sauce. SERVES 5–6.

Tortilla
➦ *Potato Omelette*

Wherever you go in Spain, from the smallest bar to the big hotel dining-room, you will find *tortilla* among the offerings. It is enjoyed hot and cold, as a snack, a first course, as picnic food—sometimes as a complete meal, with crusty bread and a glass of sherry. This version, with onion added, is very popular in Madrid.

2 tablespoons olive oil
25 g (1 oz) butter
1 large onion (preferably Spanish), thinly sliced
salt and freshly ground pepper
1 large, boiled potato, thinly sliced
5 eggs

Heat the oil and butter in a large, heavy frying pan and fry the onion over medium heat until softened, about 4 minutes. Season with salt and pepper. Spread the potato slices over the onion and season.

Beat the eggs lightly with salt and pepper to taste, pour over the vegetables and cook until beginning to set around the edges, about 1 minute. Lift the cooked edges up with a spatula and tilt the pan so the uncooked egg flows underneath. Repeat until there is no more runny egg left, but the centre of the omelette is still moist.

Invert the omelette on to a large plate, then slide it back into the pan cooked side up. Continue cooking over low heat until set and firm on the bottom, about another minute. Serve hot or cold, cut in wedges. SERVES 4.

Eggah
🍂 Vegetable Omelette

In the Lebanon, this hearty omelette is often served cold as a first course, or taken on picnics and wrapped inside Lebanese bread. If you prefer, you may certainly serve it hot from the pan for lunch or supper.

3 courgettes, thinly sliced
salt
5 tablespoons olive oil
2 leeks, trimmed, halved lengthwise and thinly
    sliced, or 2 small onions, thinly sliced
2 medium tomatoes, skinned, seeded and chopped
2 cloves garlic, crushed
2 tablespoons finely chopped parsley
freshly ground pepper
freshly grated nutmeg
7 eggs, lightly beaten

Place courgettes in a colander, sprinkle lightly with salt and let stand for 30 minutes. Pat slices dry.

Heat 3 tablespoons oil in a large frying pan, add vegetables and garlic and cook over medium heat until softened, about 8 minutes. Stir in parsley and season with salt, pepper and nutmeg. Allow to cool.

Heat the remaining 2 tablespoons oil in a 25 cm (10 inch) omelette pan over high heat. Combine vegetables and beaten eggs, pour into hot oil and cook for 1–2 minutes, or until eggs are beginning to set on the bottom. Reduce heat to moderate and cook for a further 5 minutes or until the omelette is firm underneath but still runny on top.

Place pan under a preheated hot grill for 1–2 minutes or until the top is puffed and golden. Slide on to a serving plate and allow to cool, or serve at once, cut into wedges. SERVES 4–6.

Coctel de Cafe
🍂 Coffee Cocktail

Bar-hopping or tapa-hopping is one of the irresistible excitements of Spain. Each bar has its own ambience, its own delectable assortment of *tapas* (little snacks) and its own special drinks. This recipe is from the *Boadas Bar* in Barcelona.

250 ml (8 fl oz) chilled espresso coffee
3 tablespoons Crème de Cacao (chocolate liqueur)
3 tablespoons brandy

Place all the ingredients in a cocktail shaker or screw-top jar and shake well. Pour into chilled glasses. MAKES 2 drinks.

White Sangria

Sangria is a fruit and wine punch served everywhere in Spain—as an apéritif, between-meal refresher, and with meals. It is usually made with red wine, but white wine is used at the lovely *Marbella Club Hotel* in the Costa del Sol resort of Marbella.

1 eating apple, unpeeled and finely chopped
1 orange, unpeeled and finely sliced
½ lemon, unpeeled and finely sliced
5 tablespoons Grand Marnier or Curaçao
    (orange-flavoured liqueur)
1 bottle chilled, dry white wine
450 ml (¾ pint) chilled soda water
icecubes, to serve

Place fruit and liqueur in a large jug and macerate (steep) for 2–3 hours or overnight. Add wine, stir well, then add chilled soda water. Pour over ice in tall glasses or Sangria mugs. MAKES 6–8 long drinks.

Vin à l'Orange
🍂 Orange Wine

The grand finale to a Moroccan meal is often an assortment of pastries rich in almonds, honey and sesame seeds, plus dates and figs and a glass of lemonade.

For diners who want something a little stronger than lemonade, a restaurant in Marrakesh offers this sweetened wine flavoured with orange and rum . . . almost a liqueur in flavour and consistency.

900 ml (1½ pints) dry white or red wine
225 g (8 oz) sugar
50 g (2 oz) finely grated orange rind
5 tablespoons dark rum

You need a large glass jar with a tight-fitting lid (e.g., a preserving jar) to make this drink.

Place all ingredients in the jar, stir until sugar dissolves, then seal tightly. Store in the refrigerator for 2–3 days (or up to 3 weeks), shaking the jar now and again. To serve, strain through a fine sieve into a jug and chill if desired. MAKES about 10 small glasses.

🍂 Yogurt Bliss
From Tunisia, a perfumed dessert for two. In a bowl, combine 250 ml (8 fl oz) natural yogurt, 1 teaspoon orange flower water, 1 tablespoon runny honey, ½ teaspoon ground cardamom. Fold in the skinless segments of 1 large mandarin. Serve chilled, sprinkled with blanched, slivered almonds. Serves 2.

Honey is a precious bounty to those who live off the land, and is used lavishly in the Middle East and neighbouring countries. No visitor to Turkey, Greece or the Arab world should miss the honey-saturated pastries, the sesame seed honey cakes, or the honey-sweetened meat and poultry pies. While enjoying such honeyed delights you might also like to keep in mind that the ancients regarded honey as a powerful aphrodisiac!

THE AMERICAS

Many an experienced world traveller ranks North America—Canada and the United States—top of the list for enjoyable eating out. The range of possibilities is endless, from good fast food to superb *nouvelle cuisine*, and you never seem more than a few steps from a charming restaurant. It's not a question of 'Where shall we go to eat?' but 'How are we going to choose from all the wonderful options?'

Regional specialties abound as you travel through the different states and provinces, showing the influence of ancestors from many countries. New York has some of the finest Italian restaurants, French-speaking Montreal offers a wealth of fine French restaurants, while San Francisco has a Chinatown with eating places to challenge Peking.

In North America you will also find many restaurants that serve those all-American favourites you've heard about. Don't miss hot cakes for breakfast, topped with butter and maple syrup and served with crisp bacon and sausages. Sample the glorious pies that appear on every second menu, such as blueberry, pumpkin, cherry, pecan, raisin and coconut cream. Watch for corn bread, Southern fried chicken, Maine lobster, clam chowder, Boston baked beans, Indian pudding, chicken gumbo, sourdough bread, hashed brown and Idaho baked potatoes, oyster stew, barbecued spareribs, strawberry shortcake, and the magnificent filled and frosted layer cakes.

In South America, the accent is on variety, spice, colour and excitement. Mexico, Venezuela, Colombia, Paraguay, Chile, Yucatan, Ecuador, Bolivia, Uruguay and Argentina—the very names are enough to intrigue your taste buds!

Much of Latin American cuisine is based on traditional Indian cooking, with a healthy emphasis on vegetables, fruits and grains. Then there are the influences of European conquerors and settlers (particularly the Spanish) and of Africans originally brought to the continent as slaves.

If you're like me, and regard eating as a big part of your travel adventures, you'll certainly have a wonderful time in the Americas.

The taste of American presidents has always had a profound effect on the country's eating habits. Thomas Jefferson was the first to bring a gourmet touch to the table. After years in France, he introduced Parmesan cheese, Dutch waffles, the potato delicacy now called 'French Fries', and a new icecream invention—'Baked Alaska'.

Grilled Lime Chicken

There are certain names that have always been associated with the unique magic of New York—the *Plaza* and *Algonquin* Hotels, Central Park and Times Square, *Macy's* and *Tiffany's*. A younger generation would add the name of the restaurant *Maxwell's Plum*. Keeping in mind the health-conscious needs of the 'beautiful people' clientele, many of 'Maxwell's' main dishes contrive to be light without sacrificing superb flavour. Grilled chicken with crème fraîche sauce is just one example.

6 poussins
rind from ½ lime and ½ small orange, cut in
  julienne (matchstick strips)
250 ml (8 fl oz) water
1 tablespoon sugar
4 tablespoons red wine vinegar
1 tablespoon brown sugar
250 ml (8 fl oz) Crème Fraîche (page 21)
salt and freshly ground black pepper
thin slices of lime and sprays of watercress, to
  garnish
MARINADE
1 large onion (preferably Spanish), thinly sliced
120 ml (4 fl oz) light soy sauce
6 spring onions, chopped
120 ml (4 fl oz) orange juice
5 tablespoons lime juice
120 ml (4 fl oz) Chicken Stock (page 90)
2 teaspoons finely chopped fresh ginger
3 sprigs of fresh coriander

Split the chickens down the back, remove backbones and flatten the chickens with a cleaver (Chinese chopper). Tuck the leg ends under the skin on the breast.

Combine onion, soy sauce, spring onions, orange and lime juice, chicken stock, ginger and coriander in a shallow dish and add the chickens. Marinate for 6 hours or more, covered, in the refrigerator, turning now and again. Drain the chickens, and reserve the marinade. Lightly prick the skin all over with a fork and arrange the chickens, skin side up, on a rack placed over the grill pan. Place under a preheated grill, about 15 cm (6 inches) from the heat, and grill for 12 minutes on each side.

Meanwhile, blanch lime and orange julienne for 15 minutes in boiling water and drain. In another small saucepan, bring the water and sugar to the boil, add the julienne and cook until all the liquid has evaporated. Bring the reserved marinade to the boil, add vinegar and brown sugar and simmer for 10 minutes. Purée in a blender or food processor fitted with the steel blade, return to the saucepan and stir in crème fraîche. Bring just to the simmer (don't let it boil) and taste for seasoning. Halve the chickens, arrange on a heated serving platter and spoon some of the sauce over them. Sprinkle with lime and orange julienne and garnish with lime slices and sprays of watercress. Serve rest of sauce separately. SERVES 6.

Stuffed Brioche

Key West is the southernmost point of the United States, an enchanting island or 'key' joined to the mainland by a causeway. Wonderful restaurants abound on Key West, including the palm-shaded *La Terraza de Marti*, which serves a magnificent breakfast or brunch from nine to four. Watch for brioche, baked with a cheese and ham filling—and easy to emulate at home, now many of us can buy brioche from our local French pâtisserie.

6 brioches
125 g (4 oz) bratwurst (uncooked, Continental sausages)
125 g (4 oz) ham, chopped
5 tablespoons milk
5 tablespoons double cream
75 g (3 oz) grated Gruyère cheese
1 tablespoon Cognac or brandy
salt and freshly ground pepper

Cut off the top quarters of the brioches with a serrated knife and put aside. Carefully cut out the centres from the brioches, leaving a 1 cm (½ inch) shell. Process centres in a blender or food processor fitted with the steel blade, to make crumbs.

Cut bratwurst into pieces and place in a heavy frying pan with chopped ham. Cook over moderately high heat, stirring, until bratwurst is browned and cooked through. Add milk and cream and simmer for 5 minutes. Remove from heat and stir in grated Gruyère, crumbs, Cognac or brandy and salt and pepper to taste.

Fill the brioche shells with this mixture and gently press reserved top quarters in place. Place filled brioches in lightly greased deep muffin tins or patty tins and bake in a preheated moderate oven (180°C/350°F/Gas 4) for 10 minutes until heated through. SERVES 6.

Eggs Benedict

The famous *Brennan's* restaurant on Royal Street, New Orleans, is credited with inventing Eggs Benedict, now on chic restaurant menus throughout the world.

I have enjoyed them at *Brennan's* as part of a long, lazy brunch, and also serve them at home—they're so easy, as well as delicious. *Brennan's* uses round Dutch toasts as the base, but split, toasted muffins are used in other restaurants and may be easier to find in your supermarket.

4 thick slices of ham
8 eggs
Hollandaise Sauce (page 21)
4 Dutch toasts

Grill the ham on both sides until heated through and lightly browned. Meanwhile, poach the eggs and have the hollandaise sauce prepared and warm.

Place a Dutch toast on each of 4 heated plates and cover with a slice of grilled ham. Arrange 2 poached eggs side by side on the ham and cover with sauce. SERVES 4.

Cucumber Sesame Salad

Few travellers to California can resist a visit to Disneyland. It's a bonus to find that its incredibly realistic 'worlds' of the imagination include excellent restaurants offering food in the style of each 'world'.

The *Papeete Bay Verandah* serves South Seas-style dishes such as this superb salad. It makes an interesting first course or a good accompaniment to fish.

3 cucumbers, peeled and thinly sliced
120 ml (4 fl oz) cider vinegar
2 tablespoons salt
120 ml (4 fl oz) double cream, chilled
120 ml (4 fl oz) thick Coconut Cream (page 38)
1 tablespoon sugar
1 tablespoon Chinese sesame oil
2 tablespoons snipped chives
1 tablespoon toasted sesame seeds
1 tablespoon chopped parsley

Cover the cucumber with vinegar and salt and leave to marinate for 1 hour. Drain and transfer to a serving bowl.

Whip cream until it forms soft peaks and fold in coconut cream, sugar, sesame oil and chives. Pour over the cucumber and sprinkle with sesame seeds and chopped parsley. SERVES 4.

🐚 Green Peppercorn Butter
Here's a New York idea for a superb savoury butter—serve it with grilled meats or pan-fried fish. Combine 125 g (4 oz) softened butter, 2 tablespoons crushed green peppercorns, 1 tablespoon each Dijon mustard and lemon juice and salt to taste. Shape into a cylinder, wrap in plastic film and chill. Makes enough for 6 servings.

2 hard-boiled eggs, cut into 12 wedges
12 black olives, stoned
TOPPING
8 tender, young corn cobs, husks and silky
*   threads removed*
50 g (2 oz) butter
2 tablespoons sugar
3 teaspoons salt
1½ teaspoons dried basil

Heat the oil in a large, heavy frying pan and fry the chicken fillets on both sides over medium heat until golden-brown and tender—about 2 minutes each side. Remove and cut into 12 chunks.

Add onions to oil remaining in pan and cook for 3 minutes or until softened. Add beef and stir until it is brown and crumbly. Stir in seasonings and enough water to moisten the mixture without making it too liquid. Simmer for 15 minutes, then stir in raisins and taste for seasoning.

To make the topping: cut the kernels from the corn cobs and purée in a blender or food processor fitted with the steel blade. Heat the butter in a heavy saucepan, add remaining ingredients and stir for a minute or two to heat through.

Spoon the filling into 6 individual casseroles and top each one with 2 chunks of chicken, 2 pieces of egg and 2 olives. Spoon corn topping over and bake in a preheated moderate oven (180°C/350°F/Gas 4) for 40 minutes or until a golden-brown crust forms on top. SERVES 6.

Low-Country Shrimp Pilau

The 'Low Country' of the United States is the strip of coast stretching from Wilmington, North Carolina, to Savannah in Georgia. It is rich in regional specialties, many of them with an African influence. Tiny shrimps from the Savannah River are used by restaurants serving this Low Country dish, but prawns are just as delicious.

4 rashers streaky bacon, diced
275 g (10 oz) raw, long-grain rice
2 large onions, finely chopped
2 large, ripe tomatoes, skinned, seeded and chopped
2 tablespoons lemon juice
1½ teaspoons Worcestershire sauce
1½ teaspoons salt
¾ teaspoon ground allspice
¼ teaspoon cayenne pepper
600 ml (1 pint) Chicken Stock (page 90)
750 g (1½ lb) cooked prawns, shelled and deveined

Put the bacon in a large, heavy frying pan over medium heat and brown gently. Remove with a slotted spoon and drain on paper towels.

Add rice and onions to the bacon fat and stir until onions begin to soften. Add remaining ingredients, except bacon and prawns and stir until liquid comes to the boil.

Pour the mixture into a large casserole dish, cover tightly and bake in a preheated moderate oven (180°C/350°F/Gas 4) for 20 minutes. Lightly stir in prawns and bacon, cover again and bake for a further 10 minutes or until rice is tender. Fluff up the pilau with a fork, taste for seasoning (it should be well flavoured) and sprinkle with chopped parsley. SERVES 6.

Ramos Gin Fizz

'Breakfast at *Brennan's*' is high on the list of priorities for every visitor to New Orleans. The name is a bit of a misnomer, though, for 'breakfast' is usually a leisurely early lunch that extends through the afternoon. As a prelude to the delicious food, guests usually enjoy a drink on the patio. Ramos Gin Fizz is a universal *Brennan's* favourite.

170 ml (6 fl oz) gin
2¼ tablespoons lemon juice
2¼ tablespoons simple syrup (see Note)
2 large egg whites
½ teaspoon orange flower water (from health
*   food shop or chemist)*
350 ml (12 fl oz) double cream
crushed ice

Place all the ingredients in a blender. Turn blender on high speed for 30 seconds, then off again, and repeat until mixture is creamy and frothy. MAKES 4 drinks.
<u>Note:</u> To make simple syrup, stir 50 g (2 oz) sugar into 250 ml (8 fl oz) hot water until sugar melts. Keep in a screw-top covered jar in the refrigerator.

Mrs. Trollope, mother of the English novelist, lived for some time in the USA in the 1830s. She was astounded at the size of the 'tea' served; 'more tea, coffee, hot cake and custard, hoe cake, johnny cake, waffle cake and dodger cake, pickled peaches and preserved cucumbers, ham, turkey, hung beef, apple sauce and pickled oysters than ever were prepared in any other country of the known world!'

There is a story behind Caesar Salad. Alex Cardini was chef at the San Diego racetrack in the USA. He missed his brother Caesar, who was working as a chef in cold, faraway London, so when he created this beautiful salad, he named it after his brother. The salad became famous and Caesar's name was immortalized in the food world!

Caesar Salad

There are many versions of Caesar Salad, but this is the authentic and original one—prepared for me in Mexico City by Alexander Cardini Jr., the nephew of Alex Cardini Sr. who actually created the salad. Garlic and anchovy croûtes, coddled egg, lemon dressing and freshly grated Parmesan are all essentials. The lettuce is not tossed in the dressing but gently rolled to avoid bruising. (Illustrated on page 62.)

1 cos (or romaine) lettuce
4 canned anchovies, drained
1 clove garlic, crushed
8 slices of French bread
1 egg, at room temperature
salt and freshly ground pepper
juice of 1 lemon
3 tablespoons olive oil
1 teaspoon Worcestershire sauce
3 tablespoons freshly grated Parmesan cheese

Separate lettuce leaves, wash carefully and dry. Place in a plastic bag and chill.

Mash anchovies with garlic and spread the mixture on French bread slices (these are now called croûtes). Bake in a slow oven (150°C/300°F/Gas 2) until crisp and dry. Allow to cool. Gently place the egg in boiling water for 50 seconds only.

Arrange the lettuce in a large bowl, season with salt and pepper and break the coddled egg over. Combine lemon juice, oil and Worcestershire sauce in a small bowl and beat with a fork until thick. Add to the salad with cheese and croûtes.

Gently roll lettuce leaves in dressing until each leaf is glistening. Serve at once. SERVES 2 as a light meal, 4 as a side salad or first course.

Helada de Platano

❧ *Fresh Banana Icecream*

Yucatan juts out into the Gulf of Mexico, bordering Mexico on one side and Guatemala on the other. The capital, Merida, is a city of exhilarating contrasts. You can walk from Spanish and Moorish mansions, modern buildings and a bustling plaza, to street stalls selling medicines containing staghorns, rattlesnake oil and powdered jaguar bones.

You can enjoy baked iguana (a large lizard) at a little eating house, or the offerings of international chefs at a fine hotel or restaurant—like this unusual icecream sampled at a restaurant called *Los Tulipanes.*

➥ <u>Cuban Baked Bananas</u>
Choose 4 large, ripe but firm bananas. Peel them, then brown on both sides in 25 g (1 oz) butter. Sprinkle with 50 g (2 oz) sugar mixed with 2 teaspoons ground cinnamon, then add 120 ml (4 fl oz) medium-dry sherry to the pan. Cover and simmer until the bananas are tender, about 4 minutes. Serve as a side dish with meats or as a dessert with icecream. Serves 4.

750 ml (1¼ pints) milk
225 g (8 oz) sugar
3 egg yolks, beaten
1 cm (½ inch) vanilla pod
250 ml (8 fl oz) double cream
120 ml (4 fl oz) sweet sherry
2 large, ripe bananas, mashed and sieved
25 g (1 oz) ground almonds
slivered almonds and sliced bananas, to decorate

Place the milk, sugar, beaten egg yolks and vanilla pod in a saucepan over medium heat. Stir constantly until it comes to the boil, then remove from heat at once and allow to cool. Remove the vanilla pod and stir in the cream and sherry. Process the mixture in an electric *sorbetière* until mushy, or freeze in a shallow tray until it starts to set firm around edges.

Spoon out into a bowl and beat with an electric or rotary beater until light-textured and increased in volume. Stir the bananas into the mixture with the ground almonds. Return to the freezer tray and freeze until firm. Sprinkle with slivered almonds and decorate with banana slices to serve. SERVES 6–8.

Grand Marnier Sauce

The famous New York restaurant *La Grenouille's* celebrated Grand Marnier Sauce is not difficult to make. It is rich, rather expensive, but perfect with almost any fresh fruit or fruit tart.

5 egg yolks
125 g (4 oz) plus 2 tablespoons caster sugar
120 ml (4 fl oz) Grand Marnier
250 ml (8 fl oz) double cream, softly whipped

Put the egg yolks and sugar into the top half of a double boiler or a mixing bowl that will rest snugly on top of a slightly larger saucepan. Add about 5 cm (2 inches) water to the saucepan and bring to the boil. Beat the yolks vigorously, using a rotary egg beater or hand-held electric mixer, making sure you scrape round the bottom of the bowl with the beater. Place the bowl over the simmering water but do not allow the top container to touch the water. Continue beating for 10 minutes or so until yolks are thick and a pale lemon colour. Remove the bowl from the saucepan and stir in half the Grand Marnier. Cover the surface of the sauce with plastic film and allow to cool, then chill. At serving time, fold cream into sauce and stir in rest of Grand Marnier. SERVES 8–10.

Fruit with Grand Marnier Sauce

🖎 Egg and Lemon Dressing
An unusual golden dressing from San Francisco, lovely tossed with a mixture of greens or spooned over tomato and onion slices. Beat together in a small bowl 1 large egg yolk, 3 tablespoons lemon juice, 1 tablespoon Dijon mustard and salt and pepper to taste. Add 170 ml (6 fl oz) olive oil gradually, beating until well combined. Makes about 250 ml (8 fl oz).

Burghul, Watercress and Pineapple Salad

Here's an inventive Hawaiian twist on the Middle Eastern cracked wheat salad called *Tabouleh*. Instead of parsley, there's watercress for an interesting peppery flavour—plus luscious pineapple for which the islands are so famous.

170 ml (6 fl oz) olive oil
225 g (8 oz) burghul (cracked wheat)
900 ml (1½ pints) hot Chicken Stock (page 90)
3 slices of ripe pineapple, cored and cut into
    small cubes
75 g (3 oz) coarsely chopped watercress leaves
4 tablespoons lemon juice
1 large clove garlic, crushed
salt and freshly ground pepper
watercress leaves and thinly sliced pineapple, to garnish

Heat 4 tablespoons oil in a large, heavy frying pan and add the burghul. Stir over moderate heat for 5 minutes, add the stock and bring to the boil. Cover the pan and simmer for 20 minutes or until the liquid is absorbed. Allow to cool, then place in a large bowl with the pineapple cubes and the coarsely chopped watercress.

    Whisk together remaining olive oil, lemon juice, garlic, and salt and pepper to taste. Pour over the burghul mixture and combine thoroughly. Cover the bowl, allow to stand for 2 hours, and taste for seasoning. Transfer salad to a serving plate and garnish generously with sprays of watercress and thin slices of pineapple. SERVES 6.

Sopa de Aguacate
🖎 *Avocado Soup*

The lovely old *Alemada* hotel in Mexico City makes superb soups. This one has that Spanish-Mexican flavour of ground cumin, to add to its distinction.

3 large, ripe avocados
1 clove garlic, crushed
2 tablespoons lemon juice
1 teaspoon ground cumin
220 ml (8 fl oz) milk
220 ml (8 fl oz) double cream
salt and freshly ground white pepper
thin slices of avocado, to garnish

Peel the avocados and remove seeds. Cut a few thin slices to garnish soup (squeeze over lemon to prevent them discolouring). Place remaining avocado in a bowl with garlic, lemon juice and cumin. Mash together until smooth, or mix in a blender or food processor fitted with the steel blade, then stir in the milk and cream. Season to taste with salt and pepper and chill, covered, until serving time. Adjust seasoning and serve in chilled bowls with a slice or two of avocado floating on top. SERVES 4–6.

Arroz con Pato
🖎 *Rice with Duck*

In Peru, the evening meal begins with an assortment of *entradas* or snacks. They might include mussels, tamales, grilled tid-bits on skewers, fish in lime and many more. At one such meal at the *Rosito Rios* restaurant in Lima, we sat in the open at long wooden tables and watched as the *entradas* were freshly cooked for us over glowing charcoal. There wasn't much room left for a main course, but I couldn't resist a taste of a delectable duck dish with rice.

    Just one word of caution about this recipe—with 3 chillies, the sauce will be hot! If you are not used to the heat of the chillies, it would be wise to start with one only.

1 fat duckling, weighing about 2.5 kg (5½ lb)
2 tablespoons oil
1 large onion, finely chopped
3 small, fresh or dried red chillies, or to taste,
    seeded and finely chopped
6 fat cloves garlic, crushed
4 tablespoons chopped, fresh coriander or parsley
2 teaspoons ground cumin
salt and freshly ground pepper
450 ml (¾ pint) Chicken Stock (page 90)
350 g (12 oz) raw, long-grain rice
450 ml (¾ pint) beer
125 g (4 oz) cooked green peas
sliced tomatoes, to garnish

Cut the duck into 6 serving pieces and pierce the skin all over with a fine skewer.

    Heat the oil in a large, heavy frying pan and sauté the duck pieces until brown on all sides, about 5 minutes. Transfer duck to a casserole.

    Pour off all but 3 tablespoons of fat from the pan and add onion, chillies and garlic. Cook over medium heat until vegetables are soft, about 4 minutes. Stir in coriander, cumin, salt and pepper to taste (remembering chillies are hot) and stock. Bring to the boil, stirring, then pour over the duck. If the stock doesn't cover the duck pieces, heat a little more and add to the casserole. Cover tightly and bake in a preheated moderately slow oven (160°C/325°F/Gas 3) for 1 hour or until the duck is almost tender.

Add rice and beer to the casserole, stir to combine and continue cooking until rice is tender and liquid almost absorbed, about 30 minutes. Mix in the green peas and taste for seasoning. Serve the duck and rice on a heated platter, garnished with sliced tomatoes. SERVES 6.

Empanadas
Beef Pasties

Empanadas are savoury meat pasties, popular throughout South America. I enjoyed a spicy version at the *Sheraton* hotel in San Cristobal, nestling at the foot of the snow-capped Andes. This is the chef's own recipe. *Empanadas* are made into tiny bite-size morsels for cocktail parties, into hearty ones for picnics or lunch.

EMPANADA PASTRY
500 g (1 lb) flour
2 teaspoons paprika
½ teaspoon salt
175 g (6 oz) butter, cut into small pieces
FILLING
120 ml (4 fl oz) oil
1 large onion, finely chopped
1 ripe tomato, skinned, seeded and chopped
1 teaspoon paprika
2 teaspoons flour
*1 kg (2 lb) tender steak (rump, topside, etc.),
    trimmed of fat and cut into small dice*
120 ml (4 fl oz) Beef Stock (page 77)
1 teaspoon ground cumin
salt
½ teaspoon chilli powder
2 hard-boiled eggs, finely chopped
50 g (2 oz) chopped green olives
50 g (2 oz) sultanas

To make the pastry: sift together the flour, paprika and salt. Rub the butter into the flour until the mixture resembles breadcrumbs. Gradually add enough cold water to make a fairly stiff dough. Knead lightly, wrap in plastic film and chill while preparing filling.

Heat oil in a large frying pan and gently fry onion until golden-brown. Add tomato and paprika and stir until tomato is soft. Add flour, meat, stock, cumin, salt to taste and chilli powder. Stir constantly until the mixture comes to the boil, then cover the pan and simmer for 15 minutes. Remove cover and boil rapidly for 5–10 minutes, until liquid is reduced and filling quite thick. Taste for seasoning and allow to cool.

Divide the dough into 18 pieces, each about the size of an egg. Roll each piece out to form a circle about 18 cm (7 inches) in diameter. Place about 2 tablespoons meat filling, some chopped egg and olives and a few sultanas in the centre of each circle. Spread filling out over half of the circle, leaving a margin of about 1 cm (½ inch) at the edge, and moisten the edge all round. Fold pastry over the filling (like a Cornish pasty) and press to seal, then crimp edges with the thumb and finger. Fold crimped edges back to make a firm 'hem' and arrange pasties on greased baking trays.

Bake the pasties in a preheated hot oven (200°C/400°F/Gas 6) for 15 minutes or until pastry is crisp and golden. MAKES 18.

Note: For snacks or cocktail savouries, you can make smaller *empanadas*, dividing the pastry into 30 pieces about the size of a walnut.

One of the most entrancing sights in the world is surely the floating gardens of Xochimilco, outside Mexico City. Rafts covered with soil and ablaze with flowers carry you through winding canals. Mariachi bands float past, blowing furiously, and water vendors offer an amazing array of clothes, food, drink and flowers. It's unique to Mexico—and it's unforgettable!

SILVER SERVICE AND THE GRILL ROOM

In the famous restaurants and grill rooms of the world's greatest hotels, the glamour never fades. You feel Edward VII, Dame Nellie Melba or Noel Coward may walk in at any moment! Part of the joy of eating at wonderful places like London's *Savoy* or *Connaught*, or at New York's *Plaza* or Paris's *Ritz*, lies in choosing between the *haute cuisine* style of the 'silver-service' restaurant and the less formal but gay and elegant grill. It's one of my favourite problems.

Silver Service—the art of using a spoon and fork as deftly as chopsticks to serve guests at the table—is respected among waiters as the mark of a professional and of a 'first-class' establishment.

For the guest, silver service is part of the enjoyable ritual of dining in the classic manner. For the chef, it is the opportunity for his finest presentations, with the food beautifully arranged on silver 'flats' and garnished with such delicacies as tiny tartlets or *bouchées*, mousses or aspic moulds, vegetables puréed and piped, stuffed or skilfully 'turned' to precise shapes . . . the embodiment of a style which the great chefs like Carême and Escoffier helped establish.

The behind-the-scenes picture of a great restaurant or grill room is as enthralling as the part the diners see. A grill chef cooking 20 or 30 orders, each to the specified degree of brownness outside and juiciness within, and each ready exactly when required, is a fascinating sight. Others in the kitchen are carrying out their own *tours de force* as fish are delicately poached, vegetables braised, mousses swiftly turned out, sauces finished and garnishes placed just so. All display the concentration which is indispensable to masterly cooking.

None of this means that the fine dishes of the silver service restaurant or the grill room are beyond the home cook. As with all cooking, their preparation is a matter of combining a number of quite simple steps. Use fresh, top-quality ingredients, read the directions all the way through before you start to cook, have at hand all the ingredients, utensils and accompaniments you will need, and these recipes are at your command.

In the 50s and early 60s, dishes which could be prepared at the table were especially popular. The *Maitre d'* would stand beside his *guéridon* (portable stove) and produce dazzling successes like Steak Diane.

At *The Ivy* restaurant in London, the *Maitre d'* has two versions of the origin of the dish—first, that a French chef created it for his daughter Diane, second that it was named after a Greek slang word for sauté pan, which is *dean*. I prefer the first explanation!

Coquilles St. Jacques Mistral
➧ *Scallops with Vermouth and Cream Sauce*

The last time I visited London I stayed at the *Royal Garden* hotel, whose *Royal Roof Restaurant* looks over Kensington Palace and the gardens. Thanks to the restaurant manager Mario Martinelli, I went home with recipes for several of their superb dishes, including this one. The accompaniment was wild rice, a great luxury, but Basmati rice with its distinctive nutty flavour makes a good alternative.

24 scallops, dark beards removed
175 g (6 oz) butter
2 tablespoons finely chopped spring onion
large pinch of ground saffron
4 tablespoons dry vermouth
350 ml (12 fl oz) Fish Stock (page 81)
450 ml (¾ pint) double cream
salt and freshly ground white pepper
extra 15 g (½ oz) butter
3 tomatoes, skinned, seeded and coarsely
*   chopped*
pinch of sugar
braised wild rice or Basmati rice, to serve (see
*   right)*
GARNISH
tarragon leaves
few thin slices truffle
3 teaspoons snipped chives

Pat the scallops dry with paper towels.

Melt half the butter, add chopped spring onion and cook gently until soft. Remove from heat and place the scallops on top of the onion. Sprinkle with saffron and cover with the vermouth and fish stock. Bring to the simmer and poach for 1 minute. Remove the scallops and keep warm.

Boil down the cooking liquid on high heat until it is reduced to a few spoonfuls. Stir in cream and boil until reduced by half. Season the sauce with salt and white pepper, strain it through a fine sieve and return it to the rinsed-out saucepan. Reheat and whisk in the remaining butter.

While the sauce is reducing, melt the extra 15 g (½ oz) butter, add chopped tomatoes and heat gently without cooking. Season with salt, pepper and a pinch of sugar and keep hot.

To serve, place tomato mixture in the centre of a heated serving dish and arrange the scallops round it. Pour the sauce over the scallops and garnish them with tarragon leaves and truffle slices, if using; garnish the tomatoes with chives. Serve with braised wild rice or Basmati rice. SERVES 4.

Braised Rice

Wash 75 g (3 oz) wild rice or Basmati rice in several changes of water, then dry on paper towels. Melt 25 g (1 oz) butter in a heavy saucepan, add rice and stir on medium heat for 2 minutes. Add 250 ml (8 fl oz) boiling chicken stock and cook on medium heat until steam holes appear in the rice, then cover tightly and cook on very low heat until the rice is tender—about 5 minutes for Basmati rice, 30 minutes for wild rice (check once or twice and add a spoonful of water if the wild rice is drying out). Serve at once.

Steak Diane

If you have a touch of the showman in you, why not prepare Steak Diane at the table for your guests, as it's done in *The Ivy* restaurant in London. Two steaks can be cooked at a time in an electric frypan, so in under 5 minutes 4 people are served. Have creamy mashed potatoes ready and a green salad on the table.

For each person allow the following:
1 thick slice, about 4 cm (1½ inches), fillet steak
salt and freshly ground pepper
50 g (2 oz) butter or a little more
2 tablespoons finely chopped parsley
1 clove garlic, finely chopped
2 tablespoons snipped chives (optional)
a good dash of Worcestershire sauce—about 1 tablespoon
1 tablespoon brandy

Trim all fat and gristle from the steak, then slice almost through each piece and open out like butterfly wings. Place steak between 2 pieces of plastic film and flatten out with a steak mallet or rolling pin so it looks like a large pancake—no thicker than 6 mm (¼ inch). Sprinkle lightly with salt and pepper.

Heat the butter in a heavy frying pan and when it is sizzling drop in the steak. Shake the pan by the handle to stop meat from sticking, then start timing: allow 40 seconds on the underside for rare steak, 1 minute for medium. Keep the heat high enough for the steak to brown quickly and, if necessary, add a little more butter.

Turn the steak over after the required time and sprinkle with half the parsley and garlic. Cook the other side until done to your liking (40 seconds-1 minute) and turn again. Sprinkle remaining garlic and parsley (and chives, if using them) over the top and add the Worcestershire sauce. Heat the brandy, set alight, and pour over the steak. Shake the pan to distribute the sauce, turn the steak over in it, then transfer to a hot plate and pour the pan juices over. SERVES 1.

Cailles aux Cerises
❦ Quail with Cherries

Auguste Escoffier died about 50 years ago, but there is a little of him in every good chef. I've heard even the most innovative chef confess: 'I go back to Escoffier for inspiration'. When I met this light, delicious presentation of quail with cherries in a smart London restaurant, I saluted the king of chefs whose recipe it is.

4 quail, cleaned
25 g (1 oz) butter
2 tablespoons brandy
4 tablespoons port, in which a strip of orange rind has been soaked overnight
250 ml (8 fl oz) White Stock (see right)
3 tablespoons redcurrant jelly
salt and freshly ground pepper
40 fresh poached or canned cherries, stoned
lemon juice
CROÛTES
4 slices of bread
1 tablespoon oil
25 g (1 oz) butter

Wipe the quail inside and out with damp paper towels and truss the legs and wings close to the body (see page 96).

Melt the butter in a heavy saucepan and brown the quail all over. Remove with a slotted spoon and set aside. Add brandy, port and orange rind to the pan and boil for 1 minute, stirring in all the brown crustiness that clings to the bottom of the pan. Remove orange rind, add stock and boil on high heat until the liquid is reduced to about 120 ml (4 fl oz). Stir in redcurrant jelly and season with salt and pepper to taste.

Return the quail to the saucepan, cover and simmer for 15 minutes. Add drained cherries and simmer 2 minutes longer to heat them through. Sharpen the sauce to taste with a little lemon juice.

While the quail are simmering, cut a circle from each slice of bread. Heat oil and butter together and fry the bread circles until golden on both sides. Drain on crumpled paper towels.

Remove the trussing strings and place a quail on each bread croûte. Spoon the sauce and cherries over and serve immediately. SERVES 4.

❧ Beef Stock

Place the following in a large saucepan: 1 kg (2 lb) beef bones, 500 g (1 lb) chopped stewing beef, 1 sliced carrot and onion, cold water to cover, 1 teaspoon peppercorns, 1 bouquet garni (page 16). Bring to simmering point, skim the surface, then simmer, covered, for 4–5 hours. Strain and chill. Remove fat before using.

White Stock: Use veal bones and veal in place of beef.

❦ To Clarify Stock

Strain stock, chill and remove all fat. Heat gently with 1 crushed eggshell and 1 lightly beaten egg white for every 900 ml (1½ pints) stock, whisking steadily until the mixture boils. Simmer undisturbed for 20 minutes. Line a colander with 2 layers of scalded muslin or disposable cloth, slide the egg white crust on to the cloth and slowly pour liquid through.

Vinaigrette

A classic accompaniment to grills is green salad tossed with vinaigrette (French Dressing). It's quick and easy to make in a screw-top jar: place in the jar 2 tablespoons wine vinegar, ¼ teaspoon salt, freshly ground black pepper, ½ teaspoon Dijon mustard and 90 ml (3 fl oz) olive oil or other good oil (walnut is delicious). Shake until well blended. Makes about 120 ml (4 fl oz).

Peppered Sprouts with Mushrooms

A spicy approach to sprouts! Cook 350 g (12 oz) baby Brussels sprouts in boiling, salted water until almost tender, about 10 minutes. Drain. In a frying pan, cook 1 medium onion, chopped, in 2 tablespoons olive oil until soft. Stir in ¼ teaspoon salt, 1 teaspoon cracked black peppercorns and 125 g (4 oz) sliced button mushrooms. Cook for 2 minutes, then add the sprouts and stir over moderate heat until the sprouts are tender. Serves 4.

Entrecôte Dorchester
Steak with Four Peppercorns

London has always attracted great chefs to the restaurants of its prestigious hotels, and one of the most famous is the *Grill Room* at *The Dorchester*. Now that different peppercorns are available, it seems natural that one of *The Dorchester's* inventive chefs would combine them in one dish—adding new flavour, colour and texture to the perennial favourite, Pepper Steak.

4 thick fillet or boneless rib steaks
salt
2 teaspoons each white and black peppercorns, cracked (see Note 1)
15 g (½ oz) unsalted butter
1 tablespoon oil
4 tablespoons brandy, warmed
120 ml (4 fl oz) dry white wine
120 ml (4 fl oz) double cream
15 g (½ oz) salted butter
1 tablespoon drained pink peppercorns
1 tablespoon drained green peppercorns

Trim the steaks of any gristle or excess fat and sprinkle lightly with salt. Combine cracked white and black peppercorns and press firmly and evenly into both sides of the steaks with the heel of the hand.

In a large frying pan, heat the unsalted butter and oil together. Add steaks and sauté on high heat for 3–4 minutes each side, for medium rare. (To sauté meat, place in hot fat, move each piece once to prevent sticking, then don't touch again until the meat is browned and slightly crusty underneath. Turn and repeat.)

Pour off any excess fat, add warmed brandy and set alight. Shake the pan until the flames subside. Transfer steaks to a heated platter and keep warm.

Add wine to the pan and stir over high heat, scraping up the brown crusty bits. Reduce the liquid to about 4 tablespoons, then stir in cream and any juices that have accumulated around the steaks on the platter. Cook over moderate heat until the sauce thickens slightly.

Cut the salted butter into small pieces and swirl into the sauce one piece at a time. Stir in pink and green peppercorns. Spoon the sauce over the steaks and serve immediately. SERVES 4.

Note 1: To crack peppercorns, place in a small, heavy bowl and press with the handle of a rolling pin until they crack. They should not be crushed too fine.

Note 2: This sauce is fiery, for those who like it that way. Reduce quantities of pink and green peppercorns to taste.

Coquilles St. Jacques au Safran
Scallops in Saffron Cream Sauce

Maxim's of Paris is not just another three-star restaurant, it is the quintessence of Paris. Under the glamour and glitter that have attracted generations of Royalty, stars, artists and Parisians, there is something solid and permanent. *Maxim's* is *Maxim's* and the food, like the service and atmosphere, is perfection. Here is one of the simple dishes great restaurants like *Maxim's* do so well.

1 kg (2 lb) scallops, with shells
75 g (3 oz) butter
1 shallot, chopped
large pinch of saffron
salt and freshly ground pepper
½ teaspoon Cognac or brandy
½ teaspoon dry vermouth
2 large tomatoes, skinned, seeded and chopped
125 g (4 oz) mushrooms, sliced
400 ml (14 fl oz) double cream
3 tablespoons Hollandaise sauce (page 21)

Open, wash and clean the scallops, removing them from their shells. Cook the scallops in a tightly covered frying pan with half the butter, the shallot, saffron, and salt and pepper to taste, for 4 minutes.

Remove scallops from the pan and set aside. Add the Cognac or brandy, vermouth, tomatoes and mushrooms to the pan and simmer for 15 minutes. Add the cream and remaining butter, a piece at a time. Reduce this sauce, stirring constantly.

When the sauce is smooth, add the scallops to reheat them. Bind the mixture with the hollandaise sauce. Serve at once with pilau rice. SERVES 4.

Entrecôte Dorchester

I am delighted to include in this chapter the contributions of M. Jean Valby, President of the international association of chefs, *La Chaîne des Rôtisseurs*, of which I am honoured to be the inaugural member in Australia. M. Valby's voice is an influential one in support of the classic skills and judgment, which, no matter what fashions come and go, are the foundation of fine cooking.

When the great hotels of the world are discussed, the *Savoy* of London often comes first.

The names associated with the *Savoy* since it opened in the late 1800s are among the most glittering in history: César Ritz (later to open his own *Ritz* hotels) was the first General Manager, Escoffier his *Maître Chef*. Johann Strauss conducted his waltzes in the restaurant and Pavlova danced in cabaret. Today, to lunch or dine in the *Savoy Grill* remains a grand occasion—one no visitor to London should miss.

Lamb Shrewsbury

When my daughter was studying cooking in London some 10 years ago, she wrote back of an excellent lamb dish enjoyed at *Lacy's* restaurant. She came back home, we re-created the dish, and still enjoy it today.

8 loin lamb chops, cut about 4 cm (1½ inches)
*   thick*
salt and freshly ground pepper
40 g (1½ oz) butter
1½ tablespoons flour
120 ml (4 fl oz) Beef Stock (page 77)
3 tablespoons port
2 tablespoons redcurrant jelly
¼ teaspoon dried rosemary

Ask your butcher to bone the chops and trim the tails, but to leave on the outer layer of fat. Remove the skin, wrap the fat around the meat and tie in place with string, to make noisettes. Season on both sides with salt and pepper.

Heat 25 g (1 oz) of the butter in a large, heavy frying pan and brown the chops on both sides over medium heat. Reduce the heat and cook a further 5–6 minutes on each side, or until still slightly pink in the middle. Remove strings and arrange noisettes on a heated serving plate.

Pour off all but 2 tablespoons of drippings left in the pan. Stir in the flour and cook until the mixture is smooth, stirring constantly. Take the pan off the heat and slowly stir in the stock. Return to the heat, add port, redcurrant jelly and rosemary and stir until the sauce is smooth and thickened. Swirl in the remaining butter, taste for seasoning, and spoon the sauce over the noisettes. SERVES 4–6.

Biftek Grillé Marchand de Vin

➤ *Grilled Steak with Red Wine Butter*

A restaurant's charcoal grill gives the fierce heat necessary to seal a steak quickly; this is the secret of the delicious brown crust which locks in the juices.

At home, preheat the grill for 15–20 minutes before brushing the bars with oil and putting on the steak. Choose thick cuts of tender steak—fillet, rump or sirloin—and nick the fat at 2.5 cm (1 inch) intervals to prevent curling. Grill each side for 1–2 minutes at very high heat, then turn the heat down a little or lower the meat from the heat. Continue to cook, turning once or twice, until medium rare (when the meat feels springy) or to your liking.

Steak may be seasoned with pepper before cooking but do not salt until cooked. Place the steaks on heated plates and top with *marchand de vin* butter.

Marchand de Vin Butter
120 ml (4 fl oz) dry red wine
1 tablespoon finely chopped spring onion
pinch of salt
freshly ground black pepper
50 g (2 oz) butter, softened
1 teaspoon lemon juice
2 teaspoons chopped parsley

Simmer the wine, spring onion, salt and pepper together until the liquid is reduced to 1 tablespoon. Cool. Cream the butter and gradually work in the wine and onion, the lemon juice and parsley. Form into a cylinder by rolling in plastic film, and chill. Cut into slices and place 2 slices, overlapping, on each steak. Serve immediately. SERVES 4.

Brochettes de Foie de Volaille

➤ *Brochettes of Chicken Liver*

A special recipe from M. Jean Valby, President of *La Chaîne des Rôtisseurs*.

For each person allow the following:
4 chicken livers
milk
8 small squares of bacon
8 button mushrooms
salt and freshly ground pepper
butter
8 small pieces of bay leaf
fine, soft breadcrumbs

80

Trim chicken livers, cut them in half and soak in a little milk for 2 hours (this lightens the flavour). Cook bacon in a dry frying pan for a minute or so, just until stiffened, and remove with a slotted spoon.

Drain chicken livers and dry with paper towels. Season livers and mushrooms with salt and pepper. Add a little butter to the pan in which you cooked the bacon and toss livers and mushrooms on high heat just until livers are stiffened.

Thread skewers with a piece of chicken liver, a piece of bay leaf, a square of bacon, a mushroom and so on. Brush with melted butter and roll in breadcrumbs. Grill at gentle heat, turning often, for about 10 minutes or until golden. Matchstick potatoes may be served as an accompaniment. SERVES 1.

Filets de Sole Bonne Femme
Poached Fillets of Sole with Mushrooms

Dine at *The Savoy* or *The Dorchester* in London, *Maxim's* in Paris, or *The Four Seasons* in New York City and you will find great sole dishes such as this on the menu. Dover sole is one of the finest fish in the sea and perhaps the cook's perfect fish. Its flesh is firm, white and delicate—lending itself to any number of sauces—and the fillets hold their shape beautifully, so they can be presented in elegant ways. I think they are perhaps at their delicate best when gently poached in a court bouillon of wine and aromatics, and served in a sauce made from the cooking liquid. When you master this easy recipe, you will have no problem in cooking the equally famous sole dishes which follow.

40 g (1½ oz) butter
1 small onion, finely chopped
12 button mushrooms, thinly sliced
6 fillets of sole or other fine-textured white fish, skinned
salt and freshly ground white pepper
1 tablespoon chopped parsley
170 ml (6 fl oz) dry white wine
120 ml (4 fl oz) water
SAUCE
15 g (½ oz) butter, softened
3 teaspoons flour
2 tablespoons double cream
squeeze of lemon juice

Melt the butter in a large, shallow pan and spread chopped onion and half the sliced mushrooms over the base of the pan. Arrange fish fillets, skinned side down, side by side on the vegetables and season with salt and pepper. Sprinkle remaining mushrooms and the chopped parsley on the fish and pour wine and water over.

Poach the fish, as described on page 60. Remove the fish and vegetables and keep them warm while making the sauce.

Boil the strained cooking liquid in the pan over high heat until it is reduced to about 250 ml (8 fl oz). Meanwhile, cream the softened butter with the flour to make beurre manié (page 113). Whisk beurre manié, a small piece at a time, into the boiling liquid to thicken it. Stir in cream and lemon juice to taste. Correct seasoning and spoon over the fish. Serve immediately. SERVES 6.

Filets de Sole Vin Blanc
Fillets of Sole with White Wine, Egg and Cream Sauce

Follow the recipe for Filets de Sole Bonne Femme (see left) up to the point where the fish and vegetables are removed to a heated serving platter.

Reduce the cooking liquid over high heat to about 120 ml (4 fl oz). Beat 1 egg yolk lightly with 4 tablespoons cream. Turn heat low and stir cream mixture into the cooking liquid. It will thicken slightly and turn glossy almost immediately. Do not allow to boil. Remove from heat and season with salt, freshly ground white pepper and lemon juice to taste. Spoon over the fish and serve immediately. SERVES 6.

Filets de Sole Duglére
Fillets of Sole with Tomatoes

Follow the recipe for Filets de Sole Bonne Femme (see left), but substitute 4 tomatoes, skinned, seeded and chopped, plus 1 clove garlic, crushed, for the mushrooms in that recipe. After removing fish and vegetables to a heated serving platter, reduce the cooking liquid and thicken with beurre manié as for Filets de Sole Bonne Femme. Remove from heat and swirl in an extra tablespoon of butter to finish the sauce. Spoon over the fish and serve immediately. SERVES 6.

Caper Sauce

A first cousin to tartare sauce, delicious with hot or cold fish. Combine in a bowl 250 ml (8 fl oz) Blender Mayonnaise (page 68), 250 ml (8 fl oz) sour cream, 3 tablespoons drained, finely chopped capers, 4 finely chopped spring onions and 1 tablespoon tomato paste. Season with lemon juice, salt and pepper to taste and a pinch of sugar. Makes about 450 ml (¾ pint).

Fish Stock

When fish is cooked in Court Bouillon (page 29) the poaching liquid itself makes excellent stock. Otherwise, follow this simple recipe. Place in a saucepan 500 g (1 lb) fish heads and bones, 1.2 litres (2 pints) cold water, 250 ml (8 fl oz) white wine, 1 teaspoon peppercorns, 1 slice of onion, a few slices of carrot and a bouquet garni (page 16). Bring just to simmering point, skim the surface, then simmer, covered, for 15 minutes. Strain before using. Makes about 1.5 litres (2½ pints).

Suprêmes de Volaille aux Ecrevisses

❧ *Chicken Breasts with Crayfish*

The splendid art of traditional *garniture* lives on at the *Royal Roof Restaurant* in London's *Royal Garden Hotel*. This delicate combination of chicken and crayfish is presented with a crayfish mousse and finished with a creamy chervil sauce, and truffles. For home cooks the dish is superb even without the crayfish mousse.

4 suprêmes (skinless, boneless half-breasts) of chicken
4 shelled, uncooked crayfish tails (or king prawns)
50 g (2 oz) butter
4 tablespoons Cognac or brandy, warmed
250 ml (8 fl oz) Chicken Stock (page 90)
1 tablespoon chopped fresh chervil or 1 teaspoon dried
120 ml (4 fl oz) double cream
salt and freshly ground white pepper
1 quantity Crayfish Mousseline (page 12), cooked in 4 individual moulds
8 thin slices of truffle and fresh chervil or watercress, to garnish

Trim any ragged edges from the suprêmes and cut and lift out the white sinew which runs down the underside of each. Dry suprêmes and crayfish tails with paper towels.

Heat the butter and, when sizzling, add the suprêmes. Sauté for 2 minutes on each side, then add the crayfish tails and sauté 1 minute on each side. Pour Cognac or brandy over, set alight and shake the pan until flames subside. Remove suprêmes and crayfish and keep warm.

Add chicken stock and chopped chervil to the pan and boil on high heat until reduced to about 120 ml (4 fl oz) liquid. Add cream and boil for 3 minutes longer. Season with salt and white pepper to taste. Strain the sauce through a fine sieve into a bowl, then return it to the rinsed-out saucepan and reheat.

Have ready the hot crayfish mousse. Turn the moulds out on to a heated serving platter and arrange the suprêmes and crayfish on the same platter. Coat the whole with the sauce and garnish each suprême and mousse with a slice of truffle and the platter with fresh chervil or watercress. SERVES 4.

Suprêmes de Volaille aux Ecrevisses

Cervelles au Beurre Noir

❧ *Brains with Black Butter*

European and American gourmets have always considered brains a great delicacy. This is probably the most popular way to prepare them—it is on the menu at London's *Savoy* as it was at the New York *Ritz-Carlton* in Louis Diat's day.

2 sets lamb's or calf's brains
TO BLANCH
2 tablespoons vinegar
1 teaspoon salt
5 peppercorns
½ onion, sliced
1 small carrot, sliced
4 sprigs of parsley
1 sprig of thyme or pinch of dried thyme
1 bay leaf
TO FINISH
salt and freshly ground pepper
2 tablespoons chopped parsley
1 tablespoon vinegar
12 capers
50 g (2 oz) butter

Wash the brains in cold water and remove the membrane which covers them. Soak the brains in cold water for several hours, changing the water several times. Put them in a saucepan, cover with cold water and add the ingredients for blanching. Bring the liquid to the boil, cover the saucepan and simmer for 30 minutes. Let the brains cool in the cooking liquid. Take them out only when they are to be drained for final cooking.

Drain the brains and cut each into 6 slices. Reheat in 2 tablespoons of the cooking liquid. Arrange the slices on a hot serving dish, season them with salt and pepper and sprinkle with parsley, vinegar and capers. In a small pan cook the butter until it is nut-brown. Pour the 'black' butter over the brains and serve them very hot. SERVES 4–6.

Although part of a good waiter's skill is to be unobtrusive, give yourself the pleasure of noticing his performance. He is a proud member of a profession which demands speed, dexterity, organization and a sound knowledge of food and wine. A first-class waiter combines some of the qualities of an actor, a diplomat, and, on occasion, a helpful nanny!

Crêpes

Light, delicate crêpes have a higher proportion of eggs to flour than pancakes. They are so tender they roll easily around a sweet or savoury filling, or can be folded and flambéed in luscious sauces, as in Crêpes Suzette.

150 g (5 oz) flour
pinch of salt
3 eggs, beaten
350 ml (12 fl oz) milk
1 tablespoon brandy
1 tablespoon oil

Sift the flour and salt into a large mixing bowl. Make a well in the centre and add eggs and milk. Stir from the centre with a wooden spoon, gradually drawing in flour. Beat well and stir in brandy and oil.

The batter may also be made in a blender, adding the dry ingredients to the liquid ones through the lid, with the motor running. Alternatively, make in a food processor, adding the liquid ingredients to the dry ones, through the feed tube, with the motor running.

Cover the bowl and allow to stand for 1 hour. Before using, stir the batter again and check consistency. The batter should be thin as cream—add more milk if necessary.

Heat a small, heavy frying pan—18 cm (7 inch) is ideal. Pour in a little oil and wipe it lightly over the surface with a paper towel crumpled into a ball. Pour out any excess oil. When the pan is just beginning to smoke, pour in enough batter to coat the base thinly, about 2 tablespoons, and rotate the pan to run the batter over evenly. Pour off any excess and judge the amount for your next crêpe accordingly.

Cook until bubbles appear and the batter loses its shine. Loosen edges and turn crêpe over, using a metal spatula. Cook 1 minute on the other side. Drop the crêpe out of the pan on to a tea-towel laid over a wire rack and then fold the ends of towel over the crêpe.

Repeat the process to make the remaining crêpes. The pan should not need further oiling, but wipe again with the oil-soaked paper towel if the crêpes show signs of sticking. Drop each crêpe directly on to the previous one and cover again with the ends of the towel. MAKES 18–20 18 cm (7 inch) crêpes.
Note: Crêpes may be made ahead and stored in the refrigerator or frozen. Wrap together in foil or a freezer bag the number that you will need at one time. Bring back to room temperature when needed. The crêpes will peel apart quite easily.

☙ Make a Tomato Rose
A pretty garnish for grilled meats and chicken. Peel a small, round tomato as you would an orange. Roll the tomato skin around itself to make one large or two small roses. This is quite easy to do, as the rose seems to fall naturally into shape. Add rose leaves from your garden, or blanch a few stalks of spring onion in boiling water for 20 seconds and arrange as leaves.

Crêpes Suzette

Everyone should enjoy, at least once, the classic restaurant experience of having a dish prepared and flamed at the table. What a production it is, with gleaming copper pans, leaping flames, and a waiter chosen for his expertise and showmanship!

Crêpes Suzette is among the most famous of these table dishes. At home, the crêpes may be assembled in the kitchen but flamed at the table, for a touch of restaurant theatrics.

12 Crêpes (see left)
SUZETTE SAUCE
4 sugar cubes
1 orange
75 g (3 oz) unsalted butter
few drops of lemon juice
120 ml (4 fl oz) Grand Marnier, Cointreau or
  Curaçao liqueur
120 ml (4 fl oz) brandy, warmed

If crêpes have been made ahead, warm them slightly, wrapped in foil, in a preheated slow oven (150°C/ 300°F/Gas 2).

Rub the sugar cubes on the rind of the orange until they are soaked in flavourful oil. Crush the sugar with a fork, then cream with 50 g (2 oz) of butter. Place the remaining 25 g (1 oz) of butter in a chafing dish or frying pan. Squeeze the orange and add the juice to the pan with the lemon juice and liqueur. Bring to the boil, then add the creamed orange butter and stir until dissolved.

Place the crêpes in the sauce one at a time and heat, spooning sauce over. Fold each crêpe in quarters like a handkerchief and push to the side of the pan before adding the next one.

When all the crêpes have been folded, spoon sauce over them, drizzle with warmed brandy and set alight. When flames die, serve 2 crêpes, with a little sauce, per portion. SERVES 6.

Pommes de Terre
❧ *Potatoes*

London's *Savoy River Restaurant* offers a choice of six ways with potatoes, *The Ivy* eight ways, *The Connaught* ten. A well-trained chef has at his command over 50 ways to present this favourite vegetable. Pommes de Terre Parmentier, Parisienne, Noisette and Château are some of the more stylish approaches —worthy companions to *haute cuisine* creations.

Pommes de Terre Parmentier

Peel 6–8 medium, old potatoes, trim the sides flat and cut them into 1.5 cm (¾ inch) sticks, then across into cubes. Cover with cold, salted water and boil for 4 minutes, then drain and dry gently on a cloth. Heat 75 g (3 oz) butter in a shallow pan, add the potatoes and cook on top of the stove or in a hot oven (200°C/400°F/Gas 6) until they are golden-brown, turning them occasionally with a spatula. Season with salt and pepper and sprinkle with parsley.

Pommes de Terre Parisienne

Follow the recipe for Pommes de Terre Parmentier, but use the small end of a melon baller to scoop the potatoes into little balls instead of dice.

Pommes de Terre Noisette

Prepare as for Pommes de Terre Parisienne, but do not cook in water. Dry potatoes well with paper towels. Heat 2 tablespoons oil and 50 g (2 oz) butter and, when the foam subsides, add the potatoes and sauté briskly, shaking the pan to roll them about, until golden-brown and tender. Season with salt.

Pommes de Terre Château

Peel 6–8 fairly large, old potatoes, trim the sides flat and cut them into quarters. Trim each quarter to make a barrel shape. Cover with cold, salted water, boil for 8 minutes, then drain and dry gently on a cloth. Heat 75 g (3 oz) butter in a shallow pan, add the potatoes and sauté them until tender and lightly browned. Season and sprinkle with parsley.

Pan-Fried Trout with Sage

Trout farming is now big business throughout the world, which is good news for both restaurateurs and home cooks. Excellent frozen trout are available all year round and many restaurants are preparing them in imaginative ways. I like this Brisbane way of cooking them with sage. (Illustrated on page 74.)

4 trout, cleaned, heads and tails left on
1 tablespoon finely chopped fresh sage or 1 teaspoon dried
salt and freshly ground pepper
flour for dusting
50 g (2 oz) unsalted butter
2 tablespoons oil
finely chopped parsley, to garnish
SAUCE
1 tablespoon finely chopped fresh sage or 1 teaspoon dried
50 g (2 oz) butter
lemon juice
salt and freshly ground pepper

Rinse the trout in cold water and pat dry with paper towels. Sprinkle the cavity of each trout with sage and salt and pepper. Dust lightly with flour, shake off excess, and season outside with salt and pepper.

Heat the unsalted butter and oil in a large, heavy frying pan and cook the trout for 4–5 minutes each side, or until outside is golden and flesh flakes easily when tested with a fork. Transfer to a heated platter.

Pour off the fat in the pan and add the sage and butter. Cook over gentle heat for 3 minutes, stirring; add lemon juice, salt and pepper to taste. Spoon over the trout and sprinkle with parsley. SERVES 4.

Beurre d'Ail

🐚 *Garlic Butter*

The garlic cloves are first boiled to make this French-chef version of a popular garnish for fish and baked oysters. Also good with grilled meats.

6 fat cloves garlic, peeled
125 g (4 oz) butter, softened

Cover the cloves with water, bring to the boil and boil for 5 minutes. Drain, and crush to a paste with a broad-bladed knife. Cream the butter, then beat in garlic. The butter can be forced through a pastry tube to make an attractive garnish, or chilled until firm. Allow one tablespoon for each serving.

If you are not completely happy about your grill, 'pan-grilling' gives excellent results. For this, you simply need a very heavy-based frying pan. Heat until it is very hot, then brush with oil or melted butter or a piece of beef fat. Add steaks and sear both sides quickly over high heat. Turn heat down a little and cook until done to your liking, turning once or twice.

THE INNOVATORS

Good chefs always want to serve food that is beautifully cooked and beautifully presented. Innovative chefs go a little further—they like to set themselves a challenge once they have mastered their profession. All around the world, these innovators are constantly exploring new ways to intrigue themselves as well as their patrons.

Innovation is not, however, mere novelty. The truly innovative idea, whether it's a twist on a classic recipe, a new combination of flavours or the arrangement of food on a plate, has a purpose—to delight and stimulate the eye and the palate.

The exciting creativity of the last few years—expressed in labels such as *La Nouvelle Cuisine, La Nouvelle Vogue*—has been an intriguing cross-section of the great cuisines. Chefs have travelled the world, learned from each other, taken what suits them—the Oriental way of brief cooking to preserve colour and texture, the good French tradition of composing a menu according to what's freshest and best at the market, the Japanese art of exquisite arrangement.

The new young chefs are bubbling with enthusiasm—questioning, creating, refining. They are bringing to their work a philosophy that welcomes change. Every chef worth his salt has a little bit of Escoffier and Carême in him; the past is to be loved and admired—but built upon. Today's innovative chef considers himself an artist, exploring new fields and expressing himself in an individual way.

Of course, innovative ideas can be found anywhere, from grand hotel restaurants to small eating places in the countryside.

This is a personal selection, collected from creative chefs who consider their work both a pleasure and a vocation.

For that enticing 'restaurant look' at home, try using large plates, big enough to act as a 'frame' for the food. (Even many desserts are now served on dinner plates.) If in doubt about colour, choose plain white.

Be aware of colour—use fresh herbs, lemons, tomatoes, vegetable julienne to spark a plate. Study food photographs, then add your own touches. *Voilà*—you're an innovative chef!

Petits Crèmes d'Asperges Sauce Maltaise

🕭 *Little Asparagus Creams with Maltaise Sauce*

Claude's restaurant in the Sydney suburb of Woollahra, now under the direction of Damien Pignolet and Josephine Carroll, has long been acknowledged one of the finest French restaurants in the southern hemisphere. Here is Damien's recipe for a delightfully original first course—creamy asparagus moulds with an orange-flavoured sauce.

CREAMS
1.5 kg (3½ lb) asparagus, peeled, trimmed and washed
salt
300 ml (½ pint) double cream, heated
6 egg yolks, beaten
salt and freshly ground white pepper
freshly grated nutmeg
6 lettuce leaves and 6 sprigs of coriander or parsley
SAUCE
2 tablespoons white wine
2 tablespoons white wine vinegar
6 peppercorns
½ bay leaf
juice of ½ orange
3 egg yolks, beaten
125 g (4 oz) unsalted butter, melted
1 teaspoon cold water
grated zest of ½ orange
salt

To make the creams: remove the coarse ends and cut off the tips of the asparagus about 1 cm (½ inch) below the head. Reserve the tips. Place trimmed stalks in a steamer set over boiling water, sprinkle with salt, and steam for 30 minutes. Purée stalks in a blender or food processor fitted with the steel blade.

Combine the asparagus purée, heated cream and egg yolks and season to taste with salt, pepper and nutmeg. Butter 6 small soufflé dishes (approximately 150 ml/¼ pint capacity). Divide the asparagus mixture among them. Place the dishes in a large baking dish and add enough hot water to come half-way up their sides. Bake in a preheated moderate oven (180°C/350°F/Gas 4) for 25–35 minutes or until the creams are set.

After the creams go into the oven, bring a small saucepan of salted water to the boil and cook reserved asparagus tips until tender, about 4 minutes. Drain and set aside. When the creams are cooked, remove them from the oven and allow to rest for 10 minutes.

While the creams are resting prepare the sauce.

Place wine, vinegar, peppercorns and bay leaf in a saucepan and boil over high heat until reduced to 1 tablespoon. Add orange juice and strain into the basin containing the beaten egg yolks. Place the basin over a pan of simmering water (do not let the bottom of the basin touch the water) and beat with a whisk until frothy and beginning to thicken. Gradually add the melted butter beating continuously. (As sauce thickens, add more butter, beating until all is used.) Remove from heat, beat in the cold water and add the orange zest. Stir in salt to taste.

Arrange a lettuce leaf on each of 6 heated plates (preferably white) and unmould a cream on to each. Put 3 asparagus tips on top of each cream, coat with hot sauce and garnish each plate with a sprig of coriander or parsley. SERVES 6.

Crème Topinambour
❧ *Cream of Artichoke and Scallop Soup*

This superb presentation of artichoke and scallop soup, crowned with puff pastry is a specialty of *Gravetye Manor*, a heavenly small hotel in Sussex. The Manor is an Elizabethan mansion with 30 acres of orchards, woodlands, a trout lake and one of the great gardens of England. The restaurant enjoys an international reputation in its own right. *Chef de Cuisine* is Michael Quinn, a young Yorkshireman whose outstanding flair and inventiveness are soundly based on classical training and impressive experience—a combination which produces the very best of innovative food. Small wonder that, by the time this book is published, he will be in charge of the kitchens of London's great *Ritz* hotel where his most famous predecessor was Escoffier himself.

175 g (6 oz) butter
1 kg (2 lb) Jerusalem artichokes, peeled and cut into pieces
125 g (4 oz) onion, coarsely chopped
125 g (4 oz) leek, coarsely chopped
30 scallops, dark beards removed
125 g (4 oz) flour
2.4 litres (4 pints) warm White Stock (page 77)
pinch of finely snipped chives
pinch of chopped fresh tarragon
4 tablespoons double cream
salt and freshly ground pepper
750 g (1½ lb) frozen puff pastry, thawed
1 egg, beaten

Melt the butter, add the prepared vegetables and 24 scallops and cook gently for 5 minutes. Stir in flour and cook a further 2 minutes. Remove from heat,

cool a little, and stir in stock, reserving 4 tablespoons stock. Return to moderate heat and stir until boiling, then simmer for 20 minutes.

Purée the contents of the pan in batches in a blender or food processor fitted with the steel blade, or rub through a sieve. Add herbs and cream, season with salt and pepper and allow to cool.

Poach the remaining scallops for 30 seconds in reserved stock, then drain them, cut into small dice and add to the soup. Ladle the soup into 8 deep ovenproof bowls. Roll out puff pastry, cut 8 circles to fit over bowls (pastry should be no more than 6 mm [¼ inch] thick), dampen edges of bowls and cover with pastry, pressing edges to seal. Brush with beaten egg and bake in a preheated hot oven (220°C/425°F/Gas 8) for 10–12 minutes or until pastry is puffed and brown. SERVES 8.

Crevettes à la Montaigu
❧ *Glazed Prawns in Pernod Sauce*

Chef Jean Jacques of the Melbourne restaurant, *Jean Jacques Seafood of France*, brings his own inimitable French touch to the preparation of superb seafood from Australian waters. For this first course, prawns are flamed in Pernod for a subtle hint of aniseed flavour, then folded through a creamy sauce which acquires a beautiful golden glaze after a moment under the grill.

1 kg (2 lb) shelled green prawns, or 2 kg (4½ lb) green prawns in the shell
salt and freshly ground white pepper
75 g (3 oz) butter
1 tablespoon chopped, blanched toasted almonds
1 tablespoon Pernod, warmed
250 ml (8 fl oz) Velouté Sauce (page 21)
120 ml (4 fl oz) double cream, whipped
120 ml (4 fl oz) Hollandaise Sauce (page 21)

Shell the prawns, if necessary, and remove dark veins. Season the prawns with salt and pepper.

Heat the butter in a large, heavy frying pan and sauté the prawns for 2 minutes or until they turn pink. Stir in almonds, then add warmed Pernod and set alight with a match. Shake the pan until flames die down and remove from heat.

Add the velouté sauce. Combine the whipped cream and hollandaise sauce and carefully fold into prawns. Divide the prawn mixture among 6 oval gratin dishes, or other individual flameproof dishes, and place under a preheated hot grill for 1 minute or until tops are golden and glazed. SERVES 6.

❧ Croûtons and Croûtes
Small squares or cubes of fried bread are called croûtons; larger pieces are croûtes. To make these, remove crusts from thickly sliced bread and cut bread into size required. Place enough oil (or equal parts of butter and oil) to come half-way up the sides of the bread in a frying pan and heat until it gives off a slight haze. Fry bread until golden on both sides, drain on paper towels and salt lightly. Store in an airtight container and reheat in a slow oven (150°C/300°F/Gas 2) as required.

Salad of Squid and Octopus

A dish which reflects the Mediterranean feeling of Sydney, with its sunny climate, miles of waterways and abundant seafood. It is a specialty of *Reflections*, Sydney's lovely northern beaches' restaurant created by Peter Doyle, whose artistry is not confined to the kitchen; Peter makes all of his dishes as beautiful as any picture.

1 kg (2 lb) squid, cleaned (page 31)
1 kg (2 lb) octopus, cleaned (page 31)
salt and freshly ground black pepper
2 bay leaves
6 peppercorns
25 g (1 oz) butter
1 Webb's Wonder or cos lettuce
125 g (4 oz) curly endive
90 ml (3 fl oz) Vinaigrette (page 78)
MARINADE
1 small onion, finely chopped
350 ml (12 fl oz) olive oil
2 large ripe tomatoes, skinned, seeded and chopped
4 tablespoons wine vinegar
3 tablespoons chopped parsley
3 tablespoons snipped chives
2 cloves garlic, peeled and halved
GARNISH
50 g (2 oz) carrot julienne (matchstick strips)
6 tiny tomatoes
chopped parsley

Cut the squid into julienne (matchstick strips).

Place the cleaned octopus in a saucepan with cold water to cover. Add a little salt and pepper, the bay leaves and peppercorns. Bring slowly to the boil, then turn heat very low so that the liquid just trembles. Cover and continue cooking until the octopus is tender. (This will depend on the octopus and may take 1–2 hours—test at intervals with the point of a knife.) Remove the pan from the heat and leave the octopus to cool in the cooking liquid. When cool, drain and cut into bite-size pieces.

Melt butter in a heavy saucepan and add the julienne of squid. Stir briskly over low heat until squid turns opaque—this will take only a short time. Remove from heat, turn squid into a sieve and rinse under cold water to stop further cooking.

Cook onion slowly in 4 tablespoons olive oil until soft. Add tomatoes, cover and simmer until the mixture is thick. Season lightly with salt and pepper and set aside to cool.

Mix vinegar with a little salt and pepper and beat

in the remaining cup of olive oil a little at a time. Add tomato mixture, parsley, chives and garlic. Season to taste, add the squid and octopus and mix thoroughly. Place in a covered container and refrigerate for 1–3 days—the longer the time, the better the flavour of the salad.

Wash and dry the lettuce and endive, toss in vinaigrette and heap on 6 individual plates. Pile the squid and octopus on top, garnish with carrot julienne and spoon over some of the remaining marinade. Place a tiny tomato on the side of each plate and sprinkle each salad with a little chopped parsley. SERVES 6.

Poires Fraîches Vinaigrette
🍐 *Fresh Pears with Herb Dressing*

Refreshing, beautiful to look at, simple yet subtle—a first course typical of Michael Quinn's approach to food at *Gravetye Manor* in Sussex.

6 slightly under-ripe pears, peeled
120 ml (4 fl oz) white wine vinegar
10 fresh mint leaves
10 fresh tarragon leaves
6 sprigs of mint, to garnish
SAUCE
170 ml (6 fl oz) Blender Mayonnaise (page 68)
120 ml (4 fl oz) double cream, softly whipped
1 teaspoon chopped fresh mint
1 teaspoon chopped fresh tarragon
DRESSING
170 ml (6 fl oz) white wine vinegar
1 tablespoon chopped, mixed fresh mint and tarragon
juice of 2 lemons
salt and freshly ground pepper
caster sugar
125 g (4 oz) smoked ham, cut into fine julienne
  (matchsticks)

Cover the pears with cold water, add vinegar and herbs and poach gently until pears are tender, about 10 minutes. Drain and cool; remove stalks carefully.

Make the sauce by folding all ingredients lightly together. Put in a sauceboat.

Combine all ingredients for the dressing. Cut the tops off the pears and, with a teaspoon, carefully scoop out the cores and seeds. Fill the hollows with dressing and put the tops back on. Place a sprig of mint on each in place of the stalk. Offer the sauce separately. SERVES 6.

Salad of Squid and Octopus

🐦 Chicken Stock

Place the following in a large saucepan: 500 g (1 lb) chicken bones or pieces, cold water to cover, 1 sliced carrot, 1 sliced onion, 1 teaspoon peppercorns and a bouquet garni (page 16). Bring to simmering point, skim surface, and simmer covered for 3–4 hours. Strain and chill. Lift off fat before using.

Noisettes d'Agneau aux Trois Purées

▶ *Noisettes of Lamb with Three Purées*

Michael Quinn of *Gravetye Manor*, Sussex, balances flavours brilliantly with three vegetable purées, sautéed lamb and a vermouth and butter sauce. The presentation has great style. (Illustrated on pages 86 and 87.)

8–12 noisettes of lamb (see Note)
3 tablespoons oil
50 g (2 oz) butter
4 tablespoons dry vermouth
125 g (4 oz) extra butter, softened
salt and freshly ground black pepper
PURÉES
750 g (1½ lb) each carrots, sweet potato and
*   parsnips, peeled and cut into pieces*
salt
sugar
250 g (9 oz) butter divided into 3 parts and cut
*   into cubes*
freshly ground black pepper
chopped parsley, to garnish

Prepare the purées first. Place vegetables in 3 separate saucepans, cover with cold water and add a pinch of salt to each and a pinch of sugar to the carrots. Cover and cook until tender. Drain, shake over the heat for a few minutes to dry off the vegetables, then purée separately in a blender or food processor fitted with the steel blade, or by rubbing through a sieve. Return each purée to its own saucepan over low heat and beat one-third of the butter, a piece at a time, into each. Season with salt and black pepper.

Butter a baking tray. Mould purées into egg shapes in the same manner as when shaping quenelles (page 12). As each egg shape is moulded, place it on the baking tray. When all are done, cover loosely with buttered foil and place in a preheated low oven (120°C/250°F/Gas low) ·to keep hot.

Dry noisettes on paper towels. Heat the oil and 50 g (2 oz) butter in a large, heavy frying pan until they give off a slight haze, add noisettes and sauté briskly about 4 minutes on each side or until well-browned and springy to the touch (this means the lamb will still be pink inside). Remove noisettes, cut off strings and keep warm.

To make the sauce: pour off fat from the pan, add vermouth and boil for 1 minute, stirring in the brown crustiness from the bottom of the pan. Whisk in the 125 g (4 oz) butter and season with salt and pepper.

Have heated plates ready and place 2 or 3 noisettes on each plate with a portion of each purée opposite them. Spoon a little of the sauce over each noisette and sprinkle a pinch of chopped parsley over each purée. Serve the remaining sauce separately in a heated sauce-boat. SERVES 4.

Note: Noisettes are made from a rack of lamb (with the flap left on) from which skin, excess fat and bones have been removed—your butcher will do this for you. Season inside with salt and freshly ground black pepper and, starting from the thick side, roll up tightly and tie with string at 4 cm (1½ inch) intervals. Cut through exactly half-way between strings. If using very young spring lamb, allow 3 noisettes per portion, otherwise allow 2.

Soupe de Tomates Fraîches au Pistou

▶ *Fresh Tomato Soup with Pounded Basil*

Here is an exciting recipe from Michel Guérard of France for a soup which can be served hot or cold. The *pistou* is a lovely touch.

300 g (11 oz) ripe tomatoes
1 small carrot
half a leek
1 shallot
1 clove garlic
1 teaspoon olive oil
1 sprig thyme
half a bay leaf
1 tablespoon tomato paste
1¼ litres (2¼ pints) Chicken Stock (page 90) or water
1 teaspoon salt, a pinch of pepper
PISTOU
2 teaspoons basil, pounded to a paste with
*   1 teaspoon olive oil*

Skin the tomatoes, cut them in half and press the halves lightly in the palm of your hand to squeeze out excess liquid and seeds.

Peel the carrot, leek, shallot and garlic, and chop them coarsely.

Brown them lightly in the saucepan in which you have first heated the olive oil; add the sprig of thyme and the half bay leaf. Cover them with the fresh tomatoes and the tomato paste. Moisten with the chicken stock or water. Cook gently, uncovered, for 20 minutes.

Remove the thyme and bay leaf, put the mixture into the liquidiser, purée it and strain back into the saucepan, and reheat. Add salt and pepper to taste.

Michel Guérard's name is synonymous with the culinary revolution that began in France in the 60s, and has evolved throughout the years to become *Nouvelle Cuisine*—a lighter, more wholesome, yet dazzlingly original approach to traditional French *haute cuisine*.

Serve in separate soup bowls, adding the pistou (basil and oil paste) at the last moment.

Delicious hot, this soup is also good when served iced; in which case, do not reheat it after puréeing in the liquidiser. Simply chill the mixture in the refrigerator after straining, do not add the pistou until you serve the soup, and decorate it with a little sprig of fresh basil. SERVES 4.

Petits Éclairs de Saumon ou Truite Fumée

👁 *Little Éclairs of Smoked Salmon or Trout*

This is one of *Donlevy's* (Melbourne) most exquisite ideas for a first course—little éclairs filled with luxurious smoked fish mousse and presented with a fresh cucumber and dill sauce.

1 quantity Choux Pastry (page 128)
1 egg, beaten with a pinch of salt and a dash of
*   water, for eggwash*
FILLING
225 g (8 oz) smoked salmon or smoked trout (or
*   other smoked fish such as mackerel)*
75 g (3 oz) smooth cream cheese, at room temperature
dash of Tabasco
prepared horseradish
freshly ground pepper
lemon juice
4 tablespoons double cream
1 egg white
salt
SAUCE
2 cucumbers, unpeeled, sliced lengthwise and seeded
3 teaspoons chopped fresh dill
250 ml (8 fl oz) sour cream
250 ml (8 fl oz) Blender Mayonnaise (page 68)
½ clove garlic, crushed
salt and freshly ground pepper

To make the éclairs: grease and flour a baking tray and, using a skewer, mark with parallel lines a little finger's length apart. Place the choux paste in a piping bag, fitted with a plain 1 cm (½ inch) tube, and pipe 7.5 cm (3 inch) strips between the lines, spacing them a little apart.

Brush choux strips with eggwash and bake in a preheated oven (220°C/425°F/Gas 8) for 12 minutes. Reduce heat to 180°C/350°F/Gas 4 and bake for a further 10 to 15 minutes or until the éclairs are golden-brown and feel light in the hand. Slit each éclair along one side as soon as they are removed from the oven and cool on a wire rack.

To make the filling: blend fish and cream cheese in a blender or food processor, or beat by hand, until smooth. Add a dash of Tabasco and horseradish, pepper and lemon juice to taste. Turn the mixture into a bowl, whip cream lightly and fold in. Beat the egg white with a pinch of salt until it forms soft peaks and fold into the mousse. Taste and adjust seasoning. Cover, and set aside in a cool place.

To make the sauce: slice cucumbers thinly, salt lightly and stand them in a colander for 10 minutes. Rinse, squeeze out excess liquid in a tea-towel and purée in a blender or food processor until smooth. Mix with remaining ingredients and season to taste.

Split the cooled éclairs in half and fill with the mousse. Spoon the sauce on to individual plates and place éclairs (3 per person) on the sauce. SERVES 10.

Nine-herb Salad of Hintlesham

One of the showpieces of Robert Carrier's *Hintlesham Hall* home in Suffolk, England, is the 18th-century herb garden, and some of his most innovative dishes make lavish use of fresh herbs. If you can't find traditional English herbs such as purslane and roquette for this Elizabethan-style salad, make up your own mixture and choose enough salad greens to serve 6.

mixed salad greens: iceberg, cos and mignonette lettuce
12 sprigs each of the following herbs, or your
*   own mixture: tarragon, purple and green*
*   basil, flat-leafed parsley, purslane, roquette*
Mustard Vinaigrette (see below)
1 small bulb fennel, coarsely chopped
2 tablespoons coarsely snipped chives
2 tablespoons coarsely chopped, curly parsley

Wash the salad greens and dry thoroughly in a salad dryer or with a clean towel. Cover and chill.

Cut or break the herbs into tiny sprigs, wash, drain and dry. Arrange the greens and herbs in a large salad bowl, pour the dressing over just before serving and sprinkle with fennel, chives and parsley. Toss well at the table and serve at once. SERVES 6.

Mustard Vinaigrette
Beat together 2 tablespoons wine vinegar and 1 tablespoon Dijon mustard. Add ½ teaspoon salt and a good grinding of pepper, then beat in 6 tablespoons of fruity olive oil a little at a time.
Note: Robert Carrier's trick for fruity oil is to keep 3 oil-packed black olives in the bottle of olive oil.

👁 Mignonette Bagatelle
The Innovators like to take advantage of the natural design and colours of food—like this simple salad served by Jean Luc-Lundy. For each serving, open the heart of a crisped mignonette (or Webb's Wonder) lettuce like a rose, strew over julienned beetroot and dress with walnut oil and a squeeze of lemon juice. Voilà!

Glenella Lamb with Rosemary

Glenella is a wonderful old 'born-again' guest house in the Blue Mountains of New South Wales—just a pleasant train ride west of Sydney. Since it was taken over by young Englishman Michael Manners and his wife Monique, it has won a reputation for absolutely wonderful food.

Michael, who does most of the cooking himself, originally trained at the Hotel School in Lausanne, Switzerland. Like most successful innovators, his imagination is supported by a wide knowledge of classic cuisine. This lamb dish, one of my favourites, demonstrates how the two go hand-in-hand at *Glenella*.

2 whole loins of lamb
freshly ground black pepper
2 tablespoons brandy
450 ml (¾ pint) Brown Stock (page 97)
1 tablespoon oil
15 g (½ oz) butter plus an extra nut of butter
4 tablespoons Madeira, warmed
1 sprig of fresh rosemary, chopped, or
    ½ teaspoon dried
salt
rosemary sprigs, to garnish

When you order loins from the butcher, ask him not to chine them or chop between the bones. Cut the fillets of lean meat from the bones, carefully remove all fat and gristle and tie each fillet into a neat shape with fine string. Season with black pepper, sprinkle with brandy, cover and set aside.

Simmer the stock over gentle heat until reduced to about 170 ml (6 fl oz). Set aside.

Heat the oil in a roasting pan over high heat, add the 15 g (½ oz) butter and when the foam subsides, add the lamb. Brown well all over, add Madeira and set alight, shaking the pan until the flames subside. Place the pan in the centre of a preheated, very hot oven (230°C/450°F/Gas 9) and roast for 8–10 minutes. Turn oven off, transfer lamb to a hot dish and leave in the oven for 10 minutes with door half open.

Meanwhile, add reduced stock to the pan with the rosemary; bring to simmering point, scraping up the brown bits from the bottom, season with salt to taste and strain into a small saucepan. Place the sauce over low heat.

Remove string from lamb and cut into thick slices, or cut into long thin slices (at a 60° angle) like a breast of duck.

Glenella Lamb with Rosemary

Remove the sauce from heat, swirl in the extra nut of butter and spoon on to one side of 6 heated plates. Arrange 3 overlapping slices of lamb on each of the plates. Serve at once, garnishing each plate with a sprig of rosemary. SERVES 6.

Langouste aux Mangues, Sauce au Basilic

◖ *Lobster with Basil Sauce and Mangoes*

The *Bagatelle* restaurant in Sydney's Darlinghurst is known for food that is creative in both approach and presentation, and at the same time based on the finest traditions of classic French cuisine. Fellow restaurateurs come here to eat, and overseas visitors compare it to the best that is happening in Paris and London. There could be no greater tribute to young chef Jean-Luc Lundy, co-owner of *Bagatelle* with his wife Béatrice. This lobster salad, with its beautiful combination of flavours, textures and colours, demonstrates Jean-Luc's very personal touch.

Court Bouillon (page 29)
2 small lobster tails (see Note)
2 large, ripe mangoes
SAUCE
2 tablespoons good wine vinegar
6 tablespoons olive oil
1 small clove garlic, peeled
30 fresh basil leaves
salt and freshly ground white pepper

Bring the court bouillon to the boil in a large saucepan. Add lobster tails and simmer for 6–8 minutes or until shells turn red. Remove lobster tails from the pan. When cool enough to handle, remove shells and cut flesh into slices 1 cm (½ inch) thick.

Meanwhile, make the sauce. Place vinegar, oil, garlic and basil leaves in a blender or food processor fitted with the steel blade and process until smooth. Season to taste with salt and pepper.

With a sharp knife, make a slit lengthwise around the mangoes and peel off the skin. Cut the flesh into very thin slices.

Assemble the dish on 4 large, individual plates. First, make a circle of mango slices on each plate, leaving a space in the centre. Heap medallions of lobster in the space and spoon the sauce in a ribbon around the outside of the mango slices. SERVES 4.
Note: Jean-Luc uses live green lobsters for this dish, but you can use frozen lobster tails.

◖ Blanching Nuts
Blanching simply means to remove the skin of nuts. To blanch almonds, cover them with boiling water, leave for 5 minutes, then drain and slip off skins with the fingers. To blanch hazelnuts or pistachios, roast them on a tray in a moderate oven (180°C/350°F/Gas 4) for 10 minutes. The skins can then be rubbed off with a cloth.

Smoked Duck Breasts with Ginger Butter Sauce

Young chef Tony Rogalsky is going from success to success at his beguilingly-named Melbourne restaurant, *The Hot Pot Shop*. This recipe demonstrates his originality in both approach and presentation— and with Tony's clear instructions for smoking the duck, it should not be beyond the scope of a careful home cook.

2 × 1.5–2 kg (3½–4 lb) ducks
salt
1 onion, peeled and quartered
1 unpeeled carrot, washed and roughly chopped
1 stick of celery, roughly chopped
1 bouquet garni (1 bay leaf, 1 sprig of parsley, 1
*   sprig of thyme, 1 clove and 5 peppercorns,*
*   tied in a muslin bag)*
900 ml (1½ pints) cold water
sawdust (see Note)
slices of kiwi fruit, to garnish
GINGER BUTTER SAUCE
250 ml (8 fl oz) green ginger wine
1 small piece fresh ginger (about 15 g/½ oz),
*   peeled and cut into fine julienne (matchstick*
*   strips)*
250 ml (8 fl oz) duck stock (see method)
½ teaspoon preserved red ginger (from Asian
*   food stores)*
25 g (1 oz) unsalted butter, cut into small cubes
salt and freshly ground black pepper

To Truss Poultry

Whether roasting or poaching a bird, take a moment to truss it into a neat shape. Shape the bird with both hands, tucking the neck flap underneath the folded wings at the back, and lay it breast up. Take a piece of string and place the centre below the breast at the neck end. Bring the ends down over the wings to cross underneath, then up to tie the legs and tail (parson's nose) together.

Carefully remove the breasts from the ducks, sprinkle lightly with salt, and set aside, covered. Remove thighs and drumsticks and reserve for another dish. Use the dark carcases to make stock as follows:

Break each carcase into 2 or 3 pieces and place the bones in a baking dish. Bake in the upper half of a preheated very hot oven (230°C/450°F) for 20–30 minutes, stirring bones occasionally until they are well browned. Add onion, carrot and celery and return dish to oven until vegetables are browned, about 15 minutes.

Transfer solid ingredients to a saucepan, leaving fat behind. Add bouquet garni and cold water and simmer very gently for 2 hours, skimming the surface now and again (make sure the liquid doesn't boil; it should barely quiver). Strain the stock and taste. If the flavour is not concentrated enough, return to a clean saucepan and reduce over low heat. Cool, then cover and refrigerate until the fat sets. Lift off fat, and set stock aside.

To smoke the breasts, choose 2 small flameproof baking dishes of even size, making sure one has a heavy base. Sprinkle sawdust over the surface of the heavy-based dish to a thickness of approximately 2 cm (¾ inch). Place a metal rack over the sawdust and arrange the breasts on the rack.

Invert the second baking dish over the breasts so it completely encloses them and the rack. Encase the 'smokehouse' with heavy duty aluminium foil, sealing the joins very carefully so no smoke can escape.

Place the heavy dish over medium heat until the sawdust ignites and starts smoking (small wisps of escaping smoke will indicate this). Turn heat to very low and continue 'smoking' for 15 minutes. Turn off heat but leave 'smokehouse' on stove for 5–10 minutes. When sawdust is extinguished and there is no further smoke, remove foil and baking dish cover and put the duck breasts aside in a warm place.

To make the ginger butter sauce: bring wine, ginger julienne and stock to the boil over high heat and boil rapidly until reduced by half. Add preserved red ginger. Whisk the butter gradually into the boiling liquid and season to taste with salt and pepper.

To serve, carve the duck breasts into thin slices. Arrange on a heated serving platter and pour a little hot sauce over. Garnish the edge of the platter with slices of kiwi fruit. SERVES 4.
<u>Note:</u> Tony suggests using sawdust from pine, hickory, red gum or any other wood of your choice. Sawdust is available at many barbecue outlets or timber mills, or your butcher may be able to supply some.

Lobster Tails Steamed with Marjoram

Tony and Gay Bilson were among the very first of the brilliant young chefs to bring a new dimension to Australian restaurant food. Today, their *Berowra Waters Inn*—delightfully located beside the Hawkesbury River near Sydney, and reached by boat—is a Mecca for Australian lovers of fine food and overseas visitors alike. Here is the Bilsons' recipe for lobster in a sauce flavoured with fresh marjoram.

For each serving, allow the following:

1 small lobster
2–3 sprigs of marjoram
1/2 tomato, skinned, seeded and diced
SAUCE
mirepoix (see below)
125 g (4 oz) butter
5 tablespoons dry white wine
1 teaspoon chopped fresh marjoram
5 tablespoons double cream
salt and freshly ground white pepper

Kill the lobster by freezing.

Blanch the lobster by dropping it into boiling water for 5 minutes only, then run cold water over it to stop further cooking.

Separate the tail from the head and shell the tail, leaving the meat in one piece. Make an incision on the back of the tail and open it out in a 'butterfly' shape, exposing the inside flesh.

Place the tail in a steamer with marjoram sprigs and top with tomato. Steam for approximately 7 minutes or until the inside flesh is white.

Meanwhile, make the sauce. Smash the lobster head and sauté with the mirepoix in 25 g (1 oz) butter. Add white wine and boil down until reduced by half. Add marjoram and cream and boil down again until the liquid reaches a syrupy consistency. Strain the sauce and beat in the remaining butter, seasoning to taste with salt and white pepper.

To serve, pour the sauce into a wide, shallow bowl and place the tail on top. SERVES 1.

Mirepoix

This is a mixture of aromatic vegetables and herbs. For each serving, allow 1 tablespoon each of finely diced carrot and onion, 1/2 tablespoon finely diced celery, a sprig of thyme and a small piece of bay leaf.

Seafood Blanquette

This dish is the creation of Peter Doyle, who started *Turrets* restaurant in a city pub, and has now moved to a new location on the magic northern peninsula of Sydney. His new restaurant, housed in a charming old cottage at Palm Beach, offers the same superbly cooked and original food that so quickly earned Peter a reputation as one of the best young chefs in Australia.

750 g (1 1/2 lb) green prawns, shelled
750 g (1 1/2 lb) skinless fillets of John Dory or
*   other firm, white fish*
2 cucumbers, peeled
1 canned pimiento
900 ml (1 1/2 pints) Fish Stock (page 81)
250 ml (8 fl oz) double cream of Crème Fraîche (page 21)
salt and freshly ground white pepper
lemon juice
2 tablespoons mint leaves, cut into fine strips
50 g (2 oz) butter, softened

Devein the prawns. Cut the fish fillets into *goujons*, strips about 8 × 1 cm (3 × 1/2 inch), removing any bones. Halve the cucumbers lengthwise and scoop out the seeds. Cut into large dice, then trim into olive shapes. Drop these into boiling, salted water, count to 10, drain, and refresh under cold water. Cut pimiento into julienne (matchstick strips).

Boil the fish stock rapidly in a stainless steel or enamel saucepan until reduced by half. Take out 250 ml (8 fl oz) of stock and pour into the bottom of a steamer or saucepan. Add cream to the remaining stock and boil until reduced by one-third. Set aside.

Bring the 250 ml (8 fl oz) fish stock to the boil. Place strips of fish in the top of the steamer or a metal colander and place over the boiling stock. Cover tightly with a lid or foil and steam over high heat for 2 minutes. Uncover, add the prawns, cover again and continue steaming for a further 1–2 minutes until prawns turn pink. Remove from heat and keep tightly covered.

While fish and prawns are cooking, gently reheat the cream sauce and add the cucumber and pimiento. Season with salt, pepper and lemon juice to taste and simmer for 4 minutes; add strips of mint and simmer 1 minute longer. Remove from heat and beat in the butter in walnut-size pieces, blending in each piece before adding the next.

Arrange the fish and prawns on 6 individual plates. Spoon cucumber in among the fish and prawns and spoon sauce over each serving spreading the mint and pimiento attractively on top. SERVES 6.

❧ Brown Stock
Make this in the same way as Beef Stock (page 77) but brown bones and vegetables first. Place them in a greased roasting pan, sprinkle with a little oil, and roast in a hot oven (230°C/450°F/Gas 9) until a rich brown, turning everything to brown evenly. Make sure to scrape up the brown bits from the roasting pan and add to the saucepan.

Truffled Galantine of Quail

In any discussion of Australia's innovative chefs, the name of Stephanie Alexander is one of the first mentioned. She is chef (and co-owner, with husband Maurice) of the Melbourne restaurant that bears her name. The food at *Stephanie's* certainly expresses—beautifully—this young chef's personal preferences. She likes clear, strong tastes such as fish broth, bouillon, and saffron. She believes in the concept of a well-designed total meal, so the restaurant offers a prix fixe format of several smallish courses. She abhors shortcuts, so there are no boosters, colourings, inappropriate starches or thickeners in her lovely food. And perhaps nicest of all for her patrons, she admits to a 'touch of the housewife'—she treats them as if they were guests in her own home. For a very special occasion, here is a Stephanie Alexander galantine.

🐦 To Skin and Seed a Tomato

Drop the tomato into boiling water, count to six, remove it and drop into cold water. Cut out the blossom end of the tomato with the point of a small knife. Make a nick in the skin and pull it off.

To seed the tomato, cut in half crosswise and squeeze seeds out gently.

6 quail
salt and freshly ground pepper
dash of Cognac
40 g (1½ oz) butter
350 g (12 oz) mirepoix (chopped, mixed
*   vegetables including a skinned, seeded tomato)*
1 pig's trotter
1.6 litres (2¾ pints) light Chicken Stock (page 90)
1 tiny can truffles, drained and juice reserved
port
DUCK MOUSSE
75 g (3 oz) duck livers
50 g (2 oz) pork fat, cut into small dice
50 g (2 oz) butter
75 g (3 oz) canned foie gras
3 teaspoons double cream
MARINADE
1 sprig of thyme and 1 bay leaf marinated in 4
*   tablespoons port, with salt and pepper to taste*

First, prepare the quail. Cut out the backbone with poultry shears and carefully remove rib cage with a sharp knife and fingers, leaving wings and legs intact. (Keep knife blade always angled into carcase to avoid cut fingers.) Sprinkle opened-out birds with salt, pepper and Cognac. Cover and refrigerate for a few hours.

Heat 25 g (1 oz) butter in a heavy saucepan and brown quail bones over moderate heat. Heat remaining 15 g (½ oz) butter in a small saucepan and brown mirepoix, stirring to prevent sticking. Add mirepoix to quail bones with pig's trotter and stock. Bring to the boil, then cover and simmer for 2 hours.

Strain stock into a clean saucepan and discard bones, mirepoix and pig's trotter. Boil stock rapidly until it is reduced to one-third. Cool, remove any fat particles and clarify (see page 77). Flavour with the juice reserved from the can of truffles, add port to taste and check seasoning. Cool and refrigerate. (If mixture hasn't jellied, reheat and add 1 teaspoon gelatine, stirring until gelatine dissolves.)

To make the mousse: place the duck livers and pork fat in a bowl and pour port and herb marinade over. Cover and leave for 2 hours. Remove livers and cook them rapidly in butter until browned outside but still pink inside, about 2 minutes. Remove livers with a slotted spoon and set aside.

Pour marinade into the pan, scrape up any brown bits on the bottom and boil rapidly until reduced by half. Remove thyme and bay leaf. In a food processor fitted with the steel blade, purée duck livers and pork fat with the cooking juices, then rub through a fine sieve to remove any sinews. Process the purée again, adding foie gras, then stir in cream and check seasoning. Chill until required.

To prepare the galantine: stuff each quail with 1 tablespoon of the duck mousse and sew up with white cotton thread, leaving a long tail of the thread for easy removal. Truss and cook in a preheated hot oven (220°C/425°F/Gas 8) for 10 minutes, until golden. (Don't overcook, flesh must be slightly pink.) Cool and refrigerate. When quite cold, remove the threads.

Place the quail on a rack set over a tray. Melt prepared aspic over gentle heat and place in a bowl set in another bowl filled with ice. Stir until aspic becomes thick. Rapidly spoon aspic over quail, then scatter each with a little chopped truffle. Scoop up excess aspic from tray, re-melt it, then return to bowl over ice. When thickened, spoon another layer over quail. Repeat this process of melting and thickening aspic until quail have a sufficient coating, or until all aspic is used up.

Serve quails with finger bowls, so legs and wings can be eaten in the fingers. SERVES 6.

P.S.: At *Stephanie's*, the galantine is served in a 'nest' of fresh garden herbs with a few flowers entwined for colour.

<u>Note:</u> Canned truffles and *foie gras* (goose liver pâté) are available from good delicatessens and many high class supermarkets. Your poultry shop will order quail and duck livers for you.

Truffled Galantine of Quail

Danish-born Mogens Bay Esbensen has an international background reflected in his original, eclectic approach to food: his menus are apt to be inspired by Scandinavia, the Orient, France, Italy. He has been the driving force behind some of Sydney's finest restaurants, and still delights in passing on his skills to aspiring chefs and home cooks. The Australian food scene has been enriched by Mogens' talents and enthusiasm.

Potato Bread

Innovation can take many forms. Mogens Bay Esbensen, of *Butler's Restaurant* in Kings Cross, and *The Old Bank Restaurant* in Darlinghurst, Sydney, suggests the combination of warm, old-fashioned Potato Bread served with fresh, cold butter and radishes. He adds: 'Don't forget mugs of foaming cold beer.' I think the combination is perfect for a lazy lunch on a sunny weekend.

350 g (12 oz) old potatoes
40 g (1½ oz) compressed yeast
450 ml (¾ pint) tepid water
1 kg (2 lb) white bread flour (from the health food shop)
2 teaspoons salt
1 egg yolk, beaten with 2 teaspoons water
1 teaspoon sea salt (coarse salt)
3 teaspoons poppy seeds

Boil the potatoes in their skins until tender, then peel and mash. Dissolve the yeast in the tepid water. Place the flour in a large bowl and sprinkle salt over the top. Pour the dissolved yeast into the middle and stir a little flour into it. Allow this mixture to rest for 15 minutes.

Add the mashed potatoes to the yeast and flour mixture and mix well with a wooden spoon to make a dough. Cover the bowl with plastic film and a tea-towel and leave in a warm place for 30 minutes until the dough has doubled in size.

Punch the dough down and shape into 20 balls. Place the balls on a buttered baking tray in a circular shape, close together. Place in a warm place to rise for 20 minutes.

Preheat the oven to hot (200°C/400°F/Gas 6). Brush the rolls with beaten egg yolk, sprinkle with sea salt and poppy seeds and bake for 30 minutes or until nicely browned and cooked through. MAKES 20.

Feuilleté de Petites Cigales
➤ *Shellfish in Puff Pastry*

Overseas visitors to Australian fish markets are often intrigued by what looks like a squat, miniature lobster. This is the Moreton Bay or Balmain 'Bug'— an unflattering name for one of the most succulent of all Australian sea creatures, with firm, white flesh tasting something like a cross between lobster and crab. Jean Jacques, of Melbourne's *Jean Jacques Seafood of France*, makes these little 'bugs' into a superb first course, not difficult to prepare at home.

Substituting large prawns gives you almost the same results.

3 tablespoons white wine vinegar
18 large green prawns
2 × 350 g (12 oz) packets frozen puff pastry, thawed
beaten egg yolk, to glaze
SAUCE
1 tablespoon finely chopped onion
120 ml (4 fl oz) dry vermouth
250 ml (8 fl oz) Velouté Sauce (page 21)
250 ml (8 fl oz) double cream
1 tablespoon snipped chives
salt and freshly ground white pepper

Bring a large pan of water to the boil with the vinegar. Add the prawns and cook for 5 minutes after water returns to the boil. Remove the prawns and, when cool enough to handle, cut the soft, white underside of the shell down the centre, without cutting through the meat. Remove meat in one piece, and set aside.

Roll the pastry out to 6 mm (¼ inch) thickness and cut 6 strips 15 cm (6 inches) long and 8 cm (3 inches) wide. (Reserve leftover pastry for another dish.) Chill strips for 20 minutes. Brush tops of strips with egg yolk, arrange on a lightly dampened baking tray and bake in a preheated very hot oven (230°C/450°F/Gas 9) until golden-brown and cooked through, about 10 minutes.

While the pastry is cooking, prepare the sauce. Place onion and vermouth in a small saucepan and boil over high heat until liquid is reduced by half. Add velouté sauce and cream and boil over moderate heat for 5 minutes. Turn heat to low, add the reserved meat and slowly reheat for about 5 minutes. Stir in chives. Season to taste with salt and pepper and keep warm.

Remove the pastry strips from the baking tray. Split each one in half through the middle, giving 2 pieces 15 × 8 cm (6 × 3 inches). Arrange bottom halves on 6 large, round, heated dinner plates. Place 3 pieces of the seafood on each piece of pastry, spoon a little sauce over and the rest around the pastry. Top with the second piece of pastry and serve at once. SERVES 6.

Walter's Waldorf Salad

Walter Magnus was one of the great innovative Australian chefs of a generation ago. His son Peter, who has inherited his late father's love of food and cooking, and who is a fellow member of *La Chaîne des Rôtisseurs*, was kind enough to give me Walter's special approach to a famous salad.

6 Granny Smith apples
juice of 2 lemons
6 tender sticks of celery, sliced
75 g (3 oz) walnuts, coarsely chopped
1 × 440 g (15 oz) can pineapple pieces, drained
120 ml (4 fl oz) mayonnaise, home-made if
    possible (page 68)
120 ml (4 fl oz) sour cream
2 tablespoons clear honey
salt

Peel and core the apples and cut into small cubes (about the size of a little fingernail). Place in a large bowl and toss with the strained lemon juice. Add the sliced celery to the bowl with the walnuts and pineapple.

Combine mayonnaise, sour cream and honey with salt to taste and fold through the apple mixture. Cover and chill for several hours or overnight to blend and mellow the flavours. Bring to room temperature to serve. SERVES 6.

Sorbet à la Framboise Double
🍂 *Double Raspberry Sorbet*

This vividly beautiful dessert features raspberries twice over, and is served with whole raspberries for intensity of flavour and a magical combination of textures. It is offered by Jean-Luc Lundy and his wife Beatrice, at their *Bagatelle* restaurant—a converted Victorian terrace in Sydney's Darlinghurst.

350 g (12 oz) fresh raspberries or thawed frozen
    raspberries
SORBET
5 tablespoons sugar
150 ml (¼ pint) water
300 g (10 oz) fresh or thawed frozen raspberries
2 tablespoons lemon juice
SAUCE
200 g (7 oz) fresh or thawed frozen raspberries
3 tablespoons sugar
170 ml (6 fl oz) water
1 tablespoon lemon juice

Place the sugar and water in a small saucepan, bring to the boil and boil until syrupy—about 3 minutes. Remove from heat and cool. Purée the raspberries in a blender or food processor fitted with the steel blade, then rub through a fine sieve into a bowl. Stir in cooled syrup and lemon juice.

You can process the mixture in an electric *sorbetière* until it thickens or use the following method. Pour the sorbet into a round, metal cake tin and place in a freezer until it begins to set around the edges, about 30 minutes.

From then on, stir the mixture with a spoon every 10 minutes until thick—an extra hour or so. (This constant stirring gives a smooth texture to the sorbet.) Cover and leave in the freezer until required.

To make the sauce: make a syrup by boiling sugar and water together (see sorbet above) and allow to cool. Purée the raspberries in a blender or food processor fitted with the steel blade and rub through a fine sieve. Add to the syrup with the lemon juice, cover and chill.

Arrange the dessert individually on large, flat plates, Using 2 tablespoons, scoop the sorbet into egg shapes and arrange 3 scoops on each plate in the form of a three-pointed star. Scatter fresh raspberries between the points of the star and spoon the sauce over. Serve at once. SERVES 4.
Note: For a dinner party it helps to shape the sorbet 'eggs' in advance. Placed on a metal tray they can be stored in a freezer for up to 1½ hours before serving, and transferred to the plates with a spatula or slice.

Sydney people still speak nostalgically of Le Coq D'Or restaurant in Ash Street. 'The Golden Rooster' set new standards in restaurant style, with prize-winning murals by Elaine Haxton and two dining-rooms—one serving only egg dishes. As popular as the restaurant itself was owner-chef Walter Magnus, famous for his wide smile and elegant monocle as well as his marvellously creative food.

🍂 Cheese Soufflé Savoy
Work 1 tablespoon of butter into 2 tablespoons flour, then whisk into 450 ml (¾ pint) of boiling milk. When smooth, remove from heat, add 2 tablespoons grated Gruyère cheese, 3 tablespoons grated Parmesan cheese and 4 egg yolks. Season well and fold into 6 stiffly beaten egg whites. Bake in a 1.2 litre (2 pint) soufflé dish in a preheated hot oven (200°C/400°F/Gas 6) for about 20 minutes.

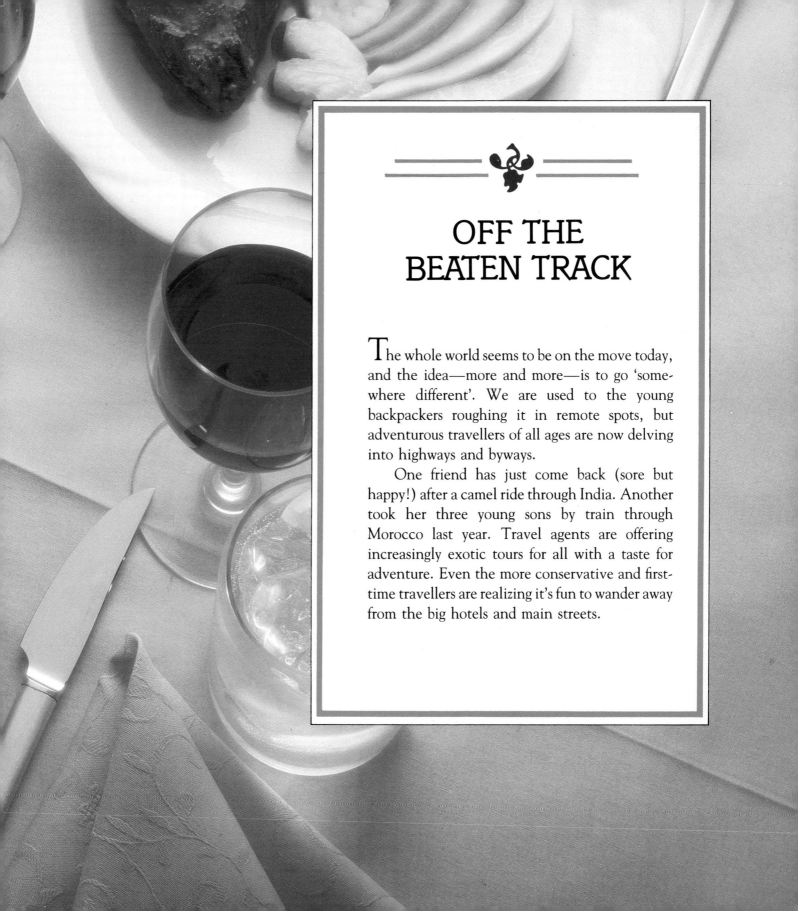

OFF THE BEATEN TRACK

The whole world seems to be on the move today, and the idea—more and more—is to go 'somewhere different'. We are used to the young backpackers roughing it in remote spots, but adventurous travellers of all ages are now delving into highways and byways.

One friend has just come back (sore but happy!) after a camel ride through India. Another took her three young sons by train through Morocco last year. Travel agents are offering increasingly exotic tours for all with a taste for adventure. Even the more conservative and first-time travellers are realizing it's fun to wander away from the big hotels and main streets.

When you go off the beaten track, whether to a different country or behind the scenes in a popular one, you certainly have more chance of meeting local people instead of other tourists. You also have the opportunity of trying the real food of the country, not 'international' versions aimed at the conservative traveller. And there is always the promise of the unexpected! In remote Norfolk Island in the Pacific, for instance, still inhabited by descendants of 'Bounty' mutineers, the system of bartering has been preserved. At one small restaurant I enjoyed fish that had just been traded by a fisherman for lemons from the restaurant's lemon tree. The salad of Trefoil greens was by courtesy of an islander who had exchanged his greens for a container of guava icecream. The icecream itself was due to nature's bounty, for the guava grows wild on Norfolk. All in all, a magic meal!

I also remember lining up for freshly grilled satés with Balinese children at Sanur Beach . . . watching them catch coconut crabs in Noumea . . . trying flying fox cooked in red wine at Vanuatu in the New Hebrides . . . the kind of experiences waiting for everyone with a touch of adventure in their bones.

I hope this chapter encourages you also to explore the memorable possibilities waiting 'off the beaten track'.

Garlic has always been credited with wonderful powers. In classic times it was eaten by athletes to ensure their best performance and by farm labourers to maintain their strength. It has been cited as a cure for fever, consumption, snake bite, worms, plague and the vapours. Even today many people believe it is wise to carry garlic or wear it threaded round the neck to ward off sickness.

Chicken Liver Terrine with Port and Brandy

Prince Edward Island, Canada's smallest province, is the setting for that charming book of our childhood, *Anne of Green Gables*. The capital, Charlottetown, has relaxed little restaurants like the *Griffin Room* that offer excellent, home-style cooking. Here is a hearty terrine you can look forward to on a visit to Charlottetown! Meanwhile, it would make an excellent first course for your next dinner party.

4 tablespoons olive oil
2 large onions, finely chopped
1 clove garlic, crushed
500 g (1 lb) chicken livers
225 g (8 oz) lean minced beef
225 g (8 oz) lean minced pork
120ml (4 fl oz) brandy
4 tablespoons port
1 tablespoon chopped fresh oregano or
  1 teaspoon dried
½ teaspoon dried rosemary
½ teaspoon dried thyme
salt and freshly ground pepper
350 g (12 oz) streaky bacon rashers, derinded

Heat the oil in a large, heavy frying pan and fry the onion and garlic over medium heat until soft, about 4 minutes.

Meanwhile, trim membranes and any dark spots from chicken livers, rinse in cold water and pat dry. Add to the pan with the onions and cook, stirring, until lightly browned on the outside but still pink inside, about 3 minutes. With a slotted spoon, transfer onions and livers to a bowl.

Add the minced beef and pork to the pan and stir until meat is crumbly and no longer pink, about 4 minutes. Add the meat to the bowl with the livers. Purée the mixture in batches in a blender or food processor fitted with the steel blade and return to the bowl. Stir in brandy, port, herbs and salt and pepper to taste.

Line a loaf pan 23 × 11 cm (9 ×4 inches) with bacon rashers, letting the ends hang over the sides. Spoon the mixture into the pan and fold bacon ends back over it. Cover the mixture with a triple layer of aluminium foil placed directly on top. Place the pan in a baking dish filled with enough hot water to come half-way up the sides, and bake in a preheated moderate oven (180°C/350°F/Gas 4) for 2 hours.

Remove terrine from the oven and allow to stand for 15 minutes, then take the pan out of the baking dish. Place a weight weighing about 2 kg (4½ lb) on top of the terrine and allow to cool. Place terrine, still weighted, in the refrigerator and chill for 2 days before removing weight and foil and unmoulding. Serve cut in thin slices with hot, buttered, whole-grain toast. SERVES 8–10.

Note: To weight the terrine, place a breadboard or tray on top and cans of food or other weights on top of the board.

Bosanski Lonac
➤ *Baked Pork and Vegetables, Bosnian-Style*

The ancient walled city of Dubrovnik, on Yugoslavia's magnificent Adriatic coast, has no big tourist hotels inside its walls; but there is a friendly tourist bureau that arranges accommodation in private homes, and restaurants serve the old regional specialties of Yugoslavia in an unchanging atmosphere that takes you back hundreds of years.

750 g (1½ lb) boneless pork, thinly sliced
4 large onions, thinly sliced
4 large potatoes, thinly sliced
4 large peppers, seeded and thinly sliced
salt and freshly ground pepper
paprika
170 ml (6 fl oz) melted bacon fat, lard or
   unsalted butter
350 ml (12 fl oz) sour cream

Grease a deep casserole dish and arrange in it the pork, onion, potatoes and peppers in layers, finishing with a layer of potatoes. Season each layer with salt, pepper and paprika and drizzle with bacon fat, lard or butter. Spread two-thirds sour cream over the top, cover the casserole and bake in a preheated moderate oven (180°C/350°F/Gas 4) for 1 hour or until tender.

Spread remaining sour cream on top and place under a preheated grill for a few minutes until lightly browned. Serve from the casserole with bread and a green salad. SERVES 6.

Biftek à la Créole
➤ *Marinated Steak Flamed with Rum*

Martinique is an enchanting flower-covered island in the Caribbean Sea, famous among other things for its dark, aged rum. At one restaurant with a view of the harbour, the chef flames a tender steak with rum and serves it with a salad of tropical fruits. (Illustrated on pages 102 and 103.)

4 pieces of tender grilling steak, cut thick
2 cloves garlic, crushed
2 tablespoons olive oil
1 tablespoon wine vinegar
salt and freshly ground pepper
5 tablespoons dark rum
Fruit Salad, to serve (see Note)

Snip the edges of the steaks to keep them flat while grilling. Combine garlic, oil and vinegar in a bowl with salt and pepper to taste and marinate steaks for 2–3 hours, turning several times.

Drain steaks, reserving the marinade, and pat dry. Grill under a preheated grill until done to your liking, brushing both sides with marinade.

Arrange steaks on a heated platter. Warm the rum in a small saucepan, pour over steaks and ignite. When flames go out, serve with fruit salad. SERVES 4.
Fruit Salad
Line a bowl with crisp lettuce. Arrange slices of fresh pineapple, paw paw, banana, mango, etc. in a pretty pattern and sprinkle with Vinaigrette (page 78).

Onion and Garlic Soup

Skiing buffs sing the praises not only of the slopes in Austria's Salzburg, but of the restorative powers of a special garlic soup served at the *Hotel Schloss Fuschl*. Don't stint on the amount of garlic—this is what makes the soup so remarkable, and delicious.

50 g (2 oz) unsalted butter
2 large onions, thinly sliced
15–20 fat cloves garlic, finely chopped
50 g (2 oz) flour
1.5 litres (2½ pints) Beef Stock (page 77)
250 ml (8 fl oz) dry white wine
120 ml (4 fl oz) sour cream
salt and freshly ground pepper
freshly grated nutmeg
croûtons (page 89) and finely chopped parsley

Melt the butter in a heavy saucepan and cook the onions and garlic over moderate heat until soft and golden, about 5 minutes. Stir in the flour off the heat, then return to heat and cook, stirring, for 3 minutes. Gradually stir in the stock and wine, bring to the boil and simmer, covered, for 20 minutes.

Strain the soup through a fine sieve into another saucepan and stir in the sour cream. Add salt, pepper and nutmeg to taste, then bring to simmering point. Ladle into heated bowls and serve topped with croûtons and chopped parsley. SERVES 6.

➤ Banana Rum Flip
I'm told this is a favourite breakfast drink in the Caribbean! Place in a blender or food processor 1 ripe banana, cut into pieces, 90 ml (3 fl oz) milk, 1 tablespoon lime or lemon juice, 1½ tablespoons caster sugar and 120 ml (4 fl oz) light rum. Whiz until mixture is smooth. Makes 2 flips.

Pork in Mustard Sauce

Liechtenstein is a tiny, independent principality on the Swiss border—not too far off the beaten track for anyone touring Europe, but with a charm and history all its own. I like this Liechtenstein way of cooking pork, with basil and mustard flavouring a creamy wine sauce.

750 g (1½ lb) pork fillet
salt and freshly ground pepper
flour for dusting
50 g (2 oz) butter
2 tablespoons olive oil
170 ml (6 fl oz) dry white wine
170 ml (6 fl oz) sour cream
1 tablespoon Dijon mustard
2 teaspoons chopped fresh basil or ½ teaspoon
   dried
1 hard-boiled egg, finely chopped to garnish

Cut the pork into 8 medallions (rounds) of equal size and, using a rolling pin, flatten slightly between 2 sheets of plastic film. Sprinkle both sides of the pork with salt and pepper and dust with flour.

Heat the butter and oil in a large, heavy frying pan and fry the medallions on both sides over medium heat until cooked through and golden-brown. This will take about 4 minutes each side. Remove the medallions to a serving platter and keep warm.

Add the wine to the pan and bring to the boil over high heat, stirring to get up the brown bits on the bottom. Continue boiling for a minute to reduce the wine by half; then stir in the sour cream and keep stirring over medium heat until the sauce is thickened.

Remove pan from heat and blend in the mustard, basil and salt and pepper to taste. Spoon the sauce over the pork medallions and sprinkle with chopped egg. Serve with sautéed potatoes and a green salad. SERVES 4.

Les Moules aux Herbes

❧ Mussels with Herbs

If you are in the Marseilles area of France, take a side trip to lovely Montpellier, where Les Frères Runel serve (among other delights) a superbly flavoured mussel hors d'oeuvre. At home, serve it as a first course or a luncheon main course. It's especially easy on the cook, as the mussels can be prepared well beforehand and grilled just before serving.

3 kg (6½ lb) mussels in the shell
500 g (1 lb) butter, softened
8 spring onions, finely chopped
4 cloves garlic, crushed
50 g (2 oz) breadcrumbs (made from day-old bread)
6 tablespoons finely chopped parsley
salt and freshly ground pepper

Scrub the mussels well in several changes of water, scrape off the beards, and soak in cold water to cover for several hours. Discard any that have broken shells or remain open. Drain and rinse under cold running water.

Arrange mussels in one layer in roasting pans and place in a preheated very hot oven (230°C/450°F/Gas 9) until shells have opened, about 8 minutes. Discard any unopened mussels.

Combine remaining ingredients until well-blended, seasoning generously with salt and pepper. Remove the top shells from the mussels and cover each mussel with the butter mixture, filling the shells to the top. Arrange in flameproof dishes and chill, covered, for 30 minutes or until ready to cook.

Place under a preheated grill and grill for 3 minutes, or until tops are golden and butter mixture bubbly. SERVES 6–8 as a first course, 4 as a main course. Note: This recipe is easy to halve.

Fochabers' Syllabub

On the River Spey in the Highlands of Scotland is the town of Fochabers, where the Baxter family makes its beautiful marmalades, jams and game soups. Many a small Highland hotel thereabouts specializes in traditional recipes like this syllabub.

4 large egg whites
175 g (6 oz) caster sugar
300 ml (½ pint) Sauternes
90 ml (3 fl oz) lemon juice
600 ml (1 pint) double cream
candied angelica or peel, to decorate

Whisk the egg whites in a large bowl until they hold soft peaks. Gradually add the sugar, whisking until stiff peaks form. Fold in Sauternes and lemon juice.

Whip the cream until it just holds its shape and fold gently into the egg white mixture. Spoon into tall wineglasses and chill overnight, or until the syllabub separates into cream at the top and liquid at the bottom of the glass. Top each dessert with a piece of candied angelica or peel. SERVES 8.

Les Moules aux Herbes

Syllabub takes its name from Sillery, a wine of the French Champagne district, which was once the best-known in England, and 'bub', Elizabethan slang for a bubbling drink. Syllabubs were once a simple mixture of wine, sweetening and milk, and were sometimes made by milking a cow directly into a bowl of wine to get the desired foamy effect.

Creamy Peanut Soup

Saint Eustatius (soon affectionately referred to by visitors as 'Statia', the local name for it) is a tiny Dutch-owned island in the Caribbean. Restaurants and inns like the *Old Gin House* offer a fascinating mixture of Dutch and West Indian food, often with French or American overtones—depending on the nationality of the chef. This creamy peanut soup demonstrates the intriguing offerings you will find on Statia menus.

200 g (7 oz) shelled, roasted peanuts
2 tablespoons peanut oil
1 large onion, finely chopped
1 teaspoon crushed aniseed
3 tablespoons soy sauce
450 ml (¾ pint) hot Chicken Stock (page 90)
350 ml (12 fl oz) scalded milk
dash of cayenne pepper
120 ml (4 fl oz) double cream
chopped peanuts, to garnish

Purée the peanuts in batches in a blender or a food processor fitted with the steel blade. Heat the oil in a large, heavy saucepan and cook the onion and aniseed over moderate heat for 5 minutes, stirring. Stir in the peanut purée little by little, then the soy sauce and chicken stock. Whisk in the hot milk in a steady stream and heat just to boiling point. Add cayenne pepper to taste and stir in the cream. Serve in heated bowls, sprinkled with chopped peanuts. SERVES 4–6.

Sugar Cones with Rum-Cream Filling

The lake-filled Varmland area of Sweden offers so much for the visitor who likes an unspoiled country holiday. It is ideal picnicking, fishing and camping country, with the bonus of comfortable hotels, economical pensions and restaurants serving such local delicacies as salmon and tender elk. At the *Hotel Bjornidet* in Torsby they also pride themselves on lovely desserts, including a crisp sugar cone filled with rum cream and jam made from local lingonberries. In your own kitchen, you can use any good, not-too-sweet berry jam.

2 eggs
125 g (4 oz) sifted icing sugar
75 g (3 oz) sifted flour

FILLING
350 ml (12 fl oz) double cream whipped with 1 tablespoon sugar
6 tablespoons berry jam
2 tablespoons dark rum
extra jam, to decorate

Beat the eggs until light and lemon coloured, then beat in icing sugar 25 g (1 oz) at a time. Continue beating until mixture is very fluffy. Add the flour in 3 lots, beating well between each addition.

Preheat the oven to very hot (230°C/425°F/Gas 8). Lightly butter a baking tray, sprinkle with flour, then tap tray on the back to remove excess flour. Pour 2 tablespoons of the batter on to the tray and form into a 13 cm (5 inch) round with the back of a spoon. Make another round in the same way. Bake the rounds in the preheated oven for 2–3 minutes or until set and golden-brown. With a spatula, quickly invert each round on to a tea-towel and, while still hot, roll into a cone. Stand the cones upright in tall glasses to cool and harden. Continue to make rounds with remaining batter, cooking only 2 at a time and shaping the cones while hot. (If rounds become too brittle to roll, return to oven for a few seconds to soften.)

Fold whipped cream, jam and rum together and chill for 1 hour.

Place the cones in long-stemmed glasses, fill each with 3 tablespoons of the cream mixture, and decorate with a little extra jam. MAKES about 16.

Mock Duck
Stuffed Steak in Mushroom Sauce

My Scottish heritage has led me to explore the high roads and low roads of Scotland. I am very fond of Dumfries in the south-west, a town where Robert Burns spent much of his time. At the *Globe Inn* in Dumfries, things are still much as they were in the 18th century—you can even stay in Rabbie's bedroom and sit in the oak chair he favoured in the bar. Here is my version of a steak dish I enjoyed at the *Globe*.

1 thick slice of topside steak, weighing about 1.5 kg (3½ lb)
salt and freshly ground pepper
STUFFING
75 g (3 oz) fresh breadcrumbs
1 small onion, finely chopped
½ teaspoon thyme
½ teaspoon dried tarragon
50 g (2 oz) cold butter, cut into small pieces
salt and freshly ground pepper

Caribbean Fruit Salad
Sublime! Place in a bowl 125 g (4 oz) each diced fresh pineapple and orange, 225 g (8 oz) each sliced bananas and hulled strawberries, 25 g (1 oz) desiccated coconut, 25 g (1 oz) each chopped dates, walnuts and sunflower seeds. Blend together 120 ml (4 fl oz) natural yogurt, 2 tablespoons honey, 2 tablespoons each orange and lemon juice and 2 slices fresh ginger (finely chopped). Pour over the fruit, toss well and chill before serving. Serves 8.

SAUCE
50 g (2 oz) butter
225 g (8 oz) mushrooms, finely chopped
3 tablespoons flour
450 ml (¾ pint) scalded milk
salt and freshly ground pepper
lemon juice

Cut the steak in half horizontally and season with salt and pepper. Combine all stuffing ingredients and spread over one slice of meat, leaving a margin of 1 cm (½ inch) around the edge. Place the other slice on top, press together, and skewer the edges securely. Put the meat in a deep casserole just wide enough to hold it comfortably.

To make the sauce: heat the butter in a heavy saucepan and fry the mushrooms over moderate heat until soft, about 5 minutes. Sprinkle flour over the top and cook, stirring, for 2 minutes. Remove the pan from the heat and add scalded milk in a stream, stirring constantly. Return to the heat and stir until sauce boils. Season with salt, pepper and lemon juice to taste.

Pour sauce over the steak and cover the casserole. Bake the casserole in a preheated moderate oven (180°C/350°F/Gas 4) for 1½ hours or until the steak is very tender.

To serve, remove skewers and cut the meat crosswise into thick slices. Taste sauce for seasoning and spoon over the meat. SERVES 6.

Schwarzwälder Eierkuchen

🖎 *Black Forest Crêpes*

Royalty and the upper classes flocked to Baden-Baden in Victorian and Edwardian days to take 'the cure' for rheumatism and a touch of distinguished gout. Today, this lovely city still offers thermal baths, the world's hottest spring, a beautiful casino, pine-scented air—and some of the finest food in Germany, at the historic *Brenner's Park* hotel. Sweet tooths should watch out for tender crêpes filled with a chocolate-cherry cream, very much in the style of the famous Black Forest Cherry Torte.

16 Crêpes (page 84)
175 g (6 oz) unsalted butter, softened
50 g (2 oz) plus 1 tablespoon icing sugar
3 tablespoons kirsch
175 g (6 oz) drained, chopped sour cherries (see Note)
200 g (7 oz) coarsely grated dark chocolate
icing sugar and chocolate curls, to decorate

Make the crêpes and keep warm. Cream butter until soft, then beat in icing sugar until the mixture is light and fluffy. Stir in kirsch, cherries and grated chocolate. Spread each crêpe with about 1 tablespoon of filling, fold into quarters, and arrange on a heated serving dish. Sprinkle with icing sugar and chocolate curls. SERVES 6–8.

Note: Sour cherries are usually sold in glass jars at good delicatessens. If unobtainable, use canned black cherries and add a good squeeze of lemon juice to the filling.

To make chocolate curls, shave thin pieces of chocolate from the side of a block of milk chocolate. Use a swivel-bladed vegetable peeler and have the chocolate at room temperature.

Chicken with Almond Sauce

Portugal's Algarve coast is justly famous for its seafood, but inland there are other culinary delights to be sought out. A spicy, nutty-textured chicken dish is the house specialty of a restaurant called *Rouxinol* (meaning 'nightingale') set high in the cool Monchique hills that rise behind the Algarve.

225 g (8 oz) blanched almonds
350 ml (12 fl oz) dry white wine
2 cloves garlic, crushed
50 g (2 oz) lard or 3 tablespoons oil
1 medium onion, finely chopped
1 small chorizo sausage, thinly sliced
1 teaspoon chilli powder
1.5 kg (3½ lb) chicken, cut into quarters
salt and freshly ground pepper
2 bay leaves

Whirl the almonds in a blender until coarsely crushed (do not allow them to become paste) or crush in a mortar. Combine with wine and garlic and allow to stand, covered, for 1 hour.

Heat the lard or oil in a deep, heavy frying pan and cook the onion over moderate heat for 3 minutes or until softened. Add the sliced chorizo and chilli powder and stir until blended. Add the chicken pieces and cook for 3 minutes, turning to coat all sides with the mixture. Sprinkle chicken with salt and pepper and add bay leaves and almond mixture to the pan. Bring to the boil, then adjust heat so mixture simmers. Cover and cook for 20 minutes, turning chicken pieces occasionally.

Uncover the pan, increase heat, and cook for 10 minutes more, or until the sauce has thickened and the chicken is tender. Adjust seasoning. SERVES 4.

It is worth spending an evening at the Casino in Baden-Baden just to enjoy its splendour— gold, crystal, Sèvres china, flowers, paintings, brocades and ornate mirrors. You need not play, just have a drink or a meal at the *Casino* restaurant (once managed by César Ritz) and imagine you're back in *La Belle Époque*.

Linguine with Courgette-Anchovy Sauce

The Isle of Capri has many little family-run eating houses. At one, on the winding road to Anacapri, the chef was an enchanting 17-year-old. She told me this was her own 'special sauce', devised on a day when the clam sauce ran out.

500 g (1 lb) linguine (see Note)
150 g (5 oz) butter
3 tablespoons olive oil
6 firm young courgettes, thinly sliced
6 flat anchovy fillets, finely chopped
3 large, ripe tomatoes, skinned, seeded and chopped
salt and freshly ground pepper
4 tablespoons finely chopped parsley
50 g (2 oz) grated Parmesan cheese

Cook the linguine in plenty of boiling, salted water until tender but still firm.

Meanwhile, heat 75 g (3 oz) butter and the oil in a large, heavy frying pan and add the courgettes. Stir over medium heat until barely tender, about 3 minutes. Add the anchovies and tomatoes and cook a further few minutes until tomatoes are softened. Taste and season with salt and pepper—be careful with the salt, as the anchovies are salty.

Drain the linguine and place in a heated serving bowl. Add the remaining butter, cut into small pieces, the parsley and grated cheese and toss to combine. Pour the sauce over and toss lightly again. Serve at once on heated plates. SERVES 6.
Note: Linguine are narrow, flat ribbons of pasta. If unavailable, use tagliatelle or other flat noodles.

Moroccan Lentils

Eating in Morocco can be an enchanting experience. A pierced bronze lamp throws spangles on the ceiling, the cushions are deep and soft, the food exotic yet delicious. This dish, which can be served hot or cold, was enjoyed in a small restaurant off the beaten track in Fez.

350 g (12 oz) brown lentils
900 ml (1½ pints) water
1 large onion, chopped
3 tablespoons olive oil
1 teaspoon salt
1 × 227 g (8 oz) can tomatoes, with their juice

Linguine with Courgette-Anchovy Sauce

4 tablespoons chopped parsley
2 fat cloves garlic, crushed
2 teaspoons ground cumin
1 teaspoon ground cinnamon
½ teaspoon cayenne pepper

Wash the lentils and place in a large saucepan with the water, onion, olive oil and salt. Bring to the boil, then simmer, covered, for 45 minutes or until most of the liquid is absorbed. Add remaining ingredients and simmer, uncovered, for 20 minutes, stirring occasionally. Taste for seasoning and transfer to a heated serving bowl. SERVES 6.
Note: As a hot dish, serve with spicy sausages, meatballs or kebabs. Cold, the lentils can be rolled inside pitta bread or served as a salad with cold meats.

Rum and Ginger Mousse

A relative of mine who lived in the Caribbean gave me this recipe from a hilltop restaurant on the island of Haiti. It uses the lovely local white rum of the Caribbean, which does so much for a dessert. Macerate pineapple in white rum or use it to flambé pineapple or bananas, as well as adding it to this easily made mousse.

1½ teaspoons gelatine
2 tablespoons cold water
4 egg yolks
75 g (3 oz) sugar
450 ml (¾ pint) double cream or evaporated milk
175 g (6 oz) finely chopped, glacé ginger
120 ml (4 fl oz) white rum
4 egg whites
pinch of salt
extra chopped ginger and whipped cream, to decorate

Soak the gelatine in cold water for 5 minutes to soften. Beat the egg yolks with sugar until thick and light. Bring the cream or evaporated milk to boiling point and add to egg yolks in a steady stream, beating constantly.

Transfer the mixture to a heavy saucepan and cook over moderate heat, stirring all the time, until thick enough to coat the back of a spoon. (Be careful not to let it boil.) Remove from heat and stir in the ginger, rum and gelatine. Whisk the egg whites with a pinch of salt until they hold stiff peaks. Stir one-third of the whites into the custard mixture, then fold in remaining whites. Divide the mousse among 6 tall glasses and chill for 2–3 hours. Decorate with whipped cream and chopped ginger. SERVES 6.

Rum is the great drink of the Caribbean—every bar offers Planter's Punch, which comes in many variations but always contains rum and fresh fruit juice. The original recipe called for 'One of sour, two of sweet, three of strong and four of weak': one part fresh lime juice, two parts sugar, three parts rum and four parts water or ice.

Strawberry Cocktail
A fruity refresher for a summer lunch party. Place in a blender or food processor 5 icecubes, juice of 1 lemon, 90 ml (3 fl oz) light rum, 2 teaspoons caster sugar and 125 g (4 oz) hulled strawberries. Blend until mixture is thick and well combined. Makes 2 drinks.

Amazing Grace
Scene: Christmas Eve, 1980, Noumea, the South Pacific.
Act 1: The towering stone Madonna emerging through the first floor level from her Pirog (native boat) welcomes us to *L'Eau Vive du Pacific* and an authentic French meal. The food, wine and service are divine.
Act 2: Printed sheets are passed around, lights are lowered, and the enchanting Polynesian and local French waitresses group to sing *Ave Maria*. The diners, eyes lowered, follow the words. Not really amazing, when you know the restaurant is so professionally run by an order of nuns!

Fish in Pernod Sauce

Visitors to America's West Coast should make time for a visit to Seattle, with its bustling waterways, fascinating history, and man-made attractions. You will find many superb restaurants in and around Seattle, including *Gérard's Relais de Lyon* in Bothel, just outside the city. Here is a typical Gérard dish—a fine Pacific fish, prepared with French flair.

50 g (2 oz) butter
225 g (8 oz) mushroom caps, thinly sliced
6 spring onions, finely chopped
450 ml (¾ pint) Fish Stock (page 81)
4 fillets firm white fish, each weighing 225 g
(8 oz), skinned and boned
250 ml (8 fl oz) double cream
4 tablespoons Pernod
extra 50 g (2 oz) chilled butter, cut into small pieces
salt and freshly ground white pepper

Heat the butter in a large, heavy frying pan and cook the mushrooms and spring onions for 5 minutes over moderate heat, stirring. Add the fish stock and bring just to simmering point. Add the fish fillets, cover and poach for 5 minutes or until they just flake when tested with a fork. Transfer fish and mushrooms to a heated platter.

Reduce the poaching liquid over high heat by two-thirds. Stir in the cream and continue cooking until the sauce is reduced by half. Lower heat to moderate and stir in the Pernod. Add the chilled butter, a piece at a time, whisking well after each addition and adding the next piece before the previous one is completely melted. Season the sauce with salt and white pepper to taste and spoon over the fish. SERVES 4.

Pot-Roasted Venison

New Zealand exports most of its venison, but a friend was lucky enough to taste it at a lodge near Lake Taupo recommended by her Maori guide. The proprietor, who was also the cook, said this method of treating venison ensures tenderness. In lieu of venison, it would be a great way of cooking a veal roast the same size.

2.5 kg (5½ lb) boneless venison roast
75 g (3 oz) butter
1 large carrot, finely chopped
1 leek or large onion, finely chopped
250 ml (8 fl oz) Beef Stock (page 77)
salt and freshly ground pepper
250 ml (8 fl oz) sour cream
MARINADE
120 ml (4 fl oz) olive oil
3 cloves garlic, crushed
1 medium onion, sliced
3 cloves
1 bay leaf
1 tablespoon salt
1 tablespoon peppercorns, cracked
1 teaspoon dried thyme
1 teaspoon allspice or juniper berries
2 slices of fresh ginger, chopped
4 sprigs of parsley
sufficient red wine to cover meat

Place the venison in a deep crockery or plastic bowl. Combine all marinade ingredients and pour over the venison. Cover and leave in the refrigerator for 3 days, turning now and again. Remove the venison from the marinade and pat dry. Strain the marinade and set aside.

Heat the butter in a large, heavy flameproof casserole or Dutch oven and slowly brown the venison on all sides. Add the carrot, leek or onion, 450 ml (¾ pint) of the reserved marinade and the beef stock. Season with salt and pepper to taste, cover tightly, and bake in a preheated moderately slow oven (160°C/325°F/Gas 3) for 1½ hours or until venison is tender.

Remove the meat to a platter and keep warm in the turned-off oven with the door open.

Reduce liquid left in casserole by rapid boiling until it measures about 350 ml (12 fl oz). Strain into a small, clean saucepan, stir in the sour cream and heat through (but do not boil). Taste for seasoning and serve as a sauce with the venison. SERVES 8.

Venison Pie

The beautiful *Horn of Plenty* restaurant in Tavistock, Devon, serves many traditional dishes, like this Venison Pie, and owner Sonia Stevenson was kind enough to provide the recipe. If you can't find venison, use good quality stewing beef (see note).

750 g (1½ lb) pickled pork, boned if necessary
  and cut into chunks
1 kg (2 lb) venison, cut into cubes
1 tablespoon tomato paste
grated zest and juice of 2 medium oranges
750 ml (1¼ pints) red wine
Beef Stock, to cover (page 77)
salt
Beurre Manié (see far right)
1 teaspoon chopped fresh marjoram
1 quantity Shortcrust Pastry (page 130)
1 egg, beaten, to glaze

Place the pork in a large saucepan and fry for a few minutes, stirring, until the fat runs. Add the cubed venison and fry until the juice runs and coats the meat with a rich, brown gravy (very important). Add the tomato paste, the orange zest and juice and the wine and mix well, scraping up the meat juices and brown bits on the bottom. Add enough stock to cover the meat and salt to taste, allowing for the saltiness of the pork and reduction of liquid during cooking. Cover the pan and simmer until meat is very tender, about 1 hour.

Strain the liquid into a clean pan and thicken to gravy consistency with pieces of beurre manié. Add marjoram, simmer 5–10 minutes and check seasoning. Place the meat in a large pie dish and cover with gravy (meat and gravy should come almost to the top of the dish). Roll pastry out to a shape about 4 cm (1½ inches) larger than the top of dish and cut a strip from the outside to fit around the edge. Dampen the top of dish, press the strip into place and dampen the top of the strip. Place the top crust in position, press firmly onto the strip and trim any excess. Cut a few slits in the top to allow steam to escape and brush with beaten egg to glaze. Place in a preheated hot oven (200°C/400°F/Gas 6) for 10 minutes, then reduce heat to moderate (180°C/350°F/Gas 4) and bake for a further 15 minutes until the pastry is golden. SERVES 8.
Note: Beef will acquire a 'gamey' taste if marinated for 24 hours. Combine 250 ml (8 fl oz) red wine, 90 ml (3 fl oz) olive oil, 1 bay leaf, ½ carrot, ½ onion, 1 teaspoon each juniper berries and black peppercorns, 2 sprigs of thyme and 4 sprigs of parsley.

Rillettes de Canard
➤ *Spiced Duck Spread*

Rillettes containing shredded pork are popular throughout France, but near Rouen, famous for its ducks, I tasted this superb variation. It keeps in the refrigerator for up to 6 weeks.

2.5 kg (5½ lb) duck, quartered
225 g (8 oz) fresh pork fat, cut into 2.5 cm (1 inch) cubes
350 ml (12 fl oz) dry white wine
2 tablespoons grated fresh ginger
1 tablespoon coarse salt (sea salt)
2 fat cloves garlic, finely chopped
45 g (1¾ oz) can green peppercorns, drained and crushed
salt and freshly ground pepper

Place duck quarters in a flameproof casserole with pork fat, wine, ginger, salt and garlic. Stir the mixture until it comes to the boil, then cover tightly and cook in a slow oven (150°C/300°F/Gas 2) for 4 hours. Set a colander over a bowl and drain the mixture, reserving the cooking liquid.

Remove skin and bones from duck and place duck meat and pork fat on a large plate. Using two forks, separate the meat and fat into shreds. When all is shredded, mix with the crushed green peppercorns and season with salt and pepper to taste.

Spoon into pottery crocks and add enough of the reserved cooking liquid to cover the mixture by 6 mm (¼ inch). Cool, cover with a lid or aluminium foil and store in the refrigerator. Serve as a first course with hot toast triangles. MAKES about 4 cups.

Pommes de Terre Sablées
➤ *Sauté Potatoes with Breadcrumbs*

The crispy, crumbly, golden outside and melting interior of good sauté potatoes depend on frequent turning as they cook – so it's not surprising that some of the best are found in small family establishments where *Maman* or *Papa* is the cook.

1 kg (2 lb) old potatoes, freshly boiled in their skins
75 g (3 oz) clarified butter or ghee
salt and freshly ground black pepper
25 g (1 oz) fresh breadcrumbs

Skin the potatoes and cut into chunky pieces. Heat a heavy frying pan, add the butter and when foaming add the potatoes. Allow them to colour before turning, then turn frequently until golden-brown. Add breadcrumbs and continue cooking and turning until crumbs are crisp and golden. SERVES 6.

➤ Beurre Manié
This 'kneaded butter' is used to thicken sauces, casseroles etc. at the end of cooking time. Work 25 g (1 oz) plain flour into 50 g (2 oz) softened butter. Place a small piece on the end of a whisk and whisk it into the simmering liquid; add more beurre manié in the same manner until the required thickness is reached. Store leftover beurre manié in a covered jar in the refrigerator.

EUROPEAN POT-POURRI

There are dishes that every traveller to Europe looks forward to. I couldn't wait to order Steak and Kidney Pudding in England . . . Wiener Schnitzel in Vienna . . . Gulyàs in Hungary. And, happily, I found I didn't have to look too far or pay too much to enjoy such well-loved dishes.

The big international hotels may serve them cooked by master chefs and lavishly presented, but they taste just as good when the proprietor of your little *pension* invites you to share a family meal.

A great delight of eating out in Europe is the discovery of food links between one country's cuisine and another. The bountiful array of appetizers called *zakuski* in Russia has its counterpart in Italy's *antipasti* table and the *tapas* served in Spanish bars. A beef stew might be flavoured with pickled pork in Germany, pickled walnuts in England, and wine and herbs in France.

Just one little word of advice—you'll get far more pleasure from your European eating experiences if you do some research before you go. Look in travel books and guides for information on food and restaurants, as well as investigating the regional cook books at your library. Make a list of the dishes that particularly interest you, and track them down.

Also, be sure to take a pocket language guide with you to restaurants. It would be a shame to pass by a dish called *bauernschmaus* on an Austrian menu, not realizing it's a superb platter of sliced hot meats and sauerkraut with savoury dumplings. Or to ignore *kurnik* in Russia, when it's a combination of layered pancakes with chicken, rice, mushroom and egg fillings. Some restaurants will have English speaking staff to advise you, but don't count on it. Take your phrase book, and take your time going through the menu.

But you're not planning a trip to Europe at the moment? Don't despair! Look for restaurants in your district that serve the food of their own countries. Good chefs take their trade secrets with them when they travel, and in today's multicultural society almost every city offers a sampling of the world's food.

Why not dine out European style at home? It's as easy as following an authentic recipe.

Steak, Kidney and Oyster Pudding

The *Spread Eagle* hotel in the small Sussex town of Midhurst is every visitor's idea of what an English pub should be: dating back to 1430, it has low beams, open fireplaces and copper pans on stone walls. It also serves some of the traditional delicacies like jugged hare, Lancashire hot pot and this suet pudding.

SUET DOUGH
125 g (4 oz) finely shredded beef suet
225 g (8 oz) self-raising flour
1 teaspoon salt
about 120 ml (4 fl oz) iced water
FILLING
125 g (4 oz) butter
750 g (1½ lb) stewing beef, cut into 2.5 cm
 (1 inch) cubes
225 g (8 oz) beef kidney, cored, skinned and cubed
1 large onion, finely chopped
2 tablespoons tomato paste
120 ml (4 fl oz) Beef Stock (page 77)
125 g (4 oz) mushroom caps, thinly sliced
4 tablespoons finely chopped parsley
2 teaspoons Worcestershire sauce
salt and freshly ground pepper
freshly grated nutmeg
GARNISH
90 ml (3 fl oz) Beef Stock (page 77)
50 g (2 oz) butter
12 oysters

Make the dough first. Place shredded suet, flour and salt in a large bowl and rub together with the fingertips until the mixture resembles breadcrumbs. Add enough iced water to form a dough, knead lightly and shape into a ball. Dust the dough with a little extra flour, wrap in greaseproof paper or plastic film and chill for at least 1 hour.

For the filling: heat 75 g (3 oz) of the butter in a large, heavy frying pan and fry the beef cubes over high heat for 3–4 minutes or until brown. (Turn them to brown evenly.) Transfer the meat with a slotted spoon to a large bowl. Add kidney to the pan and sauté for 2–3 minutes or until brown outside but still pink in the middle. Transfer to the bowl with the meat.

Add the remaining butter to the pan and fry the onion until soft, about 4 minutes; then add the contents of the pan to the steak and kidney. Stir in the remaining filling ingredients, seasoning generously with salt, pepper and nutmeg. Cool.

Roll out two-thirds of the suet dough, 3 mm (⅛ inch) thick, on a floured surface. Fit the dough into a lightly greased 1.5 litre (2½ pint) pudding basin, leaving a 2.5 cm (1 inch) overhang, and spoon the meat mixture into the centre. Roll out the remaining dough to a circle 1 cm (½ inch) larger than the top of the basin and place it in position. Bring the overhanging piece of dough up over the top round and fold the dampened edges together, pressing firmly to seal. Cover with a circle of buttered greaseproof paper.

Rinse a clean tea-towel in hot water, squeeze it dry and sprinkle lightly with flour. Drape it over the top of the pudding basin and tie tightly with string under the rim. Knot the opposite ends of the cloth together on top of the pudding and place the basin on a rack or upturned bowl in a deep saucepan. Pour in enough boiling water to come half-way up the sides of the basin and bring to the boil over moderately high heat. Cover the saucepan and steam the pudding for 5 hours, adding more boiling water as necessary to keep the required level. Remove the basin, take off the tea-towel and greaseproof paper and invert the pudding on to a hot serving platter.

To make the garnish: heat the stock with the butter. Add the oysters and poach for 2 minutes or just until the edges curl. Spoon the oysters and liquid on to the top of the pudding, letting some juices run down the sides. Cut in wedges to serve. SERVES 6.

Chicken Kiev

This is the recipe as it was created in Tsarist Russia and is enjoyed in fine Russian restaurants throughout the world today.

1 whole chicken breast, cut from a large chicken, with
    wings attached but wing tips removed
25 g (1 oz) butter, cut in half
salt and freshly ground pepper
2 tablespoons finely chopped chives
flour for dusting
1 egg, lightly beaten
50 g (2 oz) soft white breadcrumbs, rubbed through sieve
oil for deep frying

Cut the chicken breast in half. With a sharp, pointed knife remove all the bones from the breast, leaving the wing joint attached. Peel away the skin. Place the 2 pieces of breast between 2 sheets of waxed paper or plastic film and pound until thin with a steak mallet or rolling pin.

Roll each piece of butter into a cork shape and chill. Place a roll of butter at the base of each chicken breast, diagonally in line with the wing bone. Sprinkle with salt, pepper and chives. Fold the chicken flesh over the butter, then roll up towards the bone, folding the sides in as you go to enclose the butter completely inside the chicken. The flesh will adhere without skewers.

Coat each rolled breast lightly with flour, dip in beaten egg and roll in breadcrumbs. Refrigerate for at least 2 hours.

Heat the oil in a large, deep saucepan, using enough oil to cover the chicken breasts. (To test if the oil is hot enough, drop a cube of bread into it. The bread should rise to the surface immediately.)

Gently lower the chicken into the hot oil and fry for 4½–5 minutes until golden-brown. (This is the only tricky part to Chicken Kiev. The oil must be hot enough to brown the chicken breast, but not colour it too much before the chicken is cooked through. If the chicken starts to brown too quickly during this time, lower the heat.) Remove the chicken from the oil, drain on paper towels and serve immediately with potato straws—the packaged variety will do—heated in the oven. SERVES 2.

Gulyàs
➥ *Paprika Stew*

Goulash is a term covering a wide range of dishes using pork, beef, lamb, veal or game, all prepared the *gulyàs* way. One thing is certain, though—every Hungarian restaurant menu will offer at least one or two goulash dishes for you to enjoy. The *Gay Hussar* in Greek Street, Soho, London, makes a superb *Gulyàs*—they call it *Borju Pörkölt*.

50 g (2 oz) butter or lard
1 kg (2 lb) lean stewing beef or veal, cut into
    5 cm (2 inch) cubes
2 large onions, finely chopped
1 teaspoon vinegar
1 green pepper, seeded and finely chopped
2 teaspoons paprika
250 ml (8 fl oz) Beef Stock (page 77)
salt and freshly ground pepper
250 ml (8 fl oz) sour cream (optional)

Heat the fat in a large, heavy saucepan and brown the meat on all sides over high heat. Reduce heat to moderate, add the onions and stir till the onions are softened and golden-brown, about 5 minutes. Stir in remaining ingredients, except sour cream, and simmer, tightly covered, until the meat is very tender, 1½–2 hours. If desired, add sour cream and heat through. Serve with buttered noodles. SERVES 6.

➥ Pink Russian

A long, pretty summer drink. Place in a tall jug 450 ml (¾ pint) grapefruit juice, 6 tablespoons vodka and 4 tablespoons Campari. Fill the jug with icecubes and stir vigorously. Strain into 2 tall, chilled glasses and garnish with a wedge of grapefruit. Makes 2 long drinks.

If you go to Hungary you will want to enjoy Tokay, the great and justly famous wine from the village of Tokaj in the Carpathian Mountains. But there are other good wines to watch for: Balatoni Rizling and Csopaki Rizling are fine, dry whites to enjoy with fish, chicken, veal and pork. To go with a spicy *gulyàs*, try the full-bodied red wine called Egri Bikaver (bull's blood). And with the obligatory sweet pastry that finishes a meal, sip a fruity Muskotaly in a café near the Danube.

Lamb Cutlets Paloise

If you ever find yourself off the main roads in the Danish countryside, you will no doubt come across a *kro*, or a beautifully maintained traditional inn. The Danes have an adjective for such inns—they call them 'loveable'—and that is a good word to describe their unique charm and hospitality.

Ask at the *kro* if this well-loved Danish dish is on the menu—the sauce is French, but the combination of mint and lamb is international.

8 lamb cutlets or chops, cut thick
salt and freshly ground pepper
Paloise Sauce (see below)

Trim excess fat from the cutlets. Grill them on both sides under a preheated hot grill, until crisp and brown outside but still pink and juicy in the middle. (This should take 3–4 minutes each side.)

Season with salt and pepper to taste and top each cutlet with a generous spoonful of Paloise Sauce. SERVES 4.

Paloise Sauce

Make 1 quantity of Béarnaise Sauce (page 21) with chopped mint instead of tarragon and stir in 1 extra tablespoon of chopped mint. Allow to stand for 5 minutes before serving to mellow the flavours.

Miller Howe Vegetable Favourites

The *Miller Howe Hotel* in beautiful Windermere is famed for the quality of its food. One of the delights of proprietor John Tovey's table is the marvellous array of fresh vegetables—six are served with a main meat course!

Diced Turnips with Honey

500 g (1 lb) turnips
2 tablespoons or more clear honey

Peel the turnips and cut into cubes. Cook in boiling salted water until tender, about 10 minutes. Drain well and put back in the saucepan over low heat for a few minutes to dry out. Add honey to suit your taste and stir until turnips are coated. SERVES 4.

Purée of Parsnips with Toasted Pine Nuts

500 g (1 lb) parsnips
25 g (1 oz) butter
150 ml (¼ pint) double cream
2 tablespoons toasted pine nuts

Peel the parsnips and cut into pieces if large. Cook in boiling salted water until tender, about 20 minutes. Drain well, then return to the saucepan over low heat and toss in the butter. Purée with the cream in a blender or food processor fitted with the steel blade. (For an even smoother purée, pass through a fine plastic sieve.) Reheat in a saucepan that has been brushed inside with butter and serve sprinkled with the toasted pine nuts. SERVES 4.

Courgettes in Cheese Custard

John Tovey says this makes an excellent supper dish, which goes well with cold meat or grilled sausages.

1–2 tablespoons olive oil
500 g (1 lb) firm young courgettes, thickly sliced
1 medium onion, finely chopped
1 clove garlic, crushed
25 g (1 oz) butter
CUSTARD
2 eggs plus 1 egg yolk
300 ml (½ pint) double cream
125 g (4 oz) Cheddar cheese, grated
1–2 tablespoons chopped fresh herbs (parsley,
  basil, marjoram, tarragon or a mixture)
salt and freshly ground black pepper

Heat 1 tablespoon of the oil in a heavy frying pan. Add the courgette slices and toss them until they are coated with oil and beginning to soften. Remove and drain well on paper towels. Add another tablespoon of oil to the pan and fry the onion and garlic until softened. Remove and drain.

Make the custard by beating the eggs and egg yolk into the cream before adding the cheese, herbs and salt and pepper to taste.

Butter a medium-size ovenproof casserole and line it with about 1 cm (½ inch) of the custard. Bake in a preheated moderate oven (180°C/350°F/Gas 4) for about 8 minutes or until firm. Arrange the onions and courgettes on top and gently pour in the rest of the custard. Cook for a further 20–30 minutes or until set. SERVES 4.

In Holland, Denmark and Scandinavia you will be overwhelmed by the marvellous seafood and its imaginative preparation. Denmark has two of my favourites: *Gravlax*, which is fresh salmon marinated in dill, salt, sugar and peppercorns, and an exquisite smoked Baltic herring from the island of Bornholm. Ask for *Bornholmers* when in Copenhagen, for they are so fragile they cannot be exported, and this is your only chance to try one of the world's greatest delicacies.

Lamb Cutlets Paloise

Caldo Verde
❧ Green Soup

This soup is famous throughout Portugal, where the dark green vegetable called kale is often used as well as spinach. An enterprising friend obtained this recipe for me when she stayed at one of the privately owned inns called *estalagems*. She watched the cook prepare it, noting that the secret of the bright green colour is to cook the spinach no more than a few minutes after it is added to the pot.

4 large old potatoes, peeled
about 1.8 litres (3 pints) boiling, salted water
500 g (1 lb) tender spinach
3 tablespoons olive oil
salt and freshly ground pepper

Cook the potatoes in the boiling water until tender. Remove and rub them through a sieve. Leave the water in the pot. Wash the spinach thoroughly, cut away the white stalks and shred the leaves finely.

Return the sieved potato to the pot with the olive oil and spinach and cook the soup over high heat for 2–3 minutes, stirring. Season with salt and pepper to taste and serve in large bowls with plenty of crusty bread. SERVES 4.

Endive avec Jambon aux Gratin
❧ Belgian Endive with Ham and Cheese

Belgian endive is called chicory in England—but by any name the tight clumps of yellow-tipped white leaves are delicious. They can be used raw in salads, served as a vegetable, or combined with other ingredients to make main courses. I like this Brussels restaurant way of preparing endive as a lunch dish.

12 endives (chicory)
50 g (2 oz) butter
1 teaspoon sugar
salt and freshly ground pepper
1 tablespoon lemon juice
12 thin slices of ham
350 ml (12 fl oz) Béchamel Sauce (page 20)
1 egg yolk
freshly grated nutmeg
175 g (6 oz) grated Gruyère cheese

Trim the bases of the endives and remove any withered leaves. Wash under cold running water and drain.

❧ Browned Breadcrumbs
Browned crumbs make an attractive finish to vegetables, fish or chicken in a cream sauce. To make, bake chunks or slices of bread in a slow oven (150°C/300°F/Gas 2) until dry and golden-brown. Put in a paper bag and crush with a rolling pin, or process in a blender or food processor fitted with the steel blade. Store in an airtight jar, preferably in the refrigerator.

Melt butter in a heavy frying pan over low heat and sprinkle with sugar. Add the endives, turning them over in the butter, and season with salt and pepper to taste and lemon juice. Cover the pan tightly and cook over low heat for 30 minutes or until endives are tender.

Remove endives with a slotted spoon and when cool enough to handle, roll each in a slice of ham. Arrange, seam side down, in a buttered ovenproof dish just large enough to hold them in one layer.

Place béchamel sauce in a large bowl and stir into it the juices left from cooking the endives, the beaten egg yolk, a grinding of nutmeg and 50 g (2 oz) grated cheese. Spoon over the endives and sprinkle with remaining cheese. Bake in a preheated moderately hot oven (190°C/375°F/Gas 5) for 15 minutes, until sauce is bubbly and cheese golden. SERVES 6.

Waterzooi
❧ Chicken in Creamy Sauce

This is one of Belgium's favourite dishes. You can enjoy this soup-stew at restaurants throughout the country, including the elegant *La Maison du Cygne* in Brussels, close to the Grand' Place. (Illustrated on pages 114 and 115.)

1 large chicken (weighing at least 2 kg/4½ lb), trussed (page 96)
50 g (2 oz) butter, softened
6 sticks of celery, roughly chopped
3 leeks, washed, trimmed and roughly chopped
1 carrot, chopped
1 small onion, chopped
4 sprigs of parsley
3 cloves
½ bay leaf
good pinch of dried thyme
good pinch of freshly grated nutmeg
salt and freshly ground pepper
Chicken Stock, to cover (page 90)
1 lemon, thinly sliced
1 tablespoon finely chopped parsley
4 egg yolks, beaten with 4 tablespoons double cream

Rub the chicken all over with the butter and brown it in a heavy, deep saucepan, turning to brown evenly. Add vegetables and seasonings and enough chicken stock to cover. Simmer with the lid on until the chicken is tender, about 1 hour. Remove the chicken from the stock and when it is cool enough to handle, take the flesh from the bones in large pieces, discarding the skin. Keep the chicken warm.

Strain 750 ml (1¼ pints) stock into a clean saucepan, add lemon slices and parsley and heat until almost boiling. Stir a little hot stock into the egg yolk mixture, then tip back into the saucepan. Continue stirring over low heat until the sauce has thickened slightly—do not allow it to boil. Remove from heat and stir in chicken pieces. Pour into a heated tureen to serve and accompany with thin slices of buttered wholemeal bread. SERVES 4–6.

Wiener Schnitzel

There is not a restaurant in Austria that doesn't have *schnitzel* on the menu—that is, thin veal steaks (*scaloppine*) with a crisp breadcrumb coating. There are many ways of garnishing the steaks, but *Wiener* refers to the famous and decorative garnish of lemon slices, capers and anchovies. When you serve this at home, you are serving what amounts to Austria's national dish!

4 thin veal steaks
salt and freshly ground pepper
flour for dusting
1 egg, lightly beaten with a pinch of salt
75 g (3 oz) fine soft breadcrumbs
50 g (2 oz) butter
2 tablespoons oil
lemon juice
GARNISH
4 thin slices lemon
8 flat canned anchovy fillets
12 capers

Place steaks between 2 sheets of plastic film and pound as thin as possible with a smooth mallet or rolling pin. Trim ragged edges and season steaks with salt and pepper. Dust both sides with flour and shake off excess. Dip the steaks in egg and then in breadcrumbs, firming them on with a broad-bladed knife. Chill for 30 minutes to set the coating.

Heat the butter and oil in a large heavy, frying pan and when it is foaming slip the steaks into the pan. (Don't overcrowd the pan—cook them in 2 batches if necessary.) Cook on both sides over medium heat until golden-brown and crisp, about 2 minutes each side. Arrange the steaks on a heated serving platter, sprinkle with lemon juice and garnish each one with a slice of lemon topped with 2 crossed anchovy fillets and a few capers. SERVES 4
Note: Breadcrumbs made from one- or two-day-old bread and put through a sieve are the first choice for *schnitzel*.

Spätzle
🦅 *Pasta Drops*

Several countries claim these light, fluffy pasta drops as their own. Restaurants in Germany and Austria often serve them with *schnitzel*, and both Swiss and Czechoslovakian friends say they grew up with *spätzle* as part of their cuisine. *Spätzle* may also be served in pea or lentil soups, or buttered as a side dish.

350 g (12 oz) flour
3 eggs
¾ teaspoon salt
¼ teaspoon freshly ground black pepper
¼ teaspoon freshly grated nutmeg
120 ml (4 fl oz) each milk and water, mixed together
900 ml (1½ pints) simmering Beef or Chicken Stock (pages 77, 90)
75 g (3 oz) butter, melted

Sift the flour into a large bowl, make a well in the centre and break the eggs into it. Add salt, pepper, nutmeg and milk and water. Stirring from the centre out, gradually incorporate the flour into the liquid to make a smooth batter.

Hold a colander, with large holes, over a wide saucepan containing the simmering stock. Pour the batter into it, so it falls through the holes into the stock. Stir the stock gently so the *spätzle* don't stick together and cook until they rise to the surface, about 5–8 minutes. Drain well, place in a heated serving bowl and pour melted butter over. SERVES 4–6.

In Vienna, a restaurant may rise or fall on the quality of its schnitzel—a home cook is judged the same way. The colour should be golden-brown—not too light, not too dark. The breadcrumb crust should puff up in a few places, but never fall away from the veal. The outside must be crisp but not oily. In fact the final test of a schnitzel in earlier times was to sit on it for one second. If it didn't leave a fat stain on your skirt or trousers, it was perfectly cooked.

Tarte au Citron

❧ *Lemon Tart*

World-acclaimed Swiss chef Alfred Girardet presides over the kitchens of his own restaurant, the *Hotel de Ville*, in the village of Crissier outside Lausanne. In a disarmingly informal atmosphere of lace curtains and bare stone floors, you might start your meal with a blanquette of lobster and fresh salmon . . . go on to a saddle of hare with basil . . . and finish with this utterly delectable orange and lemon tart.

PASTRY
175 g (6 oz) flour
2 tablespoons caster sugar
125 g (4 oz) cold butter, cut into small pieces
1 egg yolk, lightly beaten
FILLING
4 eggs
175 g (6 oz) sugar
150 ml (¼ pint) lemon juice
120 ml (4 fl oz) orange juice
grated zest of 2 lemons (page 18)
50 g (2 oz) butter
4 tablespoons double cream
2 extra lemons, to decorate
icing sugar, to glaze

To make the pastry: sift flour and sugar together into a bowl and add the butter and egg yolk. Blend with a pastry blender, fork or two knives until well combined, then form the dough into a ball. Knead it lightly with the heel of the hand against a smooth surface to distribute the butter evenly, then re-form into a ball. Dust with flour, wrap in plastic film and chill for 1 hour.

Roll the dough out to a circle 3 mm (⅛ inch) thick on a floured surface and press firmly into a 25 cm (10 inch) flan tin with a removable fluted rim. Trim excess, by rolling a rolling pin over the top of the tin. Prick the bottom of the pastry with a fork, line with greaseproof paper and fill with dried beans or raw rice. Bake 'blind' in a preheated hot oven (200°C/400°F/Gas 6) for 10–15 minutes or until lightly browned. Take out paper and beans, and cool in the tin on a wire rack.

To make the filling: place eggs, sugar, lemon juice, orange juice and lemon zest in a bowl and beat well together. Melt the butter with the cream in a large saucepan over low heat. Add egg mixture and continue cooking until it thickens, stirring constantly—do not allow to boil.

Transfer the custard to a bowl, cover with buttered greaseproof paper and allow to cool. Pour the custard into the flan shell (still in the tin) and place on the top shelf of a preheated moderately hot oven (190°C/375°F/Gas 5) for 20 minutes.

Peel the extra lemons with a small, sharp knife and detach the segments from the membranes. Arrange the segments around the top of the tart. Cover edge of pastry with a strip of aluminium foil and sift icing sugar very generously over the filling. Place under a preheated grill for 1 minute or until the top is glazed. Remove the foil and the rim of the flan tin and serve the tart warm. SERVES 8.

Avocado with Strawberry Vinaigrette

Everybody I know who has eaten at Prue Leith's lovely London restaurant, called *Leith's*, talks about the impeccable freshness of the fruits and vegetables—many grown on Prue's own farm in Oxfordshire. In this recipe, creamy avocados and bright strawberries combine to make a first course that looks and tastes like spring.

2 large, ripe avocados
4 tablespoons salad oil
1 tablespoon lemon juice
8–10 large, ripe strawberries
sugar
salt and freshly ground pepper

Halve the avocados lengthwise, remove the stones and peel thinly. Cut into crescent-shaped slices. Combine oil, lemon juice and strawberries in a blender, adding enough strawberries to thicken the sauce and give a pretty pink colour. Add sugar, salt and pepper to taste.

Divide the sauce among 4 plates and arrange overlapping slices of avocado on top. SERVES 4.
<u>Note:</u> Failing a blender, rub the strawberries through a sieve and add to oil and lemon juice that have been whisked together.

❦ Hungarian Cucumber Salad

Refreshingly different! Thinly slice 2 large unpeeled cucumbers, sprinkle with 2 teaspoons salt and drain in a colander for 1 hour. Pat dry and combine with 4 tablespoons wine vinegar, 4 teaspoons sugar, 2 crushed cloves garlic and pepper to taste. Just before serving, toss the cucumber mixture with 1 large Spanish onion (thinly sliced and separated into rings) and sprinkle with paprika. Serves 6–8.

Tarte au Citron

Germany is a country of festivals. The most famous is Munich's *Oktoberfest*, a 16-day, non-stop feast of beer, food, singing, and foot-stamping to 'oom-pa-pa' bands. Founded in 1810 to celebrate the marriage of Crown Prince Ludwig of Bavaria, the *Oktoberfest* takes place in a gigantic fairground called *Theresienwiese*—named after Ludwig's bride, Therese.

Leberkäse

🦪 *Hot Liver Pâté*

It's one of the great national dishes of Germany—a very smooth meat and liver pâté that is steamed and served hot with mustard and crusty bread or rolls. From department store cafeterias to snack counters, *Leberkäse* is popular day and night. Some say the best *Leberkäse* is found at the stall on Munich railway station—this recipe is very close to it.

600 g (1¼ lb) lean pork, cut in pieces
450 ml (¾ pint) iced water
350 g (12 oz) pork or calf's liver, cut in pieces
1 medium onion, cut up
1 clove garlic
125 g (4 oz) bacon in one piece, derinded and
　　cut into small dice
2 eggs, beaten
2 teaspoons salt
½ teaspoon freshly ground pepper
1 teaspoon saltpetre (see Note)
1 teaspoon sugar

Mince the pork twice in a food processor fitted with the steel blade or in a hand mincer. Place in a large bowl and very gradually work the iced water into the meat. To do this, pour a little water on the meat and knead with the hands until the water is absorbed. Then add a little more water, knead again, and repeat until water is used up.

Process or mince the liver and onion with the garlic until well combined. Add liver mixture and bacon to pork mince, together with remaining ingredients, and knead very thoroughly by hand until mixture is firm and compact. Pack into a greased loaf pan or terrine, about 24 × 13 × 6 cm (9½ × 5 × 2½ inches). Brush the top of the loaf with water and set the pan in a baking dish filled with enough hot water to come half-way up the sides of the pan.

Bake on the bottom shelf of a preheated moderate oven (180°C/350°F/Gas 4) for 2½–3 hours or until the loaf is firm and has shrunk away from the sides of the pan.

Leberkäse may be served at once, or can be refrigerated until required. To reheat, cut off as many slices as you will need and place in a Chinese bamboo steamer or metal steamer. Steam over simmering water for 15 minutes or until heated through. (The slices may also be pan-fried on both sides in a little butter and served with fried onions.) SERVES 6.

Note: Saltpetre (used in curing meats and to help meat keep its pink colour) is available from some chemists. If unavailable, simply omit.

Individual Cheese Soufflés

Many people consider the finest *smörgåsbord* in Sweden is to be found at the *Operakallaren* in the Royal Swedish Opera House in Stockholm. This beautiful restaurant, spread over three floors, contains a glass-walled main dining-room, a grill room, an *Art Nouveau* bar and even a take-away food service! Try it for a total experience in good food and turn-of-the-century atmosphere. And don't miss these delectable little soufflés if they're on the menu.

4 egg yolks, lightly beaten
75 g (3 oz) freshly grated Parmesan cheese
40 g (1½ oz) plus 4 tablespoons grated Gruyère cheese
2 tablespoons Cognac or brandy
salt and cayenne pepper
400 ml (14 fl oz) double cream, softly whipped
4 egg whites, stiffly beaten with a pinch of salt

Combine the egg yolks with the Parmesan and 40 g (1½ oz) Gruyère cheese, the Cognac or brandy and salt cayenne pepper to taste. Fold in the whipped cream and then the egg whites. Divide the mixture among six 250 ml (8 fl oz) buttered soufflé dishes and sprinkle each with the remaining 4 tablespoons Gruyère cheese. Bake in a preheated hot oven (200°C/400°F/Gas 6) for 15 minutes or until soufflés are puffed and golden. Serve at once. SERVES 6.

Salzburger Nockerln
➥ *Soufflé 'Dumplings'*

The pretty Austrian town of Salzburg is famous among other things for Mozart and these golden, soufflé-like dumplings, featured on menus throughout the city. Serve them with coffee, as a dessert, or, as the Austrians often do, with a glass of champagne for a romantic late supper.

3 egg yolks
1 teaspoon flour
2 teaspoons finely grated lemon rind
5 egg whites
2 teaspoons sugar
25 g (1 oz) butter
TO SERVE
sugar
Vanilla Sauce (see below)

Preheat the oven to very hot (220°C/425°F/Gas 7).
   Mix egg yolks and flour together in a large bowl and stir in lemon rind. Whisk egg whites to a firm snow, then sprinkle sugar on top and whisk a further minute. Using a rubber spatula, fold the whisked egg whites lightly into the egg yolk mixture—do not over mix.
   Place butter in a shallow glass or pottery baking dish and heat until butter melts. Rotate the dish to coat the bottom and sides evenly with butter (wearing oven mitts to protect your hands).
   Using a large serving spoon, pile 4 masses of egg mixture into the dish—it doesn't matter if they touch each other. Bake in the preheated hot oven for 10 minutes or until the 'dumplings' are lightly browned on top and the centres are still moist but not runny. Serve at once, sprinkled with sugar, and pass a bowl of vanilla sauce. SERVES 4.

Vanilla Sauce
450 ml (¾ pint) milk
1 teaspoon vanilla
3 egg yolks
50 g (2 oz) sugar
2 teaspoons cornflour

Scald milk in the top part of a double boiler and stir in vanilla. Beat egg yolks with sugar and cornflour until light and fluffy and continue to beat while adding hot milk in a stream. Pour the mixture back into the double boiler and place over simmering water making sure water does not touch the base of the upper pan.

Cook, stirring constantly, until the custard coats the back of a metal spoon. Serve hot or cold with *Nockerln.* Also nice with stewed fruits and steamed puddings. SERVES 4.

Oliebollen
➥ *Dutch Doughnuts*

Many visitors to Europe say the best food is to be found in Amsterdam. They particularly enjoy the charming *broodjeswinkel* (snack shops), where it costs very little to sample a bowl of steaming pea soup for lunch, or chase mid-morning hunger pangs with a cup of coffee and a rich, fruity doughnut.

1 sachet dry yeast or 25 g (1 oz) fresh yeast
170 ml (6 fl oz) warm milk
½ teaspoon sugar
225 g (8 oz) flour
2 tablespoons sugar
good pinch of salt
2 eggs, beaten
1 medium tart apple, peeled and finely chopped
50 g (2 oz) raisins
25 g (1 oz) chopped, candied peel
1 tablespoon grated lemon rind
oil for deep frying
icing sugar

Stir together the yeast, warm milk and the ½ teaspoon sugar and stand for 10 minutes until the mixture has sponged. Sift flour, 2 tablespoons sugar and salt into a large mixing bowl. Using a fork, gradually stir in the yeast mixture, beaten eggs, fruit, peel and lemon rind. The dough should be soft, but just firm enough to hold its shape in a spoon. (If necessary, add a little extra flour or milk to give the right consistency.)
   Cover the bowl with a tea-towel and let the dough rise in a warm place for 1 hour or until doubled in bulk.
   Heat enough oil in a deep saucepan to give a depth of about 4 cm (1½ inches). (To test if the oil is hot enough, drop a cube of bread into it. The bread should rise to the surface immediately.) Using 2 greased tablespoons, form the dough into balls and drop them, a few at a time, into the hot oil. Fry for 3 minutes each side, or until puffed and golden-brown, then transfer them with a slotted spoon to paper towels to drain. Cover with more paper towels to keep warm. When all the doughnuts are fried, roll in icing sugar and serve immediately. MAKES about 15.

➥ German Potato Salad

Cook 6 unpeeled, medium-size potatoes in boiling salted water until just tender. Peel and slice into a serving bowl. Place in a saucepan 1 chopped onion, 120 ml (4 fl oz) chicken stock, 4 tablespoons olive oil, 1 tablespoon wine vinegar, 2 teaspoons German mustard, 1 teaspoon salt and ½ teaspoon pepper. Simmer for 5 minutes, stir in 1 tablespoon lemon juice and pour over potatoes. Cool to room temperature, stirring now and again. Serves 4–6.

Keep an eye on your waistline in Europe! Helpings are apt to be enormous and combinations rich. For example, at the famous *Michaeli Stuben* restaurant outside Bonn, a favourite dish is *Was Mutti Gerne Ist* (What Mummy Likes to Eat). This is steak covered with chicken livers and ham, topped with a rich cream sauce and served with fried potatoes and salad. If this is Mummy's kind of dish, you can imagine what Big Daddy likes to eat!

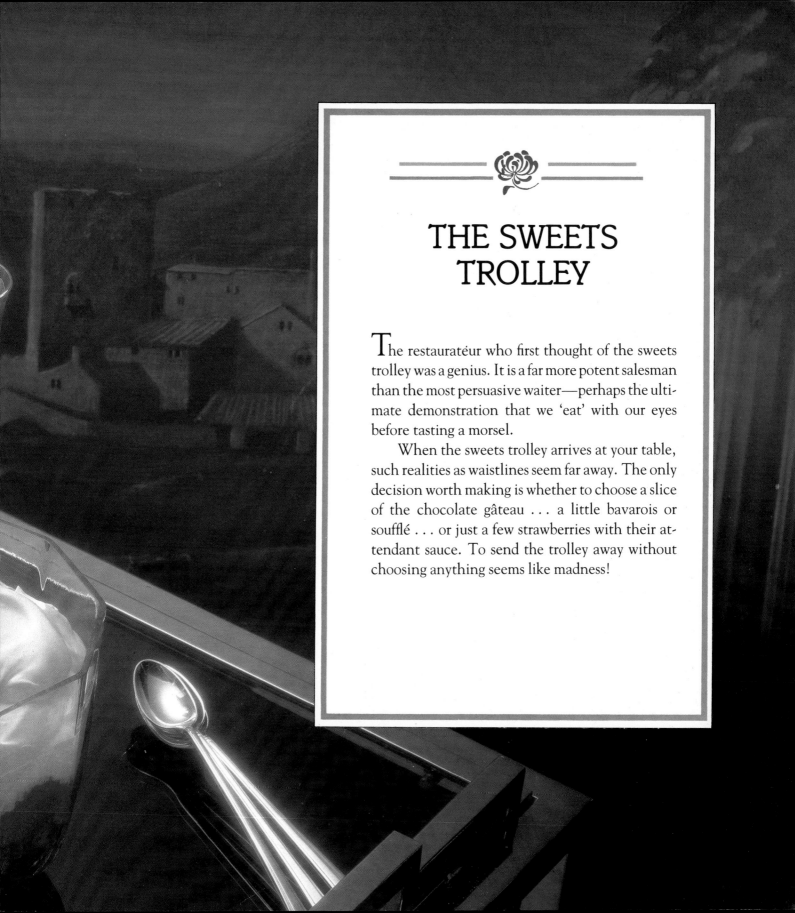

THE SWEETS
TROLLEY

The restauratéur who first thought of the sweets trolley was a genius. It is a far more potent salesman than the most persuasive waiter—perhaps the ultimate demonstration that we 'eat' with our eyes before tasting a morsel.

When the sweets trolley arrives at your table, such realities as waistlines seem far away. The only decision worth making is whether to choose a slice of the chocolate gâteau . . . a little bavarois or soufflé . . . or just a few strawberries with their attendant sauce. To send the trolley away without choosing anything seems like madness!

It's interesting to see that simple classics have pride of place on some of the most sumptuous sweets trolleys. In prestigious English restaurants like *The Dorchester Grill*, *The Savoy River Restaurant* and *Simpsons-on-the-Strand*, you find that bread-and-butter pudding, trifle, creamed rice and beautifully prepared fresh or poached fruit are starred. To order one of these is to be reminded that perfection is always in style. Fine professionalism shows—in a silken custard, in fruit precisely cut and delicately cooked, in trifles and fruit salads so carefully arranged that each portion is beautiful, right to the last serve.

It is by simple things like these that a chef's professional peers judge him, and it is here that some of his most subtle creative touches appear.

True sweets-lovers will often forego a first course in anticipation of choosing two (or more!) delights from the sweets trolley. Indeed, one of the greatest French restaurants, *Les Frères Troisgros* at Roanne, makes it almost inevitable by offering one trolley with splendid fruits, creams and custards, and a second one with magnificent pastries!

In Victorian days, recipes were popular for 'invalid cookery'. Sweets considered suitable for invalids included junkets, fruit snows, custard, blancmange and 'invalid trifle'.

The trifle was to be decorated in the early stages of the invalid's recovery with 'a very little' plain cream. As the patient became stronger, a little colour could be introduced in the form of a glacé cherry or piece of angelica. How times change! Today we know how vital it is to tempt the appetite through the eye.

Choux Pastry

This is the basis of light-as-air puffs and éclairs, and other masterpieces of the pâtissier's art.

250 ml (8 fl oz) water
125 g (4 oz) butter
½ teaspoon salt
1 teaspoon sugar
125 g (4 oz) flour
4 eggs

Put the water, butter, salt and sugar into a saucepan and bring slowly to the boil. The butter must be melted before the mixture boils. Sift flour on to a square of greaseproof paper. As soon as the water mixture boils, add flour all at once, using the paper as a funnel. Beat vigorously with a wooden spatula over low heat until the mixture comes away from the sides and begins to film the bottom of the pan.

Remove from heat and cool the choux paste to lukewarm. Beat in the eggs one at a time, thoroughly incorporating each before adding the next. If the paste is very stiff, beat an extra egg and add a little at a time until the paste is shiny and pliable, but still stiff enough to hold its shape on a spoon.

Pipe or shape the paste into round puffs, or as directed in the recipe. Bake in a preheated hot oven (220°C/425°F/Gas 7) for 12 minutes, then reduce heat to moderate (180°C/350°F/Gas 5) and continue baking for a further 15–25 minutes, depending on size, until golden-brown and light in the hand. If pastry is becoming too brown before it is cooked through, cover with a sheet of brown paper or foil.

Crème Pâtissière
❦ *Pastry Cream*

Crème pâtissière is a rich custard cream often used as a filling for cakes, éclairs, profiteroles and other luscious pastries on the sweets trolley. It is especially useful when you want to fill pastries ahead of time because, unlike fresh cream, it will not make them soggy.

Crème pâtissière can be varied with the addition of chocolate, coffee or liqueur flavourings.

250 ml (8 fl oz) milk
3 egg yolks
90 g (3½ oz) caster sugar
½ teaspoon vanilla
25 g (1 oz) flour

Bring the milk to the boil and set aside. Beat egg yolks, sugar and vanilla together until the mixture, when lifted on the beater, forms a slowly dissolving ribbon on the surface. Sift the flour over and mix well.

Add the hot milk to the yolk mixture, beating constantly. Return this mixture to the saucepan and bring to the boil, stirring constantly with a whisk. Simmer on very low heat, stirring, for 1 minute. Remove from heat, pour the custard cream into a bowl and stir until cool, then cover the surface with plastic film. Chill before using.

Profiteroles au Chocolat
☙ *Small Cream Puffs with Hot Chocolate Sauce*

One of the most irresistible, glamorous and famous of all desserts! Most restaurants fill the little puffs with *crème pâtissière*, a custard-based filling (the profiteroles don't go soggy); others, with whipped cream. Both are delicious but whipped cream makes the dessert a little easier for the home cook.

1 quantity Choux Pastry (see left)
350 ml (12 fl oz) sweetened whipped cream or
  Crème Pâtissière (see left)
icing sugar for dusting
Chocolate Sauce (see below)

Pipe or spoon choux paste on to a greased baking tray in mounds about 2.5 cm (1 inch) across, spacing them a little apart. If necessary, smooth the tops into a round shape with a damp finger. Bake in a preheated hot oven (220°C/425°F/Gas 7) for 12 minutes, then reduce heat to moderate (180°C/350°F/Gas 4) and continue baking for a further 15 minutes or until golden-brown and light in the hand. (If pastry is becoming too brown before it's cooked through, cover with a sheet of brown paper or foil.)

As soon as puffs are taken from the oven, make a hole in each one with the point of a small knife to release steam. Cool completely on a wire rack before filling.

Pipe whipped cream or *crème pâtissière* into the puffs. Pile them on a serving dish, sift icing sugar over top and serve with hot chocolate sauce. SERVES 8–10.

Chocolate Sauce
Break 175 g (6 oz) dark chocolate into pieces and place in a bowl with 6 tablespoons water and 1 tablespoon rum or brandy. Set the bowl over a pan of simmering water and stir until chocolate melts. Cook for 1 minute longer, then pour into a heated jug and serve piping hot.

Strawberries à la Ritz

When I stay in London, the lovely old *Ritz* hotel is a favourite choice, typifying the unobtrusive, traditional British style which many find so attractive. This luscious combination of strawberries and raspberries was on the menu during one of my stays in the *Ritz*. (Illustrated on pages 126 and 127.)

350 g (12 oz) ripe strawberries, gently washed
  and hulled
sugar
225 g (8 oz) ripe raspberries
170 ml (6 fl oz) double cream
candied violets or slivers of angelica, to decorate

Place two-thirds of the strawberries in a glass serving bowl and sprinkle with sugar to taste. Whirl the remaining strawberries with the raspberries in a blender or food processor fitted with the steel blade, or rub through a sieve. Spoon the purée over the whole strawberries and chill until serving time.

When ready to serve, whip the cream and spread over the fruit, masking it completely. Decorate with candied violets or slivers of angelica. SERVES 4.
<u>Note:</u> If fresh raspberries are not available, use frozen raspberries.

Poires au Sucre
☙ *Caramel Pears*

As well as their wonderful gâteaux, you can look forward to a tempting array of fruits on French sweets trolleys, like this superb dish of Caramel Pears.

50 g (2 oz) butter
6 tablespoons sugar
4 ripe pears, peeled, halved and cored
120 ml (4 fl oz) double cream
½ teaspoon vanilla
2 tablespoons kirsch

Melt half the butter in a shallow ovenproof serving dish, just large enough to take the halved pears in one layer. Sprinkle the dish with half the sugar. Place the pears cut side down in the dish. Sprinkle with remaining sugar and top each pear with a piece of butter. Bake, uncovered, in a preheated hot oven (220°C/425°F/Gas 7) for 20 minutes, basting pears several times with pan juices.

Mix together cream, vanilla and kirsch. Pour over pears and bake 20 minutes longer or until cream mixture is slightly thickened. Serve warm. SERVES 8.

☙ Sugared Fruits and Flowers
These make enchanting decorations for cakes, trifles and desserts. Use single petals of mint and rose, small whole flowers such as violets, whole fruit such as grapes and unhulled strawberries. Make sure they are perfectly dry. Beat an egg white just until frothy and paint flowers or fruits on all sides with it, using a soft paint brush. Dredge with caster sugar and place on a wire rack until egg white sets. Use as soon as possible.

Pecan Tart

At *Donlevy*'s in Melbourne, few patrons can resist this beautiful variation on a classic walnut tart. It makes a splendid large 28–30 cm (11–12 inch) tart, to serve 12 or 14 people for a dinner party.

PASTRY
50 g (2 oz) shelled pecans
150 g (5 oz) butter
75 g (3 oz) caster sugar
225 g (8 oz) flour
1 egg, beaten
FILLING
175 g (6 oz) butter
175 g (6 oz) brown sugar
120 ml (4 fl oz) warmed honey
6 eggs
75 g (3 oz) shelled pecans
DECORATION
40 g (1½ oz) dark chocolate

Grind the pecans for the pastry in a nut grinder, or process to a fine meal in a food processor fitted with the steel blade (being careful not to over process them to a paste). Cream the butter and sugar, then beat in ground pecans and flour. Beat eggs and stir in with a knife to make a soft dough—do not use all the egg unless necessary. Gather the dough into a ball with your fingertips, wrap in plastic film and chill for 20 minutes. Roll out to line a greased 28–30 cm (11–12 inch) shallow, fluted flan tin, and place in the refrigerator while making the filling.

To make the filling: cream the butter and sugar until light and fluffy, then beat in warmed honey and egg alternately. Spread the filling evenly in the pastry case and scatter the pecans over.

Bake in a preheated hot oven (200°C/400°F/Gas 6) for 5 minutes, then turn down the oven to moderately hot (190°C/375°F/Gas 5) and continue baking for a further 15 minutes or until the filling is set. (Protect the pastry sides of the tart with strips of aluminium foil if they are getting too brown.) Remove the tart from the oven and cool.

To decorate the tart, melt chocolate in a small bowl set over a pan of hot water (off the heat). Dip a fork into the chocolate and use it to drizzle fine ribbons of chocolate, in a zig-zag pattern, over the tart. Allow to set, and serve the tart at room temperature. SERVES 12–14.

Shortcrust Pastry

A classic crisp pastry for pies. Sift 125 g (4 oz) flour and a pinch of salt into a bowl. Cut 50 g (2 oz) chilled butter, margarine or lard, or a mixture, into pieces and rub into flour with the fingertips. Pour 1 tablespoon iced water over and mix to a dough with a knife—add a little more water if necessary. Turn onto a floured board, knead lightly, and chill for 30 minutes wrapped in plastic film. Use as directed in recipe. Enough for 1 thin 20 cm (8 inch) pie crust.

La Mousse Brûlée

Caramel Mousse

At *Ma Cuisine* in London's Walton Street, 'just desserts' takes on full meaning. An array of delectable temptations is brought from the kitchen to the table for consideration. It makes decisions practically impossible—*Tarte de Chez Nous*, Bread and Butter Pudding made from brioche, or this beautifully smooth caramel mousse, the author's choice!

CARAMEL
125 g (4 oz) sugar
5 tablespoons water
MOUSSE
1½ teaspoons gelatine
2 tablespoons water
5 eggs, separated
2 tablespoons caster sugar
1 teaspoon vanilla
300 ml (½ pint) double cream
TOPPING
icing sugar

First make the caramel. In a small, heavy saucepan combine sugar and 1 tablespoon water. Cook gently until sugar dissolves, then increase heat, rotating the pan gently, until a rich brown caramel forms. Remove from heat and gradually stir in remaining water to dilute the caramel. (Do this carefully at first as hot caramel may spit.) Cool for about 5 minutes.

To make the mousse: sprinkle gelatine over water and allow to sponge; then stir into caramel mixture.

Beat egg yolks, sugar and vanilla in a mixer or food processor until thick and lemon coloured. With motor still running, add the caramel mixture in a stream and beat until mixture is thick and fluffy.

Whip cream just until it holds stiff peaks and fold into the caramel mixture. In a large bowl, beat egg whites until they hold soft peaks. Gently but thoroughly fold caramel mixture into the whites.

Spoon the mixture into a large serving dish or 6–8 individual dishes and chill until set. Sift icing sugar over the top and score the icing sugar in a criss-cross pattern with a hot metal skewer. SERVES 6–8.

La Mousse Brûlée

Chocolate Velvet—The Four Seasons

One of the truly great restaurants of the world is *The Four Seasons* in New York City, where the furnishings, the menus and even the waiters' uniforms change 4 times a year to suit the seasons. On a visit some years ago, a smooth-as-velvet chocolate confection was one of the stars of the sweets trolley.

1 single-layer 20 cm (8 inch) sponge cake, bought or home-made
350 g (12 oz) dark chocolate, cut into small pieces
2 eggs, separated
2 tablespoons each kirsch, rum and Crème de Cacao
1½ teaspoons instant coffee powder
3 tablespoons crumbled marzipan
3 tablespoons melted butter
pinch of salt
3 tablespoons icing sugar
250 ml (8 fl oz) double cream, stiffly whipped
ICING
125 g (4 oz) dark chocolate, chopped
6–7 tablespoons boiling water

Split the sponge cake to make 2 thin layers. Line a 1.2 litre (2 pint) mould with pieces of sponge cut to fit, reserving the rest of the sponge.

Place the chocolate pieces in a bowl or the top of a double boiler set over hot water. Stir until the chocolate melts, then remove from heat.

Beat the egg yolks until well blended, add the kirsch, rum, Crème de Cacao and instant coffee and beat until smooth. Beat in the marzipan, melted butter and the melted chocolate until well combined. The easiest way to do this is with an electric mixer on low speed, but it can be done by hand.

Whisk the egg whites with a pinch of salt until foamy, then add the icing sugar, 1 tablespoon at a time, until stiff peaks form. Fold gently into the chocolate mixture. Fold in the cream.

Spoon the chocolate mixture into the sponge-lined mould and chill for 1 hour. Cut remaining sponge into pieces to fit the top of the mould and cover the chocolate filling completely with sponge, pressing it down slightly. Chill for a further 4 hours.

To make the icing: place the chocolate and boiling water in a bowl or the top of a double boiler set over simmering water and stir until the chocolate is smooth.

To serve, run a knife round the sides of the mould to loosen it and invert the dessert on to a flat dish. Pour the icing over the top and sides, spreading it with a broad metal spatula, and chill until set. Transfer to a pretty serving plate and cut into thin wedges to serve. SERVES 8.

Rum Cream Trifle

Trifle is still a British institution. You see it everywhere, from 'establishment' eating places like *The Connaught* and *The Ivy*, to chic newcomers like *The Neal Street Restaurant* in Covent Garden. This is an interesting version for you to try, with the cake folded through a rich egg custard set with gelatine.

1 × 20 cm (8 inch) plain sponge or buttercake
2 tablespoons dark rum
1 tablespoon gelatine
4 tablespoons water
450 ml (¾ pint) double cream
120 ml (4 fl oz) milk
3 eggs, separated, plus 2 egg yolks
4 tablespoons caster sugar
DECORATION
about 75 g (3 oz) blanched, split almonds
fresh strawberries (optional)

Break the cake into small pieces, sprinkle with rum and set aside. Soak gelatine in water to soften, then stand basin in a bowl of hot water and stir until dissolved. Heat half the cream and the milk together until bubbles form around the edge, then remove from heat. Whip the remaining cream until firm. In another bowl beat the 3 egg whites until they hold soft peaks.

Beat all the egg yolks with the sugar until thick and pale; stir in the cream mixture, then turn into a heavy saucepan. Stir over low heat until custard is thick enough to coat the back of a spoon—do not allow it to boil.

Set the saucepan on ice to cool the custard quickly, then stir in the dissolved gelatine and continue stirring until mixture is as thick as unbeaten egg white. Fold in 4 tablespoons of the whipped cream, the beaten egg whites and the rum-soaked cake. Turn into a serving bowl (a glass one looks pretty) and chill until set.

Spread, or using a piping bag and star tube, pipe the remaining whipped cream thickly over the top of the trifle and cover it with blanched, split almonds, standing them upright. If liked, surround the trifle with a ring of hulled strawberries. SERVES 8.

☙ Rich Shortcrust Pastry

A richer pastry for savoury or sweet tarts. Sift 125 g (4 oz) flour, a pinch of salt and a pinch of baking powder into a bowl. Cut 75 g (3 oz) chilled butter into pieces and rub in until mixture resembles coarse breadcrumbs. Mix 1 egg yolk with 1 tablespoon water and a squeeze of lemon juice and proceed as for Shortcrust Pastry (page 130). For sweet shortcrust, add 1 tablespoon caster sugar after rubbing in butter.

Galette Jalousie
🍂 *Glazed Pastry Sandwich*

Here is a wonderful example of what a French chef can do with a few simple ingredients. Basically, it's just a delicious pastry 'jam sandwich', but the decorative slits on the top layer of pastry, like a *jalousie* (Venetian blind), the sugar glaze and the crusty edges all add up to make Jalousie something special.

1 × 350 g (12 oz) packet frozen puff pastry,
  thawed
150–175 g (5–6 oz) best quality jam
caster sugar

Cut the pastry in half and roll each half out to a rectangle about 13 × 30 cm (5 × 12 inches). Fold one rectangle in half lengthwise and cut along the fold into narrow strips, leaving a border of about 2.5 cm (1 inch) around the edges.

Place the other rectangle of pastry on a damp baking tray. Spoon jam in a strip down the middle, leaving a border a little over 2.5 cm (1 inch) all round. Brush border with water.

Unfold the first piece of pastry and place it on top. Press the edges firmly together to seal and trim them evenly. Mark a decorative pattern with the tines of a fork around the edges, and chill the Jalousie for 40 minutes.

Brush the top lightly with water and sprinkle all over with caster sugar. Bake in a preheated, very hot oven (230°C/450°F/Gas 8) for 15 minutes or until well risen and beginning to brown. Reduce temperature to hot (200°C/400°F/Gas 6) and bake for a further 30 minutes or until pastry is golden-brown, with firm, crusty sides. (If the top is browning too much, cover loosely with foil; Jalousie needs the full cooking time to make it flaky right through.)

Cut across into slices and serve warm or cold with coffee, or as a dessert with whipped cream or custard. SERVES 6.

Bread and Butter Pudding

This favourite never loses its charm. Despite its timeless appeal, there is scope even in Bread and Butter Pudding for a chef to add his own special touch—and I particularly enjoyed the apricot finish on the pudding at *The Dorchester* in London.

250 ml (8 fl oz) milk
250 ml (8 fl oz) double cream
pinch of salt
1 vanilla pod
3 eggs
125 g (4 oz) sugar
3 soft bread rolls
25 g (1 oz) butter
2 tablespoons sultanas, soaked in hot water and
  drained
1½ tablespoons apricot jam, warmed
icing sugar, to decorate
pouring cream, to serve

Bring the milk, cream, salt and the vanilla pod to the boil, then remove from heat. Beat eggs and sugar together in a bowl and stir in scalded milk and cream mixture.

Cut rolls into thin slices, butter them on one side, and arrange in a buttered ovenproof dish, buttered side up. Sprinkle sultanas over the top, then strain milk and cream mixture over through a fine sieve.

Place the dish in a roasting pan with enough water to come half-way up the sides, and bake in a preheated moderate oven (180°C/350°F/Gas 4) for 30–40 minutes or until puffy on top and set. Spoon warmed apricot jam over and sprinkle with icing sugar. Serve the pudding warm, with pouring cream handed separately. SERVES 4.

When planning a dinner party, one shortcut I endorse is to leave the dessert to a good pâtisserie. For splendid occasions they can supply a Croquembouche or Gâteau St. Honoré . . . and they always have glistening fruit tarts, pastries and confections. Many will make something special to order, given notice. It's a shortcut I sometimes use myself!

Chocolate Roulade

My daughter Suzanne made this many times when she worked as the sweets cook at the elegant little *Cordon Bleu* restaurant in London's Marylebone Lane. The restaurant is no more, but the Chocolate Roulade lives on.

5 large eggs, separated
175 g (6 oz) caster sugar
175 g (6 oz) dark chocolate, broken into pieces
3 tablespoons cold water
extra 50 g (2 oz) grated chocolate
FILLING
250 ml (8 fl oz) double cream, chilled
1 tablespoon icing sugar
dash of vanilla

Grease a baking tray and cover with greased cooking parchment or aluminium foil. Beat egg yolks and gradually beat in sugar, continuing to beat until pale and fluffy. Place the chocolate pieces in a bowl or the top of a double boiler with the cold water. Set over simmering water and stir until chocolate melts. Cool a little, then stir the chocolate into the yolk mixture.

Whisk egg whites until they form soft peaks and fold into the yolk mixture. Spread the mixture evenly on the prepared baking tray, leaving a 2.5 cm (1 inch) margin all round. Place in a preheated moderate oven (180°C/350°F/Gas 4) and bake for 10 minutes, then reduce heat to 150°C/300°F/Gas 2 and bake 5 minutes longer. Remove from oven and cover the top with a cloth which has been wrung out in cold water. Cool, then place in the refrigerator for 1 hour.

Remove the cloth and loosen the parchment or foil from the baking tray. Dust a large sheet of waxed paper with grated chocolate, turn the roulade out onto the chocolate and carefully peel off the parchment or foil.

Whip cream with icing sugar and vanilla and spread half the cream on the roulade. Roll up like a Swiss roll, using the waxed paper to help you, onto a long, narrow board or serving platter. Decorate with remaining whipped cream and, if liked, a few whole strawberries. SERVES 6.

Creamed Rice Connaught

The sweets trolley at *The Connaught* in London includes childhood favourites with grown-up touches—like creamed rice with apricot kirsch sauce.

CREAMED RICE
50 g (2 oz) raw, short-grained rice
600–750 ml (1–1¼ pints) milk
1 vanilla pod
3 tablespoons caster sugar or to taste
120 ml (4 fl oz) double cream
1 egg white
1 tablespoon slivered, toasted almonds, to decorate
SAUCE
125 g (4 oz) sugar
2 strips of thinly peeled lemon rind
225 g (8 oz) dried apricots, soaked overnight in cold water to cover
1 tablespoon kirsch

Wash the rice and place in a large, heavy saucepan with 600 ml (1 pint) milk and the vanilla pod. Simmer very gently until the rice is soft and creamy, stirring in a little more milk from time to time if it begins to dry out. This may take 45 minutes or longer. Turn rice into a bowl, stir in caster sugar to taste, then cover and leave to cool.

Half-whip the cream; and in another bowl whisk the egg white to a soft snow. Mix the cream and egg white together and continue to whisk until the mixture holds soft peaks.

Remove vanilla pod from the rice, fold in cream mixture and turn the pudding into a serving bowl. Cover and chill.

To make the sauce: add sugar and lemon rind to apricots and simmer in the water in which they have been soaking, stirring until sugar dissolves. When apricots are soft (10–15 minutes), remove lemon rind and purée sauce in a blender or food processor fitted with the steel blade, or rub through a sieve. Thin with a little hot water if necessary to give a pouring consistency and reheat until boiling. Stir in kirsch and pour into a hot sauce-boat.

To serve, scatter toasted almonds over creamed rice and serve with the hot sauce passed separately. SERVES 6.

☙ Cooking Unfilled Pastry Shells

Unfilled pastry shells are 'baked blind' to hold their shape. Fit the pastry into the flan ring or pie tin and line it with crumpled greaseproof paper. Add enough dried beans, rice or macaroni to come half-way up the sides and bake as directed in recipe. Paper and beans are usually removed 5 minutes before the end of cooking time and the shell returned to the oven to dry out.

Profiteroles au Chocolat; Rum Cream Trifle; Pineapple in Port Wine; Chocolate Roulade; Creamed Rice Connaught

Pineapple in Port Wine

A slice or two of pineapple in orange-spiked port wine syrup is a perfect light finish to a rich meal.

1 ripe pineapple
4 tablespoons port
4 tablespoons sugar
zest of 2 oranges (page 18)

Peel, slice and core the pineapple, working on a large board. As juice collects on the board, pour it off into a cup. Set pineapple slices aside and add water to the juice, if necessary, to make 120 ml (4 fl oz).

Put the juice, port and sugar into a wide saucepan. Using a very sharp knife, cut the orange zest into the tiniest possible matchstick-length strips. Drop strips into the saucepan as you cut them. Stir the mixture over medium heat until sugar dissolves, then cook without stirring until the orange rind is translucent.

Remove the syrup from heat, add the sliced pineapple and allow to cool. Transfer to a glass serving bowl and chill until serving time. SERVES 4–6.

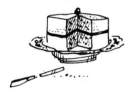

Among the many cakes listed in *Mrs. Beeton's Cookery and Household Management* are some with intriguing names. Now and again I see the point of the name—for example, 'Holiday Cake' is easy to mix. But I can't really find the starting point for 'Doodle Cake', 'Tennis Cake', or a lovely fruit cake called 'Spinster's Cake'!

Strawberry Soufflé with Kirsch

225 g (8 oz) ripe strawberries
125 g (4 oz) sugar
2 tablespoons kirsch
butter and sugar for soufflé dishes
5 egg whites
whipped double cream, to serve

Wash, hull and slice strawberries. Sprinkle with 2 tablespoons of the sugar and the kirsch, and leave to stand for 1 hour.

Butter 6 small soufflé dishes and sprinkle with sugar on the sides and bottom. Whip the egg whites until stiff, then gradually beat in remaining sugar to form a stiff meringue.

Drain the strawberries and fold through the meringue, then spoon into dishes. Stand them in a baking tin and add enough hot water to come halfway up the sides. Bake in a preheated moderate oven (180°C/350°F/Gas 4) for 15–18 minutes, or until puffed and lightly browned. Serve at once with whipped cream. SERVES 6.

Prune and Port Fool

England is famous for its 'fools', light-textured blends of puréed fruit and custard or cream. I first tasted a prune fool at a restaurant called *Crispins* in London. It is a good standby when you want an interesting dessert that requires little preparation. (Illustrated on pages 126 and 127.)

175 g (6 oz) soft, stoned prunes
250 ml (8 fl oz) water
2 strips of lemon rind
120 ml (4 fl oz) port
250 ml (8 fl oz) double cream
2 tablespoons sugar
extra whipped cream and a little grated lemon
*   rind, to decorate*

Cook the prunes in the water, with lemon rind added, until tender, about 20 minutes. Remove the rind and purée the prunes and liquid in a blender or food processor, or rub through a sieve. Cool, then stir in the port. Chill until serving time.

Whip the cream and sugar in a chilled bowl until it forms soft peaks, then fold gently into the prune mixture. Divide among 6 tall glasses and top with a spoonful of whipped cream and a little grated lemon rind. SERVES 6.

Crunchy Cinnamon Pudding

This is a classic dessert with a new and delicious twist—layers of yogurt cream between the apples and toffeed crumbs. It was created by Francis Coulson of England's *Sharrow Bay Hotel*, 1980 winner of the coveted *Egon Ronay Gold Plate Award*.

225 g (8 oz) fresh breadcrumbs
2–3 teaspoons ground cinnamon
75 g (3 oz) brown sugar
75 g (3 oz) butter
4 cooking apples, peeled, cored and quartered
120 ml (4 fl oz) water
1 tablespoon sugar
250 ml (8 fl oz) double cream
2 tablespoons caster sugar
1 small carton natural yogurt

Mix together the breadcrumbs, cinnamon and brown sugar. Melt the butter in a heavy frying pan, add the crumb mixture and stir over medium heat with a wooden spoon until crisp and toffee-like. Transfer to a plate and allow to cool.

Poach the apples in the water with the 1 tablespoon sugar. When soft, purée in a blender or food processor, or rub through a sieve; allow to cool.

Whip the cream with the caster sugar until thick, then stir in the yogurt.

In a pretty serving bowl, about 15 cm (6 inches) in diameter, make layers of crumbs, cream mixture and sweetened apple, ending with a layer of crumbs. Decorate and serve this dessert very cold. SERVES 6.

Note: You can use your own imagination with the decoration. Thin slices of unpeeled apple dipped in lemon juice would be attractive, or whipped cream and curls of chocolate or toasted, slivered almonds.

Gâteau Pithiviers

A superb confection of almond cream encased in a beautifully decorated puff pastry case is the great speciality of the French town of Pithiviers, where it is sold in the *pâtisseries* and featured in the restaurants. (Illustrated on pages 126 and 127.)

ALMOND CREAM
50 g (2 oz) butter
125 g (4 oz) caster sugar
2 egg yolks
125 g (4 oz) ground almonds
few drops of vanilla
2 tablespoons rum

PASTRY
2 × 225 g (8 oz) packets frozen puff pastry, thawed
1 egg, lightly beaten with 1 teaspoon water and pinch of salt, to glaze pastry
icing sugar

First make the almond cream. Cream butter and sugar, then beat in egg yolks, almonds, vanilla to taste, and rum. Cover and chill until the cream is firm enough to be shaped. Form into a round cake 10 cm (4 inches) across; chill again until quite firm.

Roll out half the pastry into a circle 6 mm (¼ inch) thick and, using a cake pan as a guide, cut a 20 cm (8 inch) circle from it. Roll the other half a little thicker and cut a 23 cm (9 inch) circle from it. Turn the thinner circle over on to a dampened baking tray, centre the cake of almond cream on it and brush the border with water. Place the other circle of pastry on top, cut a small hole in its centre and firmly press the top circle on to the bottom one all round the cake of almond cream.

Turn a cake pan or bowl, a little smaller in diameter than the Pithiviers, upside down on it and press into the dough to seal firmly. With a small knife, cut evenly spaced indentations in from the edge of the double thickness of pastry, then remove the pan or bowl. Place Pithiviers in the refrigerator for 40 minutes.

Brush the top surface of the Pithiviers with egg glaze and insert a small tube of buttered aluminium foil in the centre hole. Brush again with egg glaze and, with the point of a small sharp knife, cut a design of a 'cartwheel' with curved spokes from centre to edge, on the top surface. The design should be cut about 3 mm (⅛ inch) deep.

Bake the Pithiviers in the centre of a preheated, very hot oven (230°C/450°F/Gas 9) for about 15 minutes or until well risen and beginning to brown. Turn the temperature down to hot (200°C/400°F/Gas 6) and bake for a further 30 minutes or until golden-brown, with firm, crusty sides. If the top is browning too much, cover loosely with foil. Pithiviers needs the full cooking time to ensure that it is cooked and flaky all through.

Remove from the oven, turn the temperature up to very hot (240°C/475°F/Gas Maximum) and place an oven rack one position above the centre. Remove foil tube and sift icing sugar thickly over the Pithiviers. Return to the oven and bake for a few minutes, checking every 30 seconds, until sugar has melted to a glaze. Remove from the oven. Serve the Pithiviers warm or cool, cut into wedges. SERVES 8–10.

🖎 Toasting Walnuts and Almonds
Toasted nuts taste delicious eaten plain and are also used in some recipes. To toast walnuts and blanched almonds, place them in a single layer on a baking tray and roast in a moderate oven (180°C/350°F/Gas 4) for 10–12 minutes. Shake the tray from time to time, so the nuts will turn over and toast evenly. Remove them when they are golden.

🍂 Coffee Zabaglione

From New York, an exciting twist to the Italian classic dessert. Set a deep metal bowl over a pan of simmering water and add 6 egg yolks, 75 g (3 oz) sugar and 4 tablespoons dark rum. Beat the mixture with a large whisk until thick and tripled in volume. Beat in 350 ml (12 fl oz) cold, strong coffee, 4 tablespoons at a time, and continue beating until the mixture is very thick. Serve warm in stemmed glasses, with a crisp biscuit. Serves 6.

Walnut Charlotte

Wonderful desserts are a feature of the *Horn of Plenty* restaurant in Devon. I enjoyed this luscious charlotte on my own visit, and it makes a spectacular party dessert.

300 g (10 oz) unsalted butter, at room
    temperature
8 egg yolks
225 g (8 oz) icing sugar
175 g (6 oz) chopped walnuts
16–20 sponge fingers
120–250 ml (4–8 fl oz) Grand Marnier or
    other fruit-flavoured liqueur
DECORATION
ribbon, about 140 cm (55 inches) long
about 250 ml (8 fl oz) double cream, stiffly
    whipped

Cream the butter until very light, then beat in the egg yolks one by one, beating well between each addition. Sift the icing sugar over the top and blend in, then fold in the chopped walnuts. (Do not over mix when adding the sugar and walnuts or the sugar will dissolve and the mixture may become runny.)

Spoon the mixture into a 25 cm (10 inch) springform tin with a removable base and chill for 2 hours or until firm. Turn onto a chilled serving platter. Dip the sponge fingers quickly into liqueur and press around the sides. Tie in place with a pretty ribbon. Pipe or pile whipped cream on top and serve at once. SERVES 10–12.

<u>Note:</u> This quantity is excellent for a party, but may be halved. The packaged sponge fingers sold in supermarkets and often known as 'Savoyard Biscuits' are suitable. Dip them only briefly in liqueur or they may crumble.

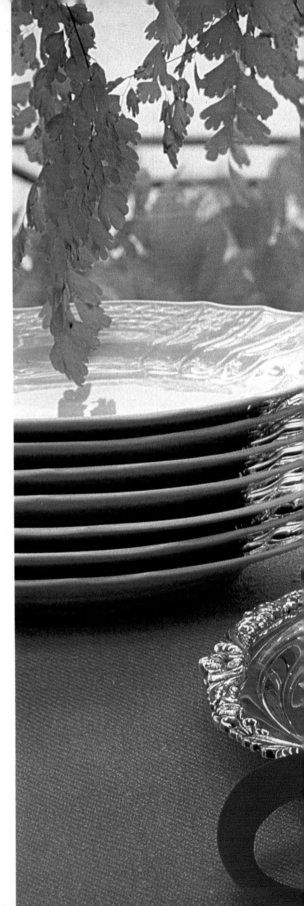

Walnut Charlotte

INDEX

ACKNOWLEDGEMENTS

Photography – Robert Golden: 2–3,
6–7, 22–3, 34–5, 50–1, 62–3, 74–5,
86–7, 102–3, 114–15, 126–7.
Norman Nicholls: 11, 14, 19, 27, 30,
39, 42, 47, 55, 59, 66, 71, 79, 82, 91,
94, 99, 107, 110, 118, 123, 131, 134,
138–9.

Illustrations by Julia Whatley.

The publishers would like to thank
Macmillan London Limited for their
kind permission to reproduce Michel
Guérard's 'Soupe de Tomates Fraîches
au Pistou' on page 92. This recipe was
first published in *La Grande Cuisine
Minceur. Les Recettes Originales de
Michel Guérard.* © Editions Robert
Laffont SA, Paris 1976. This English
translation and adaptation ©
Macmillan London Limited 1977,
translated and adapted by Caroline
Conran.